The Sustainable Corporation

A LEGAL AND BUSINESS CENTRIC APPROACH TO ESG

Travis Miller and Todd Cort
EDITORS

ABA
AMERICAN BAR ASSOCIATION
Business Law Section

Cover design by Catherine Zaccarine.

Printed in the United States of America.

27 26 25 24 23   5 4 3 2 1

ISBN: 978-1-63905-318-6

Contents

INTRODUCTION

ESG and the Twenty-Second-Century Corporation

Andrew Waitman and Travis Miller

History of the Company

An understanding of the concept of environmental, social, and governance (ESG) concerns requires an understanding of the origin of corporations. The oldest, still operating, company in the world was founded in 578 AD in Japan. Kongō Gumi was a construction company (it recently got into financial difficulty and was sold but continues to operate as a subsidiary of Takamatsu Construction Group).[1] The word "corporation" derives from *corpus*, the Latin word for body or "body of people." The essential stated rationale and benefit of a corporation is that they have the capacity to outlast their founders, contributors, and benefactors. Corporations are legal entities, authorized by the state, to organize a set of activities for a purpose. Companies today come in many different forms based on their legal jurisdiction and charter; however, this basic core tenant of permanence toward a mission remains the central tenant of a company. Due to the myriad of company structures and the disproportionate representation of corporations in ESG funds, the content of this book will focus on the corporation.

One of their most defining characteristics of a corporation is the limited legal liability with regard to its owners and operators. Two of the more famous examples of early for-profit companies are the Dutch East India Company and the British Hudson's Bay Company.[2] Each was, respectively, established by colonial interests, supported by the sovereign crown in the late seventeenth century. The purpose of these organizations was to trade and provide profits from the new

1. *Company Introduction*, Takamatsu Construction Group, https://www.takamatsu-cg.co.jp/eng/about/group/takamatsu/kongogumi.html.

2. *Trading Companies*, Encyclopedia.com (2018), https://www.encyclopedia.com/history/modern-europe/british-and-irish-history/trading-companies.

world to colonial masters, and often including the sovereign itself as shareholder. During these early incarnations of companies, the formation was permitted to allocate resources to shared goals and to provide an economic incentive to investors (the sovereign), employees, and the community/mission that the company served. As would be expected, protection of the sovereign/shareholder and profit were the core goals of the corporation.

Corporations as we know them came to being in Britain with the Joint Stock Companies Act 1844 (7 & 8 Vict. c.110) that allowed a corporation to define their own purpose. The power to control them thus passed from the sovereign government to the courts. Under the British Limited Liability Act of 1855 (18 & 19 Vict. c.133), shareholders were awarded limited liability: meaning their personal assets were protected from the consequences of the corporation's behavior or the activities of rogue employees that generated liability. In 1886, a landmark decision by a U.S. court recognized the corporation as a "natural person" under law.[3] Today, globally, the legal corporate structure would be familiar to any seventeenth-century entrepreneur. Meaning a consistency in legal structure and the rules governing corporations has remained remarkably consistent over the past 250 years. This stability echoes back to the original goal of permanence that has laid the groundwork for the immense power and wealth corporations have acquired.

The twentieth-century American principles or philosophy, articulated by Milton Friedman's essay in the 1970s *New York Times* piece called the Friedman Doctrine, became one of the most influential corporate ethics works of all time.[4] The Friedman Doctrine defines "The Social Responsibility of Business is to Increase its Profits" for its shareholders within the bounds of the law. This ethos represents a long-held American perspective of the clarity of purpose of a "for-profit" corporation. Succinctly, the Friedman Doctrine describes the purpose of the corporation is to serve the singular interests of its shareholders, which was to maximize profits. This purpose would be highly aligned with those early colonial corporate entities that were established for the benefit of the crown.

However, Friedman's premise of ignoring externalities has come under intense scrutiny recently. This scrutiny has derived from a growing alarm over the impacts corporations have had over their infinite life cycles. Friedman's perspective reflected the times they were written, well into the Cold War, known for overbearing government controls in the Soviet Union. He was concerned that a broader mandate beyond profits could open the door to corruption and allow managers to enrich themselves at the expense of investors by turning social welfare decisions into a political process. In our current context with significant environmental concerns, including climate change, unprecedented hazardous chemical releases, and conflicts of disparate societal values, free trade has generated intense scrutiny and a rethinking of the Friedman doctrine. This scrutiny has contributed toward government regulations demanding that corporations consider non-financial concerns that extend beyond profit-driven motivations. Whether the abuse of an entire ethnic population, such as the Uyghurs in the

3. *Santa Clara County v. Southern Pacific Railroad*, 118 U.S. 394 (1886).

4. Milton Friedman, *A Friedman Doctrine - The Social Responsibility of Business Is to Increase Its Profits*, N.Y. Times (Sept. 13, 1970).

Xinjiang region of China[5] or the abuse of children in Cobalt or Gold mines in the war-torn Democratic Republic of Congo, governments have issued edicts or laws that create new constraints to the pursuit of profit. The behaviors of companies and countries outside those purporting to support Western values, and even some that do, are often inconsistent or in conflict with the emancipation and empowerment ideals that are advocated by the United Nations Universal Declaration of Human Rights.

During the Cold War period from 1950 to 2000, the American *Order*, established by Bretton Woods Agreement,[6] enabled and encouraged globalization as long as a country/company agreed to play on America's side with a tacit understanding of American values and rules that were not always clearly defined, understood, or enforced. This allowed any company in any country to go anywhere at any time, protected by American hegemony, and trade with anyone else if they aligned with America and not the Soviet Union. The *Order* enabled Western Corporations to build long supply chains with profit optimization as their single, dominant ethos. This in turn resulted, in some cases, in net negative costs to society writ large, in which environmental and societal damage became a consequence of the singular preoccupation of lowest cost. As a result, modern companies would omit non-shareholder concerns from the accounting calculus of shareholder capitalism.

This doctrine led to natural inclinations for outsourcing, that is, seeking substantially lower input costs to maximize profit while seemingly reducing risk.[7] Unfortunately, the profit first pursuits often lead to questionable environmental corner cutting (waste dumping, inexpensive toxic substitutes, or inferior, sometimes carcinogenic, materials being used) and poor social and ethical employment practices (harmful working conditions, abusive employment practices combined with poverty-level pay). Consequently, selected applications to outsource often featured activities that were more regulated, higher risk, and less profitable. Rationally, these risks did not dissipate due to geographic distance; they just moved beyond the corporation's visibility, control, and liability. Massive wealth was generated by these activities, but with that extreme wealth came investors, regulators, and public demand for more accountability.

The Emergence of a New Corporate Order

The last several decades have witnessed three core converging trends that have reshaped corporate governance. Corporate profitability has reached historically unprecedented levels. Globalization has driven extreme outsourcing trends that have allowed corporations to gain access to very low-cost labor, while decoupling

5. The United Nations Office of the High Commissioner for Human Rights (OHCHR), Assessment of human rights concerns in the Xinjiang Uyghur Autonomous Region, People's Republic of China (Aug. 31, 2022) (the report concluded that "serious human rights violations have been committed," including "arbitrary and discriminatory detention of members of Uyghur and other predominantly Muslim groups," which it asserted "may constitute international crimes, in particular crimes against humanity").

6. See *Creation of the Bretton Wood System*, Federal Reserve History, https://www.federalreservehistory.org/essays/bretton-woods-created.

7. Travis Miller, Guide to Supply Chain Compliance Law and Regulations (2021).

manufacturing benefits and harms from Western consumers. Risks of non-financial concerns have entered both investor and consumer decision-making processes. Independently, each of these movements has reshaped the global business environment. However, the convergence of profitability, values/risks tied to outsourcing/globalization, and the global demand for business to consider non-financial concerns represent the most dynamic change in corporate ethos in lifetimes. The premise of this book is that the ESG movement is representative of a collective effort to rebalance the circle and quantify an approach to these non-financial considerations, such as carbon-costs into the business calculus.

This culmination of these experiences and shared history has led us to the modern context of the ESG movement that drives the purpose and relevance of this book. With increasing frequency, it seems, the Next Big Thing arrives on the global financial landscape attracting both avid proponents and fierce critics. Blockchain and Bitcoin were good examples, their benefits often touted as transformational, and their value skeptical mocked. Blockchain was introduced more than a dozen years ago, and its applications continue to evolve and improve. New innovation leveraging this technology has been nothing short of extraordinary and has drawn attention and investment globally. However, detractors frequently cite its lack of tangible broad-based value or application, claiming the application has shown no sustainable value creation capabilities to date.

Similarly, ESG falls within this theme of new ideas that has been championed by global finance, Larry Fink, specifically. ESG has the potential to vastly improve transparency in accounting, mitigate risks, and identify unique business opportunities. In today's environment, true transparency is no longer just about financial reporting; it now requires a broader disclosure of the ethical and sustainability costs included in the calculus. Impressive profits can be seen as tainted if they are produced by destroying a rainforest or violating the rights of indigenous people. At its core, ESG is about such non-financial measures and the inevitable non-financial risks embedded in these types of activities. As a result, companies that incorporate, adequately address, and mitigate such non-financial risks perform better and avoid financial concerns better than inferior peers.[8]

The specific objectives of ESG are diverse and can include reducing the emissions of carbon and toxic chemicals, avoiding human-rights abuses, and promoting fair labor practices. Within the organization, ESG is also intended to address diverse societal ills, such as issues of diversity and inclusion representation in the companies themselves. Corporations have been asked to self-reflect on difficult questions, such as "Why do only white men sit on our board of directors?" or "Is there room for diversity and inclusion?" Ideally, ESG measurements should extend to every aspect of a company, including its entire supply chain. In many ways, ESG is not dissimilar to the Enterprise Risk Management initiatives, which were introduced after the 2002 Sarbanes–Oxley legislation was passed. Both initiatives seek to identify and mitigate unreported non-financial risks to protect investors from absent or inadequate financial reporting by corporations.

8. *ESG Ratings*, MSCI, https://www.msci.com/our-solutions/esg-investing/esg-ratings.

ESG can also kick-start conversations about a company's sustainability and circular economy objectives. Its underlying philosophy is that investors, rather than simply looking for short-term profit returns, desire a long-term relationship with companies in their portfolios.

For many people and entities (consumers, investment firms, nongovernmental organizations [NGOs], and governments), the ESG agenda has become essential to doing business in the modern world. It allows companies to mitigate their negative impacts, while tracking their improvements through qualitative and quantitative measures. The largest institutional investors see these factors as compelling drivers that avoid the risk of major lawsuits against corporations within their portfolios and increase earnings through positive activities such as reducing global carbon emissions.[9] In recent years, we have seen that disparate sentiments related to socially advantageous investing create a global trade fracture into "values-based" trading zones. This means that for both companies and their investors, choices and practices should now be able to withstand scrutiny by stakeholders in diverse geographies. Naturally, for businesses, there is a certain element of self-interest in these ethical measures. While some may genuinely care about sustainability for its own sake, for instance, others may be concerned only with the improved financial performance it brings. More calculating companies just want to meet minimum sustainability standards, so they can avoid being dropped from an ESG ranking or index and receive the associated negative press. Yet, regardless of the motivation, ESG programs have emerged and will remain a driving force within corporations for decades to come.

Critics frequently cite that ESG is merely perfunctory, lacking real commitment to meaningful long-term sustainability. There are valid claims that different companies and industries have taken the liberty to cherry-pick from a wide assortment of standards and protocols. Generally, this decoupling of material non-financial risks from disclosures of social good is defined as greenwashing.[10] Moreover, since ESG-related activities have historically been voluntary, with no checks on veracity, the results are virtually impossible to compare across industries. The financial world has got used to the convenience of being able to make these global profitability and growth comparisons; so, the current ESG situation—a bewildering, inconsistent collection of changing parameters—seems like relative chaos. As a result, attempts by analysts and researchers to compare measurements of environmental impacts and its benefits can be dubious.

Rating agencies have attempted to mitigate the lack of standardization. However, the associated ranking system, published by a wide array of rating agencies, also has generated its share of grievances. Many companies, particularly those with inferior ratings, have become upset by the seemingly arbitrary

---

9. See ESG and Responsible Institutional Investing around the World, Pedro Matos, Research Foundation Literature Review (2020).

10. Statement on Environmental, Social, and Governance Disclosures for Investment Advisers and Investment Companies, SEC Comm'n Hester Peirce. (May 25, 2022). ("A key impetus for today's rulemaking is a legitimate concern about the practice of greenwashing by investment advisers and investment companies. This concern is real because advisers can mint money by calling their products and services "green" without doing anything special to justify that label.")

nature of the measures used, or by the fact that they are being ranked at all. They point out that the information about them that is used is simplistic at best or nonexistent at worst. Other companies argue that because many ESG measures are inappropriate for their particular situation, the rating agencies are giving the public misleading information about their negative environmental impacts. Overall, though, most companies have begun to take ESG seriously and are devoting some thought to their ESG programs—even if these are only modest ones.

Within each industry, ESG spans a broad set of themes, topics, and values. As mentioned earlier, one of the most important is decarbonization. The harsh realities of climate change demand action on that issue sooner rather than later and, as a result, have gained increased scrutiny by regulatory authorities. But every company, in every industry, must decide for itself which issues are most material to its own ESG progress. Such an assessment is one of the most crucial first steps in coming to terms with ESG. This fact is why a one-size-fits-all metric, produced by a rating agency, so often evokes the ire of those who have scored poorly. Relevance matters.

The Need for a Business Centric Approach to ESG

Corporate leaders face conflicting signals on the need for ESG reporting. A backlash against ESG investing has arrived, with claims ranging from political to fraudulent in nature. While more scrutiny of ESG claims is likely needed, a business-centric approach will be needed to rise to the challenges and opportunities. Effective ESG programs require more than just a policy. Businesses must utilize process-oriented output measures that can be adequately tracked and managed through qualitative and quantitative data. ESG issues are material to corporate resiliency and competitiveness today. In fact, *Harvard Business Review* has written extensively on this topic and finds that "the return on sustainability investment (ROSI), has demonstrated that embedding sustainability core to business strategy can create a competitive moat for business leaders by driving operational efficiency, innovation, employee engagement, supply-chain resilience, risk mitigation, improved sales, and other strategic business benefits."[11]

Unsurprisingly, certain industries are inherently better placed than others to perform well on ESG scores. Any extractive company, for instance, whose business is based on fossil fuels or mining should theoretically have a harder time achieving superior ESG performance rankings. Therefore, programs must be adaptable to the unique business and industry vertical being assessed. However, adaptability does not negate the need for standards and a standardized process to evaluate non-financial risk. Accordingly, business must look at norms of practice that are familiar to detect non-financial risk and to quantify what those risks and opportunities are. While there are a plethora of consultancies, advisors, and firms seeking to give advice, the fundamental processes to identify

11. Tensie Whelan, *ESG Reports Aren't a Replacement for Real Sustainability,* Harv. Bus. Rev. (July 27, 2022), https://hbr.org/2022/07/esg-reports-arent-a-replacement-for-real-sustainability.

key performance indicators (KPIs) and material concerns should not be seen as novel. Rather, corporations should relate back to base well-defined approaches that have created the durable organizational structure responsible for organizations like Kongō Gumi that have sustained for 2,500 years and counting. After all, the purpose of the corporation is and always will be to sustain: to keep something in operation; maintain, which is pragmatically directly in alignment with the goals and purpose of ESG.

An initial approach should be to benchmark against industry standardized frameworks such as the Sustainability Accounting Standards Board (SASB), the Global Reporting Initiative (GRI), Committee of Sponsoring Organizations (COSO) ESG Framework, and Task Force on Climate-Related Financial Disclosures (TCFD). Once these broad trends are established, the focus must shift to business risks and opportunities embedded in ESG. Generally, these risks are captured in a Pestle analysis that quantifies the material concerns a business will face from *P*olitical, *E*conomic, *S*ocial, *T*echnological, *L*egal, and *E*nvironmental factors. Leveraging these two standardized business methodologies creates the opportunity to perform a comparative analysis of the organizations' Strengths, Weaknesses, Opportunities, and Threats (SWOT) in relation to its peers. This analysis methodology then leverages the ability for the business to establish the most meaningful KPIs. While nothing in this approach is novel, many fail to consider and implement, it which is precisely the reason why ESG and the associated management of non-financial risk has emerged as a major management imperative.

Defining, explaining, and supporting the implementation of this business-centric approach to ESG is the core purpose of this book. The authors set up to develop a guide to mitigating legal claims of greenwashing and outright fraud, while supporting executives' decisions on where to invest time, attention, and resources in the context of ESG. Through the chapters that follow, the book's authors will identify and support the readers' ability to action critical ESG risks that investors and disparate stakeholder groups consider consequential. The journey will be challenging, transformational change always is. However, the creation of a more sustainable corporation that is less reliant on unsustainable practices and suppliers and less prone to non-financial risks is critical in a rapidly changing world and marketplace. It is our hope that this book can support you in this effort by filling a major void in existing legal and business literature and providing a powerful tool for engaging in this important endeavor.

As we embark on this polemic, the winds of economic change are blowing fiercely. With a coincident war on freedom and inflation, turbulent times have distracted the best laid business plans and priorities for rebalancing purpose and profit toward a more sustainable society. As we reach deeply into the rational and roadway ahead, we must acknowledge that business is a constant evolution of existential threats, market opportunities, and competitive dynamics. No management or investor is immune to the chaotic convergence of economic, social, geopolitical, technological, and environmental impacts buffeting the business. Fluid intelligence, granite confidence, and expansive empathy must always inform the best short-, medium-, and long-term decisions for the sustainability of the enterprise in the ever-changing context.

CHAPTER 1

Defining Environmental, Social, and Governance

Todd Cort

Definitional Confusion

Environmental, social, and governance (ESG) is relatively simple to define in principle, and yet it is confounding that consensus has proven impossible to date. The Yale Center for Business and Environment published a simple definition of ESG for practitioners[1] as "ESG (Environmental, Social, Governance) refers to the criteria that investors use to assess risks and opportunities relating to a company's environmental impact, social responsibility, and corporate governance." This definition points to several key features that are generally agreed upon in the academic and practitioner literature. First, ESG is predominantly about the priorities of investors. Second, these investors are assessing concepts of environmental impact, social responsibility, and corporate governance when looking at risks and opportunities. Finally, ESG refers to criteria for making decisions, rather than a prescribed set of topic areas.

While simple in verbiage, this definition may only confuse a stakeholder trying to organize or install a boundary on what information is or is not "ESG." This confusion can be seen in headlines around the world. Take, for example, the vilification of ESG in politics. In 2022, the legislatures and/or State Treasurers of twenty-four predominantly conservative states in the United States banned the consideration of ESG information in investment decision-making for state employee retirement funds.[2] The premise of these bans was nominal because the ESG information is not material to financial performance. Therefore, the

1. Yale Center for Business and Environment. (N.d.). *Beyond the Buzzwords: ESG*, Oct. 31, 2022, https://www.beyond-buzzwords.com/esg.

2. Eugene Grygo (2022). *24 States Forbid ESG Investing via Public Pension Funds*. FINANCIAL TECHNOLOGIES FORUM, Sept. 16, https://www.ftfnews.com/24-states-forbid-esg-investing-via-public-pension-funds/31809/.

consideration of ESG information by a fund manager would be counter to their fiduciary duty, making it illegal under securities law.

Simultaneously, activists have decried ESG as greenwashing by asset managers.[3] The premise of this complaint is that asset managers have never changed their fundamental drive to maximize shareholder returns and that consideration of ESG was merely a smoke screen to distract a rising number of concerned people away from the fact that finance was still "business as usual." Under this accusation, the benefit to the environment or society was never considered as a material factor in investment decision-making.

These two views are irreconcilable as one is premised on the idea that ESG is financially immaterial and inappropriately being considered in investing, while the other that ESG is financially material but is being ignored in investing. These two views can only exist when the definition of ESG is still under debate.

We see a similar state of debate when looking at what topic areas are included under the umbrella of ESG. Take the case of two of the predominant standards in ESG disclosure: the Global Reporting Initiative (GRI) and the Sustainability Accounting Standards Board (SASB)—now the Value Reporting Foundation (VRF). Both standards proport to provide a list of potentially material ESG issue areas for companies and both list the investment community as a key stakeholder in defining what ESG issues are material. While these standards largely agree, key issue areas are nominated as potentially material in one, but not the other. According to GRI, the telecommunications sector should consider accessibility of technology and services as a potentially material social aspect of performance.[4] SASB, however, does not nominate accessibility of telecommunications projects as material to the sector.[5] Looking wider, there is enormous discrepancy on what topic areas are included by which standard, rating, ranking system, analyst, award scheme, and reporting frameworks.

Reconciling which topic areas are included by different standards frequently comes down to understanding what is meant by "financially material." A financially material ESG topic area would be one that has impact on the financial performance of the investment or asset. However, a quick analysis reveals that the understanding of financially material depends on the values, scope, and boundaries set by the user. An investor focused on short-term financial performance, for example, may seek out only those ESG factors that have direct and demonstrable causal relationship with financial performance (such as cost savings from energy efficiency). Another investor may look at ESG factors that might be financially material over the longer term and subject to more confounding factors such as the impact of climate change on business operations through

3. Silvia Amaro. *Blackrock's Former Sustainable Investing Chief Now Thinks ESG Is a "Dangerous Placebo,"* CNBC, (Aug. 24, 2021) https://www.cnbc.com/2021/08/24/blackrocks-former-sustainable-investing-chief-says-esg-is-a-dangerous-placebo.html.

4. *GRI Telecommunications Sector Supplement.* Global Reporting Initiative. (2003). https://static1.squarespace.com/static/59dc930532601e9d148e3c25/t/59f8421e1095266e672d1851/1509442080117/gri_telecom-supplement-july-2003.pdf.

5. *Materiality Map*, Sustainability Accounting Standards Board. (N.d.). (Oct. 31, 2022), http://sasb.s3-website-us-east-1.amazonaws.com.

severe weather frequency. Finally, a third investor may look at the importance of biodiversity globally in stabilizing economies and see ecosystem protection as financially material to an individual company even though the internalization of costs from ecosystem degradation on one company would be very difficult to establish.

So, while drafting a definition for ESG is straightforward, the reality is that the definition of ESG depends on the user. Different stakeholders use the term to mean significantly different things, with significantly different objectives and a wide range of different topic areas, indicators, metrics, and criteria.

The Rise of Standards

This definitional confusion and variety of use cases has spawned a proliferation of ESG questionnaires and third-party ESG rating systems that now numbers in the hundreds.[6] While this proliferation of ESG rating services and data providers has increased the number of ESG metrics available in the investment marketplace, it has not necessarily improved the quality of the data or the comparability of the metrics across companies. A 2018 State Street study of ESG data providers observed that "there is increasingly more ESG data available today, [but] the lack of standardization poses a real challenge for investment managers. Because disclosure on ESG metrics has not been required historically, significant variation exists across the methods used by the leading ESG data providers."[7]

In the face of an expanding universe of ESG metrics and indicators, a number of voluntary disclosure standards have emerged that attempt to consolidate the space around the most material ESG factors. Given that ESG is predominantly driven by investor interests, these standards look increasingly to consolidate around the most financially material factors to satisfy investors' demand for ESG information.

Global Reporting Initiative (GRI)

The Amsterdam-based GRI was formed in 1997 to help companies and governments better understand and communicate their impact on sustainability issues such as climate change, human rights, governance, and social well-being.[8] The GRI should be credited with providing the first substantial framework for sustainability reporting. To this day, GRI has a broad reach across reporting companies and is leveraged extensively for annual corporate social responsibility reports.

---

6. Christina Wong et al. *Rate the Raters 2019, Expert Views on ESG Ratings*. SustainAbility, (2019) https://www.sustainability.com/thinking/rate-raters-2019/.

7. Jennifer Bender et al. *A Blueprint for Integrating ESG into Equity Portfolios*. 16 J INVEST MANAG. (2018). https://papers.ssrn.com/sol3/papers.cfm?abstract_id=3080381.

8. *About GRI*, Global Reporting Initiative (2020), https://www.globalreporting.org/Information/about-gri/Pages/default.aspx.

Task Force on Climate-Related Financial Disclosures (TCFD)

The Financial Stability Board formed the Task Force on Climate-related Financial Disclosures (TCFD) in 2015 to develop a consistent framework for companies to use in making voluntary climate-related financial disclosures for investors, lenders, and other stakeholders.[9] The TCFD's recommendations provide a useful structure to help companies build strategies to manage and report on the effects of climate change and therefore a useful set of topics that could be material based on the financial risks and opportunities posed by climate change. They articulate an important framework that has been adopted broadly, including by many of the signatories to the UN Principles for Responsible Investment.[10]

The TCFD's recommendations do not, however, prescribe specific reporting standards or metrics and therefore might not elicit disclosures that would enable direct comparisons across companies. The failure to specify a core set of climate change metrics and to mandate reporting methodologies limits the TCFD's value as a tool to adequately define climate aspects under the umbrella of ESG.

Sustainability Accounting Standards Board

The Sustainable Accounting Standards Board (SASB) was formed to help businesses to identify, manage, and report on the sustainability topics that are most important to investors.[11] SASB produced a set of seventy-seven industry-specific standards that target the ESG issues that generally are most financially material within an industry. The list of topic areas was determined through interviews of stakeholders and therefore is based on consensus opinion rather than empirical evidence. SASB has evolved into VRF to provide a more global perspective on ESG and to expand its assessment of materiality to include aspects of multi-capitals.

The SASB standards have become one of the dominant standards in ESG because of its historic focus on materiality to investors, and a number of ESG ratings and rankings refer to the SASB standards to define what topic areas are included in an ESG assessment. In addition, a number of commenters, including SASB officials themselves, have proposed that the SEC adopt the SASB standards in its disclosure requirements.

United Nations Sustainable Development Goals

As part of its 2030 Agenda for Sustainable Development, the United Nations adopted seventeen Sustainable Development Goals (SDGs) made specific through 169 defined policy targets.[12] The goals "recognize that ending poverty and other

9. *About the Task Force,* Task Force on Climate Related Financial Disclosures (2020), https://www.fsb-tcfd.org/about/.

10. Andy Green & Andrew Schwartz, *Corporate Long-Termism, Transparency, and the Public Interest.* Center for American Progress (Oct. 2018).

11. Sustainability Accounting Standards Board. (2018). https://www.sasb.org/.

12. *Sustainable Development Goals,* United Nations (2020), https://unstats.un.org/sdgs/.

deprivations must go hand-in-hand with strategies that improve health and education, reduce inequality, and spur economic growth—all while tackling climate change and working to preserve our oceans and forests."[13] Because the SDGs outline the greatest needs for society and the environment, they create a good road map for what topic areas might fit under the umbrella of ESG. However, unlike SASB or TCFD, the SDGs were not created with a lens on financial materiality. The SDGs therefore represent a very broad perspective on what topic areas might be included in ESG. Also, the UN SDG framework does not include any reporting requirements or metrics for companies. As such, the SDGs do not answer the need for a common reporting framework.

Edging toward a Common Definition of ESG

In response to this fragmented ESG landscape, a number of initiatives have launched with the goal of arriving at a consensus view on what is, and is not, included in ESG. The International Business Council of the World Economic Forum (WEF)[14] developed a common sustainability reporting framework designed to promote consistent corporate disclosure of ESG information. It specifically proposed the adoption of two sets of metrics drawn from existing frameworks, including SASB, GRI, TCFD, and the CDP (Carbon Disclosure Project). The core metrics are a set of twenty-two mostly quantitative measures in four categories: governance, planet, people, and prosperity. The proposed "expanded metrics" encourage reporting companies to provide further company-specific disclosure encompassing the entity's broader value chain and impacts.[15]

The WEF is not alone in trying to harmonize the topic issues included under the ESG banner on behalf of companies and investors. In April 2020, the International Organization of Securities Commissions (IOSCO) published a report designed to "help achieve a degree of international consistency and harmonization, thereby assisting investors and issuers with the cross-border and global nature of sustainable instruments."[16] Other efforts have also been created or drafted by the International Monetary Fund (IMF)[17] and CFA Institute.[18]

Most recently, the Carbon Disclosure Standards Board, GRI, CDP, International Integrated Reporting Council, and SASB collaborated to form the

---

13. *The 17 Goals.* United Nations Department of Economic and Social Affairs. (2020). https://sustainabledevelopment.un.org/?menu=1300.

14. *Toward Common Metrics and Consistent Reporting of Sustainable Value Creation.* World Economic Forum. (2021). https://www.weforum.org/stakeholdercapitalism.

15. *Toward Common Metrics and Consistent Reporting of Sustainable Value Creation.* World Economic Forum. (2020). http://www3.weforum.org/docs/WEF_IBC_ESG_Metrics_Discussion_Paper.pdf.

16. *Sustainable Finance and the Role of Securities Regulators and IOSCO.* International Organization of Securities Commission. (April 2020). https://www.iosco.org/library/pubdocs/pdf/IOSCOPD652.pdf.

17. International Monetary Fund, *Climate Change: Physical Risks and Equity Prices in* Global Financial Stability Report: Markets in the Time of COVID-19 (Apr. 2020), https://www.imf.org/en/Publications/GFSR/Issues/2020/04/14/global-financial-stability-report-april-2020#Chapter5.

18. *CFA Institute Publishes Consultation Paper on ESG Disclosure Standards for Investment Products.* CFA Institute. (Aug. 19, 2020). https://www.cfainstitute.org/en/about/press-releases/2020/cfa-institute-publishes-consultation-paper.

International Sustainability Standards Board (ISSB) under the auspices of the International Financial Reporting Standards Foundation. The group issued a draft exposure standard in early 2022.[19] The ISSB standard has gained considerable traction among investors and EU regulators due to its emphasis on financial disclosure practices even though the standard is still in development.

Defining ESG Today

In the absence of a de facto standard for ESG reporting, the definition of ESG remains somewhat elusive. However, a practical definition is possible that, while not universal to different users and stakeholders, likely meets the needs of the majority:

> ESG refers to a set of environmental, social and governance topics (and associated metrics) that are material to companies and investors. Many, but not all, ESG topics will bear a direct or indirect relationship with financial performance of the company or investor. While the list of topics will depend on the operating realities as well as the values of the individual company or investor, the potential topics are well represented by reporting standards such as the Global Reporting Initiative and Sustainability Standards Accounting Board/Value Reporting Foundation and include areas such as climate change, ecosystem protection, emissions, health and safety, human and labor rights, diversity and inclusion, privacy, product responsibility, ethics and corruption.

The precise definition of ESG will depend on the company or investor that is seeking to understand material risks and opportunities. Indeed, the major standards dictate that companies would assess this materiality themselves before deciding what topics should and should not be considered with ESG. Therefore, it is incumbent on the company and its advisors to understand not only what ESG issues are material, but why these ESG issues are considered to be material.

Leveraging Existing Business Processes to Navigate the Maze

An emerging approach to navigating this maze of disparate ESG standards, regulations, and requirements has been put forward by Tensie Whelan that is logical and pragmatic.[20] Whelan suggests that companies should use their initial

---

19. *Exposure Draft and Comment Letters: General Sustainability-Related Disclosures*. International Financial Reporting Standards Foundation. (2022). https://www.ifrs.org/projects/work-plan/general-sustainability-related-disclosures/exposure-draft-and-comment-letters/.

20. Tensie Whelan, *ESG Reports Aren't a Replacement for Real Sustainability*, Harv. Bus. Rev. (July 27, 2022).

and ongoing materiality assessments to perform a Pestle analysis that takes into account impactful reporting standards, disclosure laws, and stakeholder needs.[21] This approach leaves stakeholders with a model that considers the Political, Economic, Social, Technological, Legal, and Environmental concerns that threaten the prosperity and business continuity of the user. This model closely resembles the ISO 14001 and 9001 standards that are well established in manufacturing businesses.[22] Specifically, it supports the establishment of a legal registry of material ESG concerns that both identify applicability to the business and relevancy to business operations and stakeholders. From a practical perspective, this model seems to articulate a common approach to one of the most difficult challenges posed by ESG to the practitioner—getting started and articulating the concerns to management is a coherent process-based way.

Political

A political ESG concern relates to the specific geographies where a company has operations and/or business dealings. Political concerns dictate what activities a company can do to remain within the good graces of lawmakers in the countries where the company operates. The associated business risk to not considering this non-financial impact is being targeted by these political elites in a similar fashion to how Disney has been impacted by Governor Ron DeSantis' political positions.[23]

Economic

An economic ESG concern relates to a macro- or microeconomic factor that is beyond an individual companies' control that may impact a company in a way that is not described in its traditional financial filings. For example, the Russian war against Ukraine and the uncertainty related to the degree to which the EU will be impacted by energy has caused the Euro to fall to its lowest level against the U.S. dollar is recent history.[24] These market exchange factors may either benefit positively or negatively a company based upon how it receives payments from its customers. Moreover, these types of macroeconomic issues are frequently not reported in financial disclosures.

Social

Human perception of brands can have enormous impact on the likelihood the customers will purchase a company's products. These impacts are often very visible in either a positive or negative way, for example, the value generated by Nike's

21. Francis Aguilar, Scanning the Business Environment (1967).

22. Ruth Hillary, ISO 14001: Case Studies and Practical Experience (2017).

23. Michael Kranish, *How DeSantis Used Disney's Missteps to Wage War on Corporate America* Wash. Post (Oct. 19, 2022).

24. Megan Cerullo, *Euro Drops to 20-Year Low, Falling below a Dollar* Money Watch, (Sept. 5, 2022).

Colin Kaepernick advertising campaign[25] versus the lawsuits and press against Chevron associated with polluting Amazon tribe's land during exploration for oil.[26] These social pressures have quantifiable impacts on revenue and returns to investors, yet they frequently are not disclosed in any detail in financial disclosures. Consequently, non-financial disclosures and ESG are a natural place for investors to turn to understand a company's strategies and approach to mitigating the associated impacts.

Technology

All companies are currently in the middle of a global digital transformation that is requiring the adoption and reconsideration of technology. These concerns range from privacy to security laws that can impact core business functions like storing prospect and customer personal identifiable information to cookies present in Google Analytics.[27] The wide range of hacking, zero-day exploits, and privacy laws only furthers the need to consider a company's relationship with technology and articulate its steps and strategies to manage both the risks and opportunities posed by its efforts.

Legal

Laws are the gateway to market access. A company that does not follow the law of the country where it sells its products or services will eventually not be able to sell its products. Whether the laws prohibit the import of goods from China's Xinjiang region due to forced labor concerns[28] or eliminate the use of toxic substance in goods,[29] these non-financial concerns are critical to a company's ability to sell products. However, the multitier supply chains and difficulty in identifying indirect impacts often result in efforts and concerns not being adequately disclosed to investors via traditional financial mechanisms.

Environmental

Climate change, chemicals, and waste will likely prove to be the dominant risks to human society over the next several decades. Companies will be regulated by the laws that emerge to drive and influence behavior for decades to come. However, a qualitative and quantitative analysis of these impacts requires an in-depth analysis of operations, impacts, and stakeholders that does not fit within traditional

25. Angelico LaVito, *Nike's Colin Kaepernick Ads Created $163.5 Million in Buzz Since It Began* CNBC, (Sept. 16, 2018).

26. Rex Weyler, *Steven Donziger: The Man Who Stood Up to an Oil Giant and Paid the Price,* GREENPEACE (Feb. 26, 2020) (discussion of history of the $9.6 billion judgment against Chevron).

27. Decision of the Austrian Data Protection Authority (DPA) of 22 (Dec. 2021).

28. Uyghur Forced Labor Prevention Act (UFLPA) was signed into law by President Biden on Dec. 23, 2021.

29. The Toxic Substances Control Act (15 U.S.C. 2601–2692) consists of Public Law 94-469 (Oct. 11, 1976; 90 Stat. 2003) and the amendments made by subsequent enactments.

financial disclosures. As has been described in the above, many standards seek to provide frameworks, but only the business can know its true impact. Moreover, only the business can position itself proactively to avoid becoming the next case study in environmental disaster like the Exxon Valdez or BP oil spill.[30]

Once a Pestle analysis is complete, the next step in a materiality assessment is to prioritize what needs to be done first. An analysis of the Strengths, Weaknesses, Opportunities, and Threats (SWOT) can be leveraged to benchmark against peers and assess the non-financial risks posed by internal and external impacts. A well-structured ESG program must consider both the strengths and weaknesses of internal programs, as well as the opportunities and threats posed by external factors that influence the company's existence. This analysis requires quantifiable and qualitative data that align to the core and critical non-financial concerns identified from a materiality assessment. These data must be aligned and measured against key performance indicators (KPIs) that will meet the disclosure needs of the company and its core stakeholders.

In this context, a strength should be considered an area where a company's internal program excels, whereas a weakness is an area where a company's external program lacks in comparison to its peer group/competitors. In contrast, an opportunity is an area where a company's third-party (suppliers and indirect partners) programs excel, whereas a risk represents an area where those third-party programs lag compared to peers and competitors. This approach is practical, familiar, and adaptive to businesses. Moreover, the approach allows ESG practitioners to both describe their approach to management and defend what they quantified as material and worthy of evaluation and disclosure.

30. Duane A. Gill et al., *The Exxon Valdez and BP Oil Spills: A Comparison of Initial Social and Psychological Impacts*, 56 Am. Behav. Sci. (Aug. 5, 2011).

CHAPTER 2

Drivers behind the Environmental, Social, Governance Movement

Todd Cort and Travis Miller

ESG reporting will impact all companies in some manner over the course of the next several decades.[1] Despite the ubiquitous requirement to perform a materiality assessment, identify concerns, and disclose, it seems to be true that no two companies see the issues in precisely the same way. This paradox means that ESG disclosure requires a mix of standardized strategies and customized responses to meaningful business questions that offer investors and interested parties the ability to compare often dissimilar companies. Coupled with growing consumer and business customer interest, ESG efforts have adapted to a series of mega-trends that are changing the culture within businesses.

Standardizing Sustainability Reporting

Research on sustainability reports by standards organizations such as the Global Reporting Initiative (GRI) and World Business Council for Sustainable Development (WBCSD) indicates that companies generally report on a common broad set of issues. These commonly reported issues include greenhouse gas (GHG) emissions, water consumption, employee health and safety, and diversity, but the data lack comparability because the reports use different measurement and reporting methodologies.[2] As a result, corporate reports use

1. See Larry Fink, *The Power of Capitalism: Larry Fink's 2022 Letter to CEOs*, BLACKROCK (2022).

2. World Business Council for Sustainable Development. *Reporting Matters: Navigating the Landscape: A Path Forward for Sustainability Reporting.* (2019). https://www.wbcsd.org/Programs/Redefining-Value/External-Disclosure/Reporting-matters/Resources/Reporting-matters-2019; *About Sustainability Reporting.* Global Reporting Initiative. (2020). https://www.globalreporting.org/information/sustainability-reporting/Pages/default.aspx.

different definitions, scopes, units of measurement, measurement time frames, and other methodological elements. For example, while most companies report on employee health and safety, some report the number of sick days, while others report the number of injuries, number of accidents, time lost due to injury, or number of fatalities.[3] The same disparities in reporting methodology are found in the reporting of environmental data and, specifically, carbon accounting.[4]

Investors and non-financial data consumers are demanding consistency and comparability in the data tracked. However, companies are faced with the reality that reporting frameworks alone are imperfect vehicles for denoting important differences among companies. Accordingly, a professional group of consultants, attorneys, and marketing professionals has emerged to provide a tailored narrative about a company's unique context. For exactly these reasons, applying an appropriate framework is challenging, not only for companies but also for data aggregators, regulators, and investors. To manage the variability, a business must select a reporting framework that recognizes the need for (1) a "core" set of ESG metrics that apply to all companies, (2) a structure of industry-defined metrics that would be common to all companies within a sector, and (3) a platform for company-specific disclosures.

A Rethinking of Globalization Is Underway

The term "globalization" has only become commonplace over the last few decades.[5] The practice itself can best be described as a rapid expansion of outsourcing and the economic advantage of producing products to low-cost countries. Outsourced business practices generally involved the most regulated, least profitable, and most dangerous activities.[6] The consequence of this phenomenon has been the displacement of the Western manufacturing base to countries with a lower cost of labor and per unit production. More recently, regulation has reshaped to focus on product stewardship, the importation of goods, and

3. We conducted a study in 2018 comparing the sustainability reports of forty-eight large food and beverage firms. These reports used at least seven different metrics relative to health and safety, and five different methodologies to calculate turnover. When reporting on employee well-being, fifteen of the forty-eight firms addressed employee satisfaction, ten addressed turnover, and forty-five addressed employee training.

4. As for environmental metrics, the European Securities Market Association reviewed 937 sustainability statements and found, "Among the more frequently disclosed KPIs of a more general relevance were electricity consumption, water consumption, carbon/CO_2/greenhouse gas emissions, waste emissions and noise emissions. Whereas these KPIs were quite common among issuers in the sample, ESMA observes that issuers used a variety of measurements (e.g. CO_2 emissions were disclosed in terms of total emissions, total emissions at constant production, emissions per ton of production, tons of emissions per production hour and emission intensity ratio). While ESMA acknowledges that metrics will vary to a certain extent according to industry and sector, the plethora of metrics does somewhat hamper comparability across issuers." See European Securities and Markets Authority. *Report: Enforcement and Regulatory Activities of European Enforcers in 2019* (2020). (ESMA32-63-846). https://www.esma.europa.eu/sites/default/files/library/esma32-63-846_2019_activity_report.pdf.

5. See *Globalization*, Stanford Encyclopedia of Philosophy, http://plato.stanford.edu/entries/globalization/#3.

6. See Travis Miller, *Know Thy Product: The Global Expansion of Product Stewardship Laws' Impact on Environmental Law*. GEO. INT'L. ENV. L. REV. (May 8, 2015).

the behavioral practices performed in the production of goods by suppliers.[7] These regulations have shifted the burden of compliance onto the supply chain and the importer of finished goods. Consequently, companies seeking to import products into regulated markets must maintain complex databases evidencing compliance with the environmental laws that impact the products that will be permitted to enter such markets.

Modern society relies on a complex web of global manufacturing and industrialization processes to make goods. The industrialization tied to outsourcing and globalization has provided the fuel to transform cultures and their economies from agrarian societies to modern economies.[8] These "industrial revolutions" have materialized across many countries and created a divide between economies that have undergone this process, developed economies, and those still undergoing the transition, emerging economies. During the transition, external agents and controlling elites have the ability to rapidly create wealth that leads to a significant wealth gap. These wealth gaps have fueled economic equality movements, the creation of unions, and a greater attention to corporate social responsibility (CSR) that is encapsulated in and underpins the ESG movement.

Management of these escalating risks requires adaptation by industry and well-informed corporate counsel who can respond proactively to these challenges.[9] ESG laws now abound and are focused and targeted at transparency and regulation of products, the production of products, and the policies deployed in the production of products and services. As a result, corporate actors can no longer view CSR programs exclusively through the lens of strategic marketing or public relations programs. Rather, corporations must carefully consider disclosures in respect to the considerations to the legal requirements of environmental, health, safety, sanctions, trade, labor practices, and competing disclosure requirements.[10] To effectively deploy and monitor programs of this nature, counsel requires technology-enabled teams that have sufficient understanding and capability to track, balance, and respond to these competing requirements.

In totality, these regulations have created market forces and legal obligations that frequently demand rapid changes and coordinated efforts from suppliers, contract manufacturers, distributors, logistics providers, customers, and solution providers. In this context, the regulated community is entering the enforcement stage of emerging legal structures that warrant increased attention by counsel and senior executives. As a result, a growing need has emerged to have

---

7. Nicole C. Kibert, *Extended Producer Responsibility: A Tool for Achieving Sustainable Development*, 19 J Land Use 2, 503, 510–11 (Spring 2004).

8. Richard D. Fitzgerald, *The Social Impact of the Industrial Revolution*, Global Issues in Context, http://find.galegroup.com/gic/infomark.do?&idigest=fb720fd31d9036c1ed2d1f3a0500fcc2&type=retrieve&tabID=T001&prodId=GIC&docId=CX3408502115&source=gale&userGroupName=itsbtrial&version=1.0 (last visited Mar. 30, 2016) (providing an overview of NEIL SCHLAGER, SCIENCE AND ITS TIMES: UNDERSTANDING THE SOCIAL SIGNIFICANCE OF SCIENTIFIC DISCOVERY, 378–81 (Josh Lauer, 1st ed. 2000)).

9. Michael R. Harris, *Environmental Deliberative Democracy and the Search for Administrative Legitimacy: A Legal, Positivism Approach*, 44 U. Mich. J.L. Reform 343, 343–82 (2011).

10. Travis Miller, *The Lawyer's Corporate Social Responsibility Deskbook: Practical Guidance for Corporate Counsel and Law Firms* (2019).

internal and external expertise dedicated to the supply chain compliance function within most businesses. These supply chain compliance professionals have emerged over the last decade as a critical component of managing the emerging risks associated with outsourcing and/or globalization strategy. To mitigate risk, companies have attempted to extend and shift the burden of compliance onto the supply chain and the importer of finished goods through warranties, contracts, and/or certifications of compliance. To accomplish this burden shifting, complex databases that can track, evaluate, and disclose due diligence records must be maintained and accessible by key personnel. These databases establish chains of custody and support the identification of where supply chain breakdowns are occurring through systematic record keeping.

The associated process of implementing records systems that allow corporations to evaluate and manage data extends beyond the four corners of the organization. The evaluation of suppliers, business partners, and customers, in turn, has forced corporations to rethink legacy perceptions of what a supply chain network is. The emerging regulatory regimes targeted at product stewardship (Restriction of Hazardous Substances [RoHS][11]; Registration, Evaluation, Authorisation and Restriction of Chemicals [REACH][12]; Conflict Minerals) and the regulation of supply chain disclosures (Uyghur Forced Labor Prevention Act [UFLPA], Federal Trade Commission (FTC) Green Marketing Guide, California Supply Chain Transparency Act) will drive these liabilities.[13] These regulations' end goal is to place the same burden and scrutiny onto the brand owner as exists for domestically produced products. As such, it is both prudent and necessary for corporations to evaluate their manufacturing strategies and conclude whether the associated cost advantages of outsourcing production to other regions outweigh the burdens of the new regulatory demands. It is no longer sufficient to benefit from the value created from globalization. Rather, ESG initiatives demand that trusted networks of suppliers and partners are leveraged that adhere to a consistent system of values and legal principles to access Western markets.

A Global Focus on ESG Risk by Investors

While interest in sustainability issues broadly continues to grow, the urgency around climate change risks and opportunities has rapidly intensified. A 2020 report of the Climate-Related Market Risk Subcommittee, Market Risk Advisory

---

11. Directive 2002/95/EC of the European Parliament and of the Council of Jan. 27, 2003, on the restriction of the use of certain hazardous substances in electrical and electronic equipment, http://eur-lex.europa.eu/legal-content/EN/TXT/?uri=CELEX:32002L0095.

12. Regulation (EC) No. 1907/2006 of the European Parliament and of the Council of December 18, 2006, concerning the Registration, Evaluation, Authorization and Restriction of Chemicals (REACH), establishing a European Chemicals Agency, amending Directive 1999/45/EC and repealing Council Regulation (EEC) No. 793/93 and Commission Regulation (EC) No. 1488/94 as well as Council Directive 76/769/EEC and Commission Directives 91/155/EEC, 93/67/EEC, 93/105/EC, and 2000/21/EC, http://eur-lex.europa.eu/legal-content/EN/TXT/?uri=CELEX:32006R1907.

13. Dion Wiggins & Diane Morello, *Outsourcing Backlash: Globalization in the Knowledge Economy*, Gartner (Jul. 31, 2003).

Committee of the U.S. Commodity Futures Trading Commission (CFTC report) declared that "Climate change poses a major risk to the stability of the U.S. financial system and to its ability to sustain the American economy. Climate change is already impacting or is anticipated to impact nearly every facet of the economy, including infrastructure, agriculture, residential and commercial property, as well as human health and labor productivity."[14] These sentiments have been further reinforced by global consensus among climate scientists that has been a documented, highly detailed warning annually articulated and published by the Intergovernmental Panel on Climate Change (IPCC).[15]

The State Street Global Advisors letter reinforces the growing sentiment in the investment world that ESG issues now matter to many mainstream investors. Bank of America Merrill Lynch issued a report in 2018 noting the expansion of the Bank's focus on ESG issues over the prior several years.[16] The report declared, "ESG is too critical to ignore. Asset potential is substantial: we conservatively estimate that flows into ESG-type funds over the next few decades could be roughly equivalent to the size of the S&P 500 today."[17] The report furthermore drew a correlation between good environmental scores and financial performance, citing a study of S&P 500 companies between 2005 and 2017, which concluded that "ESG is a better signal of earnings risk than any other metric we have found."[18]

A survey by Bloomberg and the Morgan Stanley Institute for Sustainable Investing came to a similar conclusion.[19] Based on written questions and interviews with 300 U.S. asset managers, each with at least $50 million in assets under management, this survey concluded that sustainable investing is "here to stay," with 89 percent of the participants declaring it to be a permanent feature of the investment landscape and 63 percent projecting growth in sustainable investments among asset managers over the next five years.[20] Eighty-two percent of respondents viewed strong ESG performance as central to improved profitability and investment returns.[21] Similarly, Ernst & Young conducted a survey of 260 institutional investors that found a "notable consensus that ESG information is critical to investor decision-making . . . [and] ESG information plays an increasingly important role in the investment decision-making process."[22]

14. *Managing Climate Risk in the U.S. Financial System.* Report of the Climate-Related Market Risk Subcommittee, Market Risk Advisory Committee of the U.S. Commodity Futures Trading Commission. (2020, Sept. 9). https://www.cftc.gov/sites/default/files/2020-09/9-9-20%20Report%20of%20the%20Subcommittee%20on%20Climate-Related%20Market%20Risk%20-%20Managing%20Climate%20Risk%20in%20the%20U.S.%20Financial%20System%20for%20posting.pdf.

15. IPCC 6th Assessment Report. (2022). https://www.ipcc.ch/report/ar6/wg2/.

16. *Environmental, Social & Governance (ESG): The ABCs of ESG.* Bank of America Merrill Lynch. (2018, Sept. 10).

17. *Id.*

18. *Id.*

19. Bloomberg & Morgan Stanley Institute for Sustainable Investing. (2019). *Sustainable Signals: Growth and Opportunity in Asset Management.* https://www.morganstanley.com/assets/pdfs/2415532_Sustainable_Signals_Asset_Manager_2019_L.pdf.

20. *Id.*

21. *Id.*

22. Matthew Nelson. *Does Your Nonfinancial Reporting Tell Your Value Creation Story?* EY. (Nov. 29, 2018). https://www.ey.com/en_gl/assurance/does-nonfinancial-reporting-tell-value-creation-story.

In what might be seen as the strongest signal of the shifting foundations of the investment world and the growing importance of sustainability issues, Larry Fink, CEO of BlackRock, the world's largest asset manager, declared in his 2020 letter to CEOs that "climate change has become a defining factor in companies' long-term prospects" and as a result, we are "on the edge of a fundamental reshaping of finance."[23] Written just prior to the outbreak of the COVID-19 pandemic, Fink went on to say, "The evidence on climate risk is compelling investors to reassess core assumptions about modern finance. Research from a wide range of organizations . . . is deepening our understanding of how climate risk will impact both our physical world and the global system that finances economic growth." Fink emphasized the need for higher quality and more consistent ESG disclosures across companies. He further observed that more expansive sustainability analysis by investors would lead to greater capital allocation to companies that are transparent about their ESG performance and associated strategies.

Investors have taken note of the outperformance by sustainability-focused funds, when compared with their relevant benchmarks.[24] A number of analysts project that ESG-screened funds will continue to outperform their conventional benchmarks and will continue to draw investors looking for long-term outperformance and lower volatility.[25]

In 2022, some backlash emerged to the premises of ESG investing. Specifically, some have pointed to ESG as a violation of fiduciary duty in that it would distract a financial manager from their primary duty of maximizing return.[26] This perception led nineteen State Attorneys-General in 2022 to initiate investigations into fund management firms that used ESG information as part of investment strategies for state pension plans.[27] On the opposite side of the ESG backlash is the idea that ESG funds have over-promised on the beneficial impact to society and the environment that can be achieved. These people argue that ESG investing is merely greenwashed "business as usual."[28] Both of these forms of backlash make the same assumption—that ESG and financial performance are mutually exclusive despite the rising evidence of a relationship. They also highlight the broad range of

23. Larry Fink. (2020, Jan. 28). *A Fundamental Reshaping of Finance.* BlackRock. https://www.blackrock.com/corporate/investor-relations/larry-fink-ceo-letter.

24. Madison Darbyshire, *ESG Funds Continue to Outperform Wider Market,* Fin. Times (April 2, 2020), https://www.ft.com/content/46bb05a9-23b2-4958-888a-c3e614d75199; C. McCabe. (2020, May 12). ESG investing shines in market turmoil, with help from big tech. *The Wall Street Journal.* https://www.wsj.com/articles/esg-investing-shines-in-market-turmoil-with-help-from-big-tech-11589275801?mg=prod/com-wsj.

25. Michael Copley et al. *ESG Funds Remain Relative Safe Havens in Coronavirus Downturn.* S&P Global Market Intelligence. (May 19, 2020). https://www.spglobal.com/marketintelligence/en/news-insights/latest-news-headlines/esg-funds-remain-relative-safe-havens-in-coronavirus-downturn-58679570; Christopher Copper-Ind. *ESG Fund Flows Increase 37-Fold in Three Years: Research.* International Investment. (May 21, 2020). https://www.internationalinvestment.net/news/4015493/esg-fund-flows-increase-fold-research.

26. Jedd Rubenfeld & William P. Barr, *ESG Can't Square with Fiduciary Duty,* Wall St. J. (Sept. 6, 2022), https://www.wsj.com/articles/esg-cant-square-with-fiduciary-duty-blackrock-vanguard-state-stree-the-big-three-violations-china-conflict-of-interest-investors-11662496552.

27. Jacob Hupart. *19 State Attorneys-General Participate in Investigation of ESG Ratings.* Mintz, (Sept. 12, 2022). https://www.jdsupra.com/legalnews/19-state-attorneys-general-participate-2763196/.

28. Hans Taparia, *One of the Hottest Trens in the World of Investing is a Sham,* N.Y. Times (Sept. 29, 2022), https://www.nytimes.com/2022/09/29/opinion/esg-investing-responsibility.html.

investment strategies that fall under the banner of "ESG" which have created confusion in the marketplace to date. They also highlight the need for a more complete understanding of ESG and its relationship to financial performance.

Investors and Customers Want Broader and Deeper ESG Disclosure

While investors' calls for ESG disclosure grow louder, many fund managers and investment advisors express concern that they are not receiving the information that they need from companies. ESG data providers are being asked to incorporate sustainability factors fully into their investment processes.[29] A recent report from the CFTC articulated that "the lack of common definitions and standards for climate-related data and financial products is hindering the ability of market participants and regulators to monitor and manage climate risks. While progress has been made in this area thanks to voluntary disclosure frameworks and work by foreign regulators, the lack of standards, and differences among standards, remains a barrier to effective climate change risk management."[30]

State Street's 2020 letter to directors found that "fewer than 25% of the companies we've evaluated have meaningfully identified, incorporated, and disclosed material ESG issues into their strategies."[31] The WBCSD, a Geneva-based consortium of multinational companies, hosted a series of investor roundtables to understand the information that investors need to properly incorporate companies' ESG performance into their investment processes.[32] Investors want companies to clearly discuss ESG-related risks. Investors are further seeking qualitative and quantitative metrics that demonstrate good governance and effective internal controls that mitigate identified risks.

There is a noted lack of available non-financial information. The associated lack of information has led to a gap in valuation models, due to the lack of comparability of ESG reporting across companies. As a result, investors are calling for standardized narrative explanations that provide context for the provided metrics. Standards organizations have heeded the calls for guidance on standardization. For example, the Carbon Disclosure Standards Board (CDSB), a London-based nonprofit organization, committed to getting companies to provide more climate-change-related information in their ongoing financial reports. The CDSB further found that even companies offering disclosures pursuant to

---

29. Andy Green & Andrew Schwartz. *Corporate Long-Termism, Transparency, and the Public Interest.* Center for American Progress. (Oct. 2018). https://cdn.americanprogress.org/content/uploads/2018/10/01140758/DisclosureReport.pdf.

30. CFTC Report, supra, note 13.

31. Cyrus Taraporevala. *CEO's Letter on Our 2020 Proxy Voting Agenda.* State Street Global Advisors. (Jan. 28, 2020). https://www.ssga.com/us/en/individual/etfs/insights/informing-better-decisions-with-esg.

32. *Enhancing the credibility of non-financial information: The investor perspective.* World Business Council for Sustainable Development and PwC. (2018). https://docs.wbcsd.org/2018/10/WBCSD_Enhancing_Credibility_Report.pdf.

the European Union's Non-Financial Reporting Directive fail to provide investors the information they need to properly evaluate ESG factors. The CDSB report specifically noted, "Substantive improvements are still required in the quality, comparability, and coherence of disclosures in order for the Directive to achieve its objective of providing investors and wider stakeholders with relevant, consistent and decision-useful disclosures."[33]

There is a gap between the corporate sustainability information that investors seek and the information they are receiving. This gap has led to the emergence of ESG-driven activist shareholders who are working to bring new ESG information to the boards of major companies. However, activists typically have their own agendas that do not necessarily support mainstream investors to gain the analytically rigorous ESG data. As a result, the presence and absence of qualitative and quantitative data required to distinguish risks and value differentiation between the sustainability leaders and laggards remain elusive. As the State Street letter noted, activists sometimes "focus on specific or narrow ESG issues in piecemeal fashion—often creating confusion for investors, boards, and company leadership *without fundamentally tackling the ESG issues material to long-term shareholder performance*."[34] Preston goes on to note that what investors really need is "rich contextual information" that highlights true sustainability leaders and ensures "a future where high-quality companies are aligned with planetary and societal needs."

The information gap between investors and companies has also spawned a proliferation of ESG questionnaires and third-party ESG rating systems. The admirable aim of these tools is to provide more robust ESG information to the markets. A report by the U.S. Chamber of Commerce Foundation found that some companies have been asked to complete more than 250 surveys related to their ESG performance, with wildly different criteria. This process has left some companies "dazed and confused" and has required them to dedicate teams of employees to fill out surveys or respond to third parties about ESG matters.[35] There is also significant risk in contradiction, as there now exist more than 600 different ESG ratings that seek to meet investor demand for sustainability information and analyses of companies.[36] Standardization of ratings and consolidation of the ratings market seems far off.

The proliferation of ESG ratings services and data providers has increased the number of ESG metrics available in the investment marketplace. However, it has not necessarily improved the quality of the data or the comparability of the

---

33. *Falling Short? Why Environmental and Climate-Related Disclosures under the EU Non-financial Reporting Directive Must Improve.* Climate Disclosure Standards Board. (2020). https://www.cdsb.net/sites/default/files/falling_short_report_double_page_spread.pdf.

34. Taraporevala, *supra* note 31.

35. *Corporate Sustainability Reporting: Past, Present, Future.* U.S. Chamber of Commerce Foundation. (2018). https://www.uschamberfoundation.org/sites/default/files/Corporate%20Sustainability%20Reporting%20Past%20Present%20Future.pdf.

36. Aiste Brackley et al. *Rating the Raters Yet Again: Increasing ESG Scrutiny Makes Current Rate the Raters Study Even More Crucial.* SustainAbility Institute by ERM. (2022). https://www.sustainability.com/thinking/rating-the-raters-yet-again-increasing-esg-scrutiny-makes-current-rate-the-raters-study-even-more-crucial/.

metrics across companies. The different ratings have been criticized for inconsistency and deeply divergent conclusions as to who the ESG leaders really are. A recent State Street study of ESG data providers observed that "there is increasingly more ESG data available today, [but] the lack of standardization poses a real challenge for investment managers. Because disclosure on ESG metrics has not been required historically, significant variation exists across the methods used by the leading ESG data providers."[37] The U.S. Securities and Exchange Commission (SEC) Chairman Jay Clayton has expressed concern over the quality and reliability of ESG ratings, particularly by ratings providers who combine their analyses of the separate environmental, social and governance factors into one aggregate ESG score that can be "significantly over-inclusive and imprecise."[38]

Investors are drowning in incoherent ESG information that does not tangible relate to core business risks like Total Addressable Market (TAM); Earnings Before Interest, Taxes, Depreciation, and Amortization (EBITA); or Brand Value. As Dan Esty has noted, the ESG metrics available today do not meet investor needs.[39] As he explains, the existing reporting is haphazard with significant methodological inconsistencies across companies. The data aggregators often accept corporate reporting without any attempt to (1) normalize disparate data, (2) investigate or validate the information provided, (3) distinguish between missing data and poor performance, or (4) explain their approaches to filling data gaps. ESG rating agencies regularly assign scores to companies based on their proprietary analysts' subjective judgments in a manner that is neither transparent nor well explained. This lack of consistency creates substantial doubt about whether the existing sustainability scorecards mean. Rather, they have proven highly subjective and seem to lack the qualitative and quantitative metrics requested by investors.

Investors need *high-resolution, current* ESG metrics that (1) offer a perspective on a company's ability to transform its business model in response to the emerging *sustainability imperative*,[40] (2) illuminate the management team's *strategy* for addressing climate change and the emergence of a clean energy economy as well as other sustainability issues, (3) track a company's evolution toward a sustainable future, (4) highlight carbon exposure and the risk that certain lines of revenue or asset values will diminish as market expectations and requirements change, and (5) gauge *green revenue* and a company's capacity to be a *solutions provider* in response to climate change and other sustainability challenges.[41]

---

37. Jennifer Bender et al. A Blueprint for Integrating ESG into Equity Portfolios. 16 J Invest Manag 1. (2018). https://papers.ssrn.com/sol3/papers.cfm?abstract_id=3080381.

38. Jay Clayton. (2020, May 27). *Remarks at Meeting of the Asset Management Advisory Committee.* U.S. Securities and Exchange Commission. https://www.sec.gov/news/public-statement/clayton-amac-opening-2020-05-27.

39. Daniel Esty, *Creating Investment Grade Sustainability Metrics in* Values at Work: Sustainable Investing and ESG Reporting (Daniel Esty and Todd Cort eds., 2020).

40. David A. Lubin & Daniel C. Esty, *The Sustainability Imperative,* Harv. Bus. Rev. (May 2010), https://hbr.org/2010/05/the-sustainability-imperative.

41. Daniel Esty & David Lubin, *Toward a Next Generation of Corporate Sustainability Metrics in* Values at Work: Sustainable Investing and ESG Reporting (Daniel Esty & Todd Cort eds., 2020); David Lubin & Daniel Esty, *Bridging the Sustainability Gap,* MIT Sloan Mgmt. Rev. (June 17, 2014), https://sloanreview.mit.edu/article/bridging-the-sustainability-gap/.

A Company's Value Is Being Tied to Its ESG Program

While there continues to be a lack of methodological consistency in ESG reporting, there is no lack of investments flowing into ESG funds.[42] However, limited validation of the ESG data and critical gaps in the corporate sustainability disclosures are creating a potential significant risk of securities fraud, coined greenwashing. Investor trust in ESG metrics and the associated value of the organizations being funded may well be misplaced. Specifically, if the purpose of the ESG funds is to grant the investor the ability to steer capital toward companies addressing society's sustainability challenges, current disclosure practices are inherently inadequate. Moreover, they will depend on the development of new ESG reporting frameworks that offer investment-grade ESG data. Consequently, this mantra has been the recent drumbeat of the U.S. SEC's guidance concerning materiality. As Commissioner Lee notes in note 19 of her speech, Shelter from the Storm: Helping Investors Navigate Climate Change Risk (Mar. 21, 2022), there could be doubts about the materiality of information, but explaining that, "particularly in view of the prophylactic purpose" of the securities laws, and "the fact that the content" of the disclosure "is within management's control, it is appropriate that these doubts be resolved in favor of those the statute is designed to protect," namely, investors.[43]

Socially responsible investors (SRIs) have long worked to align their portfolios with their *values*. Large pension funds, sovereign wealth, and institutional investors steer clear of owning shares of corporate bad actors, including big polluters. Interest in ESG funds has recently emerged as a trend among a broader group of mainstream equity investors. Some of these *value* investors (defined by the fact that they *do care* about their portfolio returns) want to put their money into sustainability leaders. It has become an expectation that these companies will outperform the market over time. Others simply want to mitigate risk by dumping shares of companies that they fear will underperform in the years ahead as climate change and other sustainability concerns become more salient. Others have elected to invest to support a sustainable future with varying degrees of willingness to have this tilt in their portfolio produce volatility or "tracking error," even if this results in reduced returns compared with benchmark investment vehicles.[44]

Evidence of sustainability's move from the margins of the investment world to the mainstream can be seen in the groundswell of interest in the United Nations Principles for Responsible Investment (UNPRI). This initiative strives to integrate sustainability, including environmental responsibility, into the financial

---

42. Patturaja Murugaboopathy and Anurag Maan. *Global sustainable fund assets hit record $3.9 trillion in Q3, says Morningstar*, Reuters (Oct. 2021), https://www.reuters.com/business/sustainable-business/global-sustainable-fund-assets-hit-record-39-trillion-q3-says-morningstar-2021-10-29/.

43. TSC Industries, Inc. v. Northway, Inc., 426 U.S. 438, 448 (1977).

44. Tracking error (sometimes called "active risk") is defined as the divergence between a particular portfolio and the baseline investment framework against which it is benchmarked.

arena by requiring investors to adopt six guiding principles.[45] In 2016, the UNPRI reported over 1,700 signatories including almost 1,200 investment managers and asset owners representing over $59 trillion in assets under management (up from $4 trillion in 2006).[46] In another gauge of this trend, the Global Sustainable Investment Alliance (GSIA) reported that $6.57 trillion of U.S. assets under management are invested in *sustainable*, *responsible*, or *impact* investment strategies. This total represents an increase of 76 percent since 2012.[47] In a similar vein, the U.S. Forum for Sustainable and Responsible Investment Foundation identified $8.10 trillion in U.S.-domiciled assets that apply various ESG criteria in their investment analysis and portfolio selection.[48] Sustainability in fixed income markets is also growing, including the rise of green bonds[49] and associated standards for labeling.[50]

Thought leaders are adding momentum to mainstream investor interest in sustainability. Michael Bloomberg has regularly called on companies to report more fully on their climate change impacts. Larry Fink, the CEO of BlackRock, the world's largest asset manager, issues a highly disseminated annual letter to corporate leaders arguing for more attention to environmental and social elements of corporate performance. Nevertheless, *sustainable investments* still represent a relatively small percentage of total assets under management. Moreover, a significant percentage of sustainable investments are in narrowly cast SRI negative screened or exclusionary funds. These funds generally only exclude participants who do not meet certain criteria, rather than focus or channel investments toward ESG-promoting initiatives. As a result, only about 10 percent of assets under management in the United States targeted toward more broadly defined sustainable investments.[51]

The focus on sustainable investing thus seems to be more discussion than broad-based action at present. Despite growing *interest* in sustainability, many investors and even more investment advisors remain wary of making sustainability the core factor in portfolio decisions. A BNY (Bank of New York) Mellon survey suggests that investment managers often perceive a trade-off between

45. The Six Principles of Responsible Investing are as follows: (1) We will incorporate ESG issues into *investment analysis* and decision-making processes; (2) we will be active owners and incorporate ESG issues into our ownership policies and practices; (3) we will seek appropriate disclosure on ESG issues by the entities in which we invest; (4) we will promote acceptance and implementation of the principles within the investment industry; (5) we will work together to enhance our effectiveness in implementing the principles; and (6) we will each report on our activities and progress toward implementing the principles. "PRI Six Principles," accessed Jun. 7, 2016, https://www.unpri.org/about/the-six-principles.

46. *Greening Institutional Investment,* UNPRI (2016), https://www.unpri.org/environmental-social-and-governance-issues/greening-institutional-investment/296.article.

47. *2014 Global Sustainable Investment Review,* GSIA (2015), http://www.gsi-alliance.org/wp-content/uploads/2015/02/GSIA_Review_download.pdf.

48. *Report on US Sustainable, Responsible and Impact Investing Trends* 2016, US SIF (2016), https://www.ussif.org/files/SIF_Trends_16_Executive_Summary(1).pdf.

49. TAlbert Desclee et al., *ESG Ratings and Performance of Corporate Bonds,* 26 J. Fix. Inc. 21 (2016).

50. *Green Bond Highlights 2017,* Climate Bonds Initiative (2018), https://www.climatebonds.net/files/reports/cbi-green-bonds-highlights-2017.pdf.

51. *2016 Global Sustainable Investment Review,* GSIA (2017), https://www.ussif.org/files/Publications/GSIA_Review2016.pdf.

ESG emphasis and stock market performance.[52] Our own interviews (discussed below) of participants in various aspects of the sustainable investment world corroborate both *rising interest* in sustainability and *ongoing doubt and uncertainty* among mainstream investors about ESG funds. This tension brings us to the puzzles that lie at the heart of this book. What is ESG? How can diverse businesses be consistently evaluated? What steps should a business and investors take to respond to global concerns and investor's needs?

> ESG's definition includes environmental, socioeconomic, and governance issues that both affect or are impacted by business—leading to the following broad ESG definition:The term that has emerged globally to describe the environmental, social, and corporate governance issues that investors are considering in the context of corporate behaviour. No definitive list of ESG issues exists, but they typically display one or more of the following characteristics: Issues that have traditionally been considered non-financial or not material; a medium- or long-term horizon; qualitative objects that are readily quantifiable in monetary terms; externalities (costs borne by other firms or by society at large) not well captured by market mechanisms; a changing regulatory or policy framework; patterns arising throughout a company's supply chain (and therefore susceptible to unknown risks); a public-concern focus.[53]

The value in identifying ESG issues that investors need to have addressed relies upon a four-step process that underpins the structure and format of this book:

1. The business must establish which ESG activities materially affect a company's market value and access to markets of key importance.
2. The business must deal with divergent definitions of what sustainability means and the corresponding lack of clarity about the goals of sustainability-oriented investors. This activity generally requires the adoption of frameworks and alignment to chosen industry standards.
3. The business must deal with the lack of coherence in ESG methodologies that drives skepticism over the validity of ESG metrics. Alignment to standards and tools that support regulatory compliance is generally a best practice.
4. The business should take strategic steps with its end goal in mind. The foundations for better integration of sustainability into investment decisions are formalizing. To best take advantage of these trends, corporations must monitor and rely upon data-driven decisions and nonfinancial disclosures.

---

52. Gregory Stewart, Scott Berard, and Ed Fruscella, *Trends in Environmental, Social, and Governance Investing*, BNY Thought Leadership Series (2012).

53. Daniel C. Esty & Todd Cort, *The Data Challenges Which Remain in* Sustainable Investing: Revolutions in Theory and Practice (Cary Krosinsky and Sophie Purdom eds. 2008).

While ESG data providers have begun to recognize these issues, the ultimate influencer of behavioral change will likely come in the form of government-mandated ESG reporting.[54] Once the financial or non-financial regulatory community mandates a framework that would standardize (and perhaps simplify) ESG data and presentation methodologies, companies will adapt to the guidance. These mandates will also offer a greater degree of investor confidence that the metrics have been validated and can be trusted as a basis for cross-company comparisons. Such a structure would give investors what they really *need*: a reliable set of core, mandatory ESG indicators that can be supported by qualitative and quantitative metrics. The value of comparability across companies makes benchmarking possible. This measurable gauge will improve the ability to connect non-financial metrics to stock market results. Consequently, it would create incentives for greater focus in the business world on ESG performance and capital flow toward more sustainable enterprises.

In the interim, this book seeks to establish a series of normative data that most companies must consider. The work is pragmatic in nature and should serve as a guidance for counsel, investors, and ESG practitioners to support their own materiality assessments and corporate ESG evaluation frameworks. In furtherance of this effort, we offer the following key terms and definitions that will be used throughout the book and can be referred to in order to align the various authors' statements, references, and recommendations (see Table 1).

Table 1: Key Terms and Definitions.

Term	Definition
ESG	Environmental, social, and corporate governance—representing the core subcategories of sustainability issues that investors want to track and which might affect an investment's financial performance.
Material (materiality)	Information that significantly impacts investor decision-making. Defined by the U.S. Supreme Court as information that presents "a substantial likelihood that the disclosure of the omitted fact would have been viewed by the reasonable investor as having significantly altered the 'total mix' of information made available" (Bean and Thomas, 1990).
Metric	In the context of this article, *metric* refers to a gauge or measurement that tracks company-scale performance of an issue or indicator of interest.
Use case	As used here, "use case" refers to the purposes to which sustainability metrics are being put—recognizing that investors, market analysts, and academics may use the same ESG datasets to assess very different dimensions of sustainability.

54. Daniel Esty & Todd Cort, *Corporate Sustainability Metrics: What Investors Need but Don't Get*, 8(1) J Environ Invest (2017).

CHAPTER 3

ESG Investment Strategies

Todd Cort, Caleb Lee, and Annabelle Xing

Introduction

Much of the variability, confusion, and controversy associated with ESG investing can be traced back to the question of "What constitutes ESG investing?" Different stakeholders and investment firms answer this question in very different ways. While one investor may see ESG information as financial risk and part of a traditional return-maximization investment strategy (i.e., ESG integration), another may see ESG investing as an approach that excludes assets based on environmental or social impact of the asset (i.e., negative screening). Not only is the breadth of ESG investment strategies wide, the variety of financial products that are currently offered under the umbrella of ESG is proliferating rapidly.

It is therefore worthwhile to organize and understand the different investment strategies that can be included under the term "ESG." This chapter looks at the different investment strategies within ESG and groups them into five distinct types: ESG Integration, Screening, Shareholder Action, Thematic Investing, and Values First and Impact Investing. While each of these can be an investment strategy in and of itself, a given investment manager can also combine strategies within a portfolio or as part of a larger portfolio positioning strategy.

ESG Integration

The integration of ESG factors refers to "'the systematic and explicit inclusion by investment managers of environmental, social and governance factors into traditional financial analysis' in order to enhance investment decision-making."[1] In

1. Ricardo Boffo & Robert Patalano. *ESG Investing: Practices, Progress and Challenges*. OECD Paris, (2020). https://www.oecd.org/finance/ESG-Investing-Practices-Progress-Challenges.pdf.

conjunction with fundamental analysis, ESG integration investors will use their evaluation of ESG factors to generate more profitable returns and, as a secondary goal, influence companies into more ethical and sustainable behavior.

An ESG integration strategy takes slightly different forms for managed equities and fixed income assets. For actively managed equities, the consideration of ESG data can help investors better identify and quantify risks and opportunities to assets. Assessing the mechanisms by which environmental or social factors can create or deplete financial value can be done at all stages of decision-making, including idea generation, company analysis, investment case, and portfolio construction. As ESG factors are further integrated into general investment practices, asset owners and portfolio managers can begin measuring the specific impact of ESG on valuations and returns.

For fixed income assets, ESG integration can involve analyzing issuer exposure to material climate change risk (or other ESG risk) and financial implications, pricing the risk, and determining whether the bond represents good investment value. The result is a more informed assessment of issuer credit risk and creditworthiness. ESG can be considered for corporate bonds at a sector and company level. It can also be considered for government, municipal, and supranational bonds, focusing on exposure and resilience to climate change impacts. Climate change represents the predominant risk considered in ESG-integrated bonds, and credit rating agencies such as S&P have work underway on sovereign risk and climate change.

A multitude of studies have indicated that this method of assessing a firm's financial viability and capturing long-term returns on investments is highly effective. The University of Oxford and Arabesque Partners reviewed over 200 different ESG studies and found that 80 percent of studies demonstrate a positive correlation between sustainability and stock performance, and 90 percent show that firms with stronger ESG performances undertake lower costs of capital.[2] Similarly, a Deutsche Bank meta-study concluded that ESG factors correlate with superior risk-adjusted returns at the securities level, especially when investors amalgamate ESG into other promising and well-executed strategies.[3] A similar meta-study out of New York University confirmed these findings in 2021.[4]

ESG Screening

Screening is the process of evaluating companies and projects against a set of determined standards or values. In general, screening comes in the three forms of negative/exclusionary screening, positive/best-in-class screening, and

2. Gordon L. Clark et al. *From the Stockholder to the Stakeholder: How Sustainability Can Drive Financial Outperformance.* SSRN (2015).

3. Gunnar Friede et al., *ESG and Financial Performance: Aggregated Evidence from More Than 2000 Empirical Studies.* 5 J Sustain. Fin. Invest. 210–33 (2015).

4. Ulrich Atz et al., *The Return on Sustainability Investment (ROSI): Monetizing Financial Benefits of Sustainability Action in* Companies in Sustainable Consumption and Production, Volume II (Ranjula Bali Swain & Susanne Sweet eds. 2021).

norms-based screening. Each of these types of screens are employed using ESG information and asset characteristics.

Negative Screening

Negative/exclusionary screening refers to the exclusion from funds or portfolios of certain companies, sectors, issuers, or countries for engaging in activities deemed not investable. Investors may draw on various norms and values to determine exclusion criteria. A variety of ESG characteristics have been employed for negative screens such as product categories (tobacco, fossil fuels), company practices (human rights violations, animal testing), and controversies (South African apartheid, Sudan). Shariah screening, guided by Islamic tenants, is another subcategory of negative screening. While negative screening is sometimes referred to as "values first" or "ethical investing" for its more philanthropic emphasis on adherence to values over financial performance, we have separated values-first investing below as investors can take a values-first approach to investing without incorporating negative screens.[5]

Positive Screening

Positive/best-in-class screening is the practice of including certain companies and sectors in funds and portfolios for achieving positive ESG performance relative to their peers and ratings above some quantitative threshold. For example, many investors may select from companies with stocks that score in the top 25 to 50 percent on a sustainable investment (SI) metric.[6] Positive screening processes strengthen the sustainability profiles of portfolios with companies known for healthy labor practices, gender equity, environmental initiatives, climate resilience, etc. Since negative and positive screening are two sides of the same coin, investors often run these two tests in parallel.

Norms-Based Screening

Norms-based screening refers to the evaluation of companies and sectors based on adherence to institutional and international standards. Relevant standards include those issued by the United Nations, such as the seventeen Sustainable Development Goals (SDGs) and the UN Guiding Principles on Business and Human Rights, UNICEF, the Organization for Economic Co-operation and

5. Iván Arribas et al. *Negative Screening and Sustainable Portfolio Diversification.* Entrepreneurship and Sustainability Center 6, no. 4, 1566–86. (2019). https://doi.org/http://doi.org/10.9770/jesi.2019.6.4(2); Cary Krosinsky, *The Seven Tribes of Sustainable Investing in Evolutions in* Theory and Practice (Cary Krosinsky & Sophie Purdom eds., 2016).

6. Positive Screening, Robeco. 2021. https://www.robeco.com/en/key-strengths/sustainable-investing/glossary/positive-screening.html#:~:text=Positive%20screening%20is%20the%20process,selected%20for%20sustainable%20investing%20portfolios.

Development (OECD), and the International Labor Organization (ILO).[7] Investments that violate these norms may be excluded, while other investments may be weighted according to the degree of compliance exhibited.

Shareholder Action and Corporate Engagement

When investors and shareholders call upon corporations, policymakers, and outsourced fund managers to create positive change, this is referred to as Shareholder Action or Corporate Engagement. Shareholders will seek to influence corporate behavior directly (e.g., communicating with boards or senior members of companies) and indirectly (filing or co-filing shareholder proposals and proxy voting). Recent studies show that ESG shareholder resolutions rose 22 percent between 2021 and 2022 in the United States, indicating unprecedented levels of shareholder engagement and interest over sustainability.[8] The US SIF Forum for Sustainable and Responsible Investment reviewed ESG-related shareholder proposals filed between 2018 and 2020 and found investors to be most concerned about corporate political activity, labor and equal employment opportunity, and climate change/carbon emissions.[9]

Advocacy on the political level occurs through regulatory and policy change. Investors partnered with the Principles for Responsible Investment (PRI), a UN body for sustainable investment guidelines, to launch "Carbon Action," a collaborative engagement program for corporate climate lobbying in the United States, Canada, Australia, and Europe.[10] In May 2022, the Securities and Exchange Commission (SEC) declared a proposal for greater market-wide ESG disclosure and metrics, largely in response to growing investor demand for corporate transparency.[11] Due to its institutional power, shareholder engagement and advocacy is often seen as one of the most influential ESG investment strategies.

Thematic Investing

Some ESG investment managers will seek out specific solutions, projects, and companies tackling ESG issues. This is termed as "sustainability themed" or "thematic investing." Sustainability-themed sectors include renewable energy, water and waste management, cleantech, sustainable agriculture and forestry, health

7. Krosinsky, *supra* at note 5.

8. Rachel Layne. *Climate Shareholder Resolutions Flood into Proxy Season for a Record Year.* FORTUNE. (June 6, 2022). https://fortune.com/2022/06/06/climate-shareholder-resolutions-flood-into-proxy-season-for-a-record-year/.

9. *Global Sustainable Investment Review 2020.* Global Sustainable Investment Alliance. (2020).

10. Cary Krosinsky, *On Reducing Emissions and Developing a Climate Change Strategy in Sustainable Investing: Revolutions in* Theory and Practice (Cary Krosinsky & Sophie Purdom eds., 2016).

11. *Statement on ESG Disclosures Proposal.* U.S. Securities and Exchange Commission, May 25, 2022. https://www.sec.gov/news/statement/gensler-statement-esg-disclosures-proposal-052522.

products, and green infrastructure. As these ESG innovations are more commonly represented in the investment world through climate bonds or start-ups, thematic investing tends to be dominated by venture capital, private equity, or mutual funds.[12] Thematic investing seeks positive intentionality by nature, so values-first funds will adopt a gender-lens or renewables-tilt when researching for portfolio investments.

Values First and Impact Investing

The final category of ESG investing is impact investing, which is a form of investing based on moral or ethical values and can sometimes result in reduced returns (values-first investing). This entails investing with the goal of producing a positive social impact and financial returns paired with the measurement of the environmental and social performance of each investment. Impact investing is most prominent among private investors such as closed-end private equity and venture capital funds and debt funds more broadly. As an increasingly popular investment strategy, impact investing is used by a wide variety of managers from large firms such as Morgan Stanley and Blackstone to investors in microfinance. One of the greatest difficulties with this form of investment lies within its hallmark characteristic of measuring the impact of specific investments. Investors often have varying definitions and metrics curated to their own priorities and goals, and as such, each fund's method of impact investing can be fairly differentiated. One example of how investors may measure the specific positive social outcome from certain funds can be found in access to essential services. To measure access to financial services, health care, and education, a fund may choose to track the number of individuals with bank accounts, the number of patients served at health-care facilities, and the number of students enrolled in school.

Following the 2008 financial crisis, many economists, regulators, and members of the industry searched for a way to structurally modify existing markets and investing strategies to avoid excessive risk-taking that overly focuses on the short term and pure profit. Some aspired to establish a larger mission of social and environmental development in addition to financial returns, and thus invented impact investing. Within impact investing, social impact bonds and private equity are the two most prominent asset vehicles. While microfinance has garnered the most capital and notice from investors, sectors involving access to medicine, housing, and education have become increasingly popular.[13]

There are two types of impact investors: (1) Investors who willingly accept lower financial returns to accomplish greater social impact and (2) investors who will not make concessionary returns. Because most socially conscious investors are of the second type, investees must develop sustainable business models that are both financially sound and demonstrably beneficial to positive social or

12. *Global Sustainable Investment Review 2020*, Global Sustainable Investment Alliance. (2020).
13. Krosinsky, *supra* at note 10.

environmental development.[14] Case studies exist that demonstrate a relationship between impact investing strategies and financial return under certain conditions. The Global Impact Investing Network (GIIN) 2020 Annual Impact Investor Survey reported that 88 percent of impact investors met or exceeded their financial expectations and 99 percent met or exceeded their impact expectations.[15] An investment in Dodla Dairy, a firm that both produces and processes milk for over 220,000 smallholder farmers in rural India, was estimated to increase the farm families' income by nearly 73 percent. With the increased stability in income, smallholder farmers can begin making longer term investments, thereby increasing their milk yields and again their income.[16] Another investment is a financial literacy program, EverFi, which was estimated to have saved $105 million dollars over five years.[17] Another study by Cambridge Associates and GIIN found that impact investing's top-quartile returns reached 9.7 percent or higher, which matches the average return of the top 10 percent in the S&P 500.[18]

ESG and Smart Beta Strategies

Traditional portfolio management differentiates between two categories: active and passive. Active investing involves investors or fund managers making active decisions to outperform the market or some designated benchmark. Detailed and time-consuming research to identify market inefficiencies, build up unique investment strategies, and time the market strategically is at the core of active investing.[19] Thus, fund managers charge hefty management fees for their time and expertise. The term "alpha" measures how much a portfolio manager outperforms the market in managing portfolio returns.

On the other hand, passive investing aims to replicate the returns of a market index as closely as possible. That is, portfolios and funds will balance their investments to mirror the weightings and constituents of an index (e.g., S&P 500, NASDAQ, NYSE). Stock selection in passive investing can often be automated and portfolios generally require less active maintenance, hence the lower management fees. The term "beta" quantifies the volatility of a stock relative to the market's index, so passive investing is often known as "beta investing."

Most market indexes traditionally are market capitalization weighted, meaning that a handful of companies with very high market capitalization—the

---

14. Edward T. Jackson & Karim Harji. *Assessing Impact Investing*. The Rockefeller Foundation. (2014). https://www.rockefellerfoundation.org/wp-content/uploads/Impact-Investing-Thematic-Briefs-FINAL.pdf.

15. *Global Sustainable Investment Review 2020*. Global Sustainable Investment Alliance. (2020).

16. Chris Addy et al., *Calculating the Value of Impact Investing: An Evidence-Based Way to Estimate Social and Environmental returns*. 97 Harv. Bus. Rev. 102–9 (2019).

17. *Id.*

18. *Private Equity & Venture Capital Impact Investing*, Cambridge Associates and Global Impact Investing Network. (2021). https://www.cambridgeassociates.com/wp-content/uploads/2022/02/PEVC-Impact-Investing-Benchmark-Statistics-2021-Q1.pdf.

19. Sher Mehta. *Active vs Passive Investing*. Financial Edge (Apr. 16, 2021). https://www.fe.training/free-resources/portfolio-management/active-vs-passive-investing/.

product of number of shares outstanding the current stock price—flood the index and do not offer the intended exposure to a well-diversified U.S. market. For example, Apple and Microsoft would be overrepresented and weighted more heavily, despite some small or midcap-sized companies generating better returns.

Smart beta offers a third option in between active and passive investing. Over the last twenty years, smart beta has risen in popularity as an alternative investment strategy to mainstream portfolio management strategies of alpha and beta. Smart beta modifies the weights of index components (i.e., by either over- or underweighting stocks based on their exposure in some benchmark index) according to various rules and metrics. In this way, smart beta compensates for the unequal weighting of traditional indexes and aims to improve returns, reduce risk, and provide portfolios and funds—a systematic exposure to specific factors and market segments.[20]

The rules and metrics that determine modified weights bifurcate smart beta strategies into two broad categories of factor investing and alternative weighting investing. Factor strategies focus on exposing the portfolio to one or more risk factors, such as value, size, momentum, low volatility, quality, and dividend yield. Alternative weighting diversifies portfolios by concentrating on specific risk premiums like equal weight, minimum variance, max diversification, and max Sharpe ratio.[21] Smart beta investors leverage a mix of these factors and weights with proprietary indexes to develop unique portfolios.

Smart beta ESG strategy emerges from the nexus of growing sustainability consciousness and smart beta interest. In general, attitudes toward ESG have shifted toward a long-term approach focused on minimizing risk and maximizing return.[22] Investors who once held a tokenistic mindset on ESG are now integrating it more seriously into core investment strategies. In a survey of 500 global institutional investors, FTSE (Financial Times Stick Exchange) Russell reports that the strongest investment incentive among surveyed investors lies in "avoiding long term risk" and not for "sustainable good."[23]

Asset managers also cite ESG risks as key to their fiduciary responsibility. Since companies that score poorly on ESG criteria face a higher probability of underperforming in the long term—whether due to social pressure, resource shortages, media coverage, etc—investors increasingly recognize the fiduciary duty in selecting and justifying certain portfolio responsibilities.[24] For example, a thorough labor practices screening may be part of a fiduciary duty because it minimizes the firm's reputational risks to be involved in child labor, corruption, and workplace discrimination.

---

20. Gökhan Kula et al., *Beyond Smart Beta: Index Investment Strategies for Active Portfolio Management* (2017).

21. Federica Ielasi et al., *Integrating ESG Analysis into Smart Beta Strategies.* 12 *Sustainability* 1–22 (2020), https://doi.org/http://dx.doi.org/10.3390/su12229351; FTSE Russell. "Alternatively Weighted and Factor Indexes."

22. Buffo & Patalano, *supra* note 1 at 6–7.

23. *Sustainable Smart Beta Investing for Institutional Investors*, Clear Path Analysis. (2017). https://content.ftserussell.com/sites/default/files/research/clear-path-analysis-sustainable-smart-beta-oct-2017.pdf, 7.

24. *Id.* at 18.

Smart beta's inherent framework of balancing risk and return and multifactored combination of weights facilitates the incorporation of ESG concerns as new investment metrics and factors. Smart beta ESG investors consist of large institutional investors, sovereign wealth funds, and large private equity holders. A study by FTSE Russell confirms that large asset owners are pioneering sustainable smart beta, with over 80 percent of asset owners with an AUM (assets under management) of 10 billion USD or higher having implemented ESG factors into investment strategies.[25] Geographically, European and North American investors have the highest adoption rates.[26]

Three popular techniques for incorporating ESG include negative or best-in-class screening, individual ESG metrics, and climate tilts.[27] Many smart beta investors value individual ESG metrics to develop sector-specific portfolios or analyze companies across different industries. Popular ESG metrics—such as carbon, water, and waste—tend to be dominated by environmental data, since social and governance data are often more qualitative and harder to systematically quantify.[28]

Like any other weighted factor, firms often collect data from independent third-party analytics groups, governments, or company research to develop proprietary ESG factors.[29] As shown in the case studies below, the five discussed umbrellas of ESG investment appear in various combinations to form the ESG "factors" of a smart beta strategy.

AXA Investment Managers (AXA IM), a French responsible investment fund, centers their smart beta strategy around best-in-class ESG integration. Stocks first pass through four filters of desired factor exposures (quality of earnings, low volatility) and undesirable risks (speculative value, financial distress), are each awarded a score, and then evaluated based on their cumulative score sum. The list is then diversified with a weighing scheme to avoid overrepresentation of high market cap companies and underperforming small companies.

Finally, the short-listed companies are each assigned ESG scores determined by AXA's proprietary framework of six factors: resource scarcity, climate change, shifting demographics, regulation, company impact, and community expectations. AXA then builds a range of ESG subscores with their own data and raw ESG data from external providers. Certain sectors will have higher relevance for ESG (e.g., there are higher social considerations for labor conditions in retail industries and higher environmental considerations for industrials' and energy), so different sectors will carry adjusted weighting. Companies with outstanding

25. *Smart Sustainability: 2020 Global Survey Findings from Asset Owners*. FTSE Russell. (2020). https://radius-global.com/wp-content/uploads/2020/08/P4_200030_Smart-Sustainability_2020_v03.8.pdf, 3–4.

26. Doug Morrow et al. (2018). "Smart Beta and ESG." Aberdeen Standard Investments, 4.

27. *Id.*, 21–2.

28. *Id.*, 23.

29. Balázs Stempler. *ESG Investing: The Use of ESG Ratings in a Smart Beta Strategy*. 20 Finan. Econ. Rev. 91–116. (2021). https://doi.org/http://doi.org/10.33893/FER.20.2.91116.

ESG scores both within and across their respective verticals are then considered for final investment.[30]

Calvert Investments, one of the largest sustainable investment firms in the United States, developed a smart water index for their smart beta strategy. The Calvert Global Water Research Index (CALH2O) universe is composed of companies that "manage water use in a sustainable manner and are actively engaged in expanding access to water, improving water quality, promoting the efficient use of water, or providing solutions that address other global water challenges." CALH2O is an example of a sector-focused index leveraging thematic investing in water and norms-based screening adhering to UN SDG principles.[31]

The index universe consists of publicly listed companies in the utilities, infrastructure, and technology sector filtered by market cap, float-adjusted market cap, and a 20-day average trading volume. Companies were filtered again by those that generated over 30 percent of their total revenue from water-related business activities. Calvert then searches specifically for innovative water solutions, examining for companies with technological breakthroughs in water-intensive industries (i.e., food waste, paper, and semiconductors) and generating financially material signs of water efficiency and water impact. The index is asset-class agnostic, so firm researchers' source for financially material ESG signals across all asset teams and later balances selected companies by weighting them with a modified market cap according to sector. Calvert rebalances the CALH2O index quarterly, with annual adjustments made for maximum weighting per security and emerging markets.[32]

Swiss bank J. Safra Sarasin is an example of financial institutions that collect their own ESG data rather than pulling data from third-party sustainable analytics firms. Researchers in their Sustainable Investing Laboratory analyze ninety-six governance indicators that span across industries (instead of environmental or social indicators which are often industry specific). The bank then runs a series of performance and robustness measures for downside protection and upside opportunities.[33]

Smart beta exchange-traded funds (ETFs) present another ESG investment option. Large banks and financial institutions have recently begun rolling out ESG alternatives to well-established ETFs. Invesco launched the Invesco ESG S&P 500 Equal Weight ETF (RSPE), the ESG spin on the smart beta ETF known as Invesco S&P 500 Equal Weight ETF (RSP). RSPE leverages the S&P Dow Jones

30. Lise Renelleau et al. *Joining Financial and Long-Term Sustainable Performance Objectives.* A Practical Guide to ESG Integration for Equity Investing. UN Principles for Responsible Investment, 44–5, (2016). https://www.unpri.org/listed-equity/a-practical-guide-to-esg-integration-for-equity-investing/10.article.

31. Calvert. *Calvert Global Water Research Index.* (2022). https://www.calvert.com/Calvert-Global-Water-Research-Index-CALH2O.php.

32. Andreas G. F. Hoepner & J. Streur. (2016). "Constructing a Smart Water Index." A Practical Guide to ESG Integration for Equity Investing. UN Principles for Responsible Investment, 46–7, https://www.unpri.org/download?ac=10.

33. J. Safra Sarasin. (2021). "Our Sustainability Analysis." https://www.jsafrasarasin.com/internet/com/com_our_sustainability_analysis; Andreas G. F. Hoepner & Pierin Menzli. (2016). "Feeding Governance Insights into Smart Beta Strategies." A Practical Guide to ESG Integration for Equity Investing. UN Principles for Responsible Investment, 48–9, https://www.unpri.org/download?ac=10.

Industrial (DJI) ESG Scores to select best-in-class ESG leaders from each sector in the S&P 500 Equal Weight Index.[34] iShares, the largest ETF provider by BlackRock, holds a range of ESG ETFs. From Paris-aligned climate ETFs of the MSCI World and S&P 500 indexes to the Aging Populations ETF (AGED) and the Global Forestry & Timber ETF (WOOD), iShares covers both a range of sustainable and thematic funds.[35] Smart beta ESG ETFs offer investors the same diversification and risk mitigation benefits of a core holding strategy for an index fund but with an augmented ESG tilt.

ESG largely still remains a niche investment technique, with around less than 30 percent of asset managers running smart beta strategies also leverage ESG information.[36] Nevertheless, smart beta investors are advancing a movement for financially material and standardized ESG data. Indeed, confusion on definitions and data limitations on accurate forecasting prevent mainstream investors from fully utilizing existing ESG data.[37] Smart beta investors of all types will increasingly demand transparent and high-quality data to reflect their range of beliefs across sustainability into their investments.

ESG and Fixed Income

Investors increasingly want to understand the impacts of long-term ESG risks on their medium- and long-term bonds. Thus, ESG ratings and standards are becoming an integral cornerstone of a potential investment's security valuation. Fixed income assets are often attractive to sustainably inclined investors because investors can allocate capital to sustainable issues more directly, unlike purchasing equities from mainly secondary trades. Moreover, the "use of proceeds" documents of fixed income assets offer greater transparency into how the capital invested funds a project, enabling investors to target impact investments with greater certainty.

In recent years, the fixed income market has mirrored ESG trends in equity markets. Investor focus on risk mitigation has shifted the market from negative screening and values-based investing toward best-in-class and ESG integration.[38] There is also heavy reliance on third-party analytics firms for standardized and systematic bond credit ratings (e.g., prominent rating agencies that have

34. Invesco Ltd. (2021). "Pioneer of Smart Beta Launches ESG S&P 500 Equal Weight ETF." PR Newswire, Nov. 17. https://www.prnewswire.com/news-releases/pioneer-of-smart-beta-launches-esg-sp-500-equal-weight-etf-301426057.html.

35. *iShares Ageing Population UCITS ETF.* iShares. (2022). https://www.ishares.com/uk/individual/en/products/284218/ishares-ageing-population-ucits-etf?switchLocale=y&siteEntryPassthrough=true; *IShares Global Timber & Forestry ETF.* iShares. (2022). https://www.ishares.com/us/products/239752/ishares-global-timber-forestry-etf.

36. Morrow et al., 21.

37. FTSE Russell, "Smart Sustainability: 2020 Global Survey Findings from Asset Owners," 17.

38. Ali Edelstein, *Developments in Sustainable Fixed Income in* Sustainable Investing: Revolutions in Theory and Practice (Cary Krosinsky & Sophie Purdom eds., 2016).

incorporated ESG factors into rating methodologies like S&P Global Ratings, Fitch Ratings, and Moody's).

ESG considerations in fixed income assets can be examined through two main lenses: bonds and the credit assessments evaluating bonds. Fixed income bonds generally break down into sovereign, corporate, government, and municipal. Accordingly, practitioners in each bond category have unique approaches to analyzing ESG risks on credit assessments.

ESG considerations are not widespread in sovereign and government debt analysis due to the cross-border gap in knowledge. The greater difficulty in sourcing ESG data of a country compared to that of a company—especially in drawing absolute and relative ESG performance—exacerbates the low uptake in ESG factors. Research also suggests that certain ESG risks are less material for sovereign debt compared to their impact on corporate bonds.[39] Well-known ESG data sources on sovereign entities include the Freedom in the World Survey, the Fragile State Index, the Environmental Performance Index, and the Energy Trilemma Index.

Corporate credit analysis aims to integrate ESG scores into traditional credit analysis. Drawing third-party and proprietary ESG scores, analysts look at the impact of ESG issues on methods like profitability, solvency ratios, and liquidity risks.[40] ESG risks are further considered in an issuer's capacity, their ability to service and pay its debt obligations and liabilities. Credit analysts and rating agencies increasingly consider whether a company's failure to address present ESG risks will result in future fines, inability to comply with regulations, or reputational risks.[41]

Credit analysis for the sub-sovereign bond market focuses on bodies from regions, provinces, states, or municipalities that issue bonds. The U.S. sub-sovereign market consists primarily of municipal bonds. Since local social and economic changes more immediately impact a municipality than the federal government or a corporation, ESG factors have long been considered to identify a municipality's financial risk and strength of operations.[42] For project revenue bonds, rating agencies more heavily weigh project-specific ESG factors to assess proper use of proceeds.

ESG considerations also vary by their relevance to asset categories. That is, regime stability and political freedom are most applicable to sovereign debt of all bond types, employee relations and board auditing are most material to corporate, and air pollution and carbon emissions are generally relevant for most classes.

39. "Guidance and Case Studies for ESG Integration: Equities and Fixed Income," CFA Institute and UN Principles for Responsible Investment. 2018, 19–20; Mervyn Tang. *Sustainable Sovereigns in* Sustainable Investing Handbook (2018).

40. *Guidance and Case Studies for ESG Integration*, CFA Institute. (2018). 18–19.

41. Victoria Collin, *ESG in Credit Analysis*, Financial Edge (2022), https://www.fe.training/free-resources/esg/esg-in-credit-analysis/#:~:text=What%20is%20%E2%80%9CESG%20in%20Credit,its%20ability%20to%20service%20debt.

42. *Guidance and Case Studies supra* note 39 at 21.

In the ESG investment space, bonds that address an ESG issue can be collectively categorized by either their "use of proceeds" or "general purpose." Use of proceeds ("UoP") bonds to the exclusive allocation of cash raised for financing eligible projects and is otherwise known as "GSS" (green, social, or sustainable) bonds, covering green bonds, social impact bonds, and sustainable bonds. General purpose bonds focus on Key Performance Indicators (KPIs) and Sustainability Performance Targets (SPTs) identified by the bond issuer and are generally sustainability-linked bonds (SLBs).

In general, ESG bonds are issued in voluntary compliance with the International Capital Market Association (ICMA) Principles for global markets. In 2021, 98 percent of sustainable bonds globally were aligned with ICMA Principles, worth around 998 billion USD.[43] ICMA Principles encompass the Green Bond Principles (GBP), the Social Bond Principles (SBP), the Sustainability Bond Guidelines (SBG), and the Sustainability-Linked Bond Principles (SLBP). These principles do not define what GSS bonds and SLBs are but rather encourage transparency and disclosure among issuers in ESG bond markets and act as an international standard.

Bonds regardless of their issuer's jurisdiction can be categorized as one of the following types of ESG bonds.

Green Bonds

Bonds are labeled as "green" if they are either secured on approved green projects or the proceeds exclusively finance or refinance green projects not included in the collateral of the bonds themselves. In July 2022, ICMA refreshed GBP to provide greater standardization in green bonds. The updated GBP distinguishes between "standard green use-of-proceeds" bonds—where the cash raised is ring-fenced for financing climate-friendly projects—and "secured green bonds"—bonds collateralized by one or more specific projects (e.g., covered bonds and asset-backed securities).[44] Examples of eligible projects for green bond issuance include renewable energy and energy efficiency, green infrastructure, wastewater management, and clean transportation. The World Bank Green Bonds Program and the Prairie Waters Project in Aurora, Colorado, are strong examples.[45]

Social Impact Bonds

Bonds are "social" bonds if the proceeds finance or refinance social projects or activities that achieve positive social outcomes and/or address a social issue. Although not exclusively meant for target populations, social bonds frequently

---

43. "Sustainable Bonds Based on GBP, SBP, SBG and SLBP in 2021." ICMA. (2021). https://www.icmagroup.org/assets/documents/Sustainable-finance/GBP-infographic.pdf?vid=2.

44. *Green Bond Principles* ICMA. (2021). Jun., 2–4 https://www.icmagroup.org/assets/documents/Sustainable-finance/2022-updates/Green-Bond-Principles_June-2022-280622.pdf.

45. *What You Need to Know about IFC's Green Bonds*, The World Bank. (2021). https://www.worldbank.org/en/news/feature/2021/12/08/what-you-need-to-know-about-ifc-s-green-bonds; CFA Institute. "Guidance and Case Studies for ESG Integration," 158–9.

target issues that "threaten, hinder, or damage the well-being of society or a specific target population."[46] Examples of social project categories include access to essential services (health care, education), affordable housing, employment generation through SME (small and medium-sized enterprise) financing and microfinance, food security and sustainable food systems, and supported expenditures like research and development. In the last two years, COVID-related bonds emerged as a new subclass of social bonds, focused on alleviating COVID-19-related social issues for at-risk populations.[47]

Sustainability Bonds

Sustainability bonds are any type of bonds where proceeds are exclusively applied to finance or refinance a combination of both green and social projects and are in accordance with both GBP and SBP guidelines. Due to the increasing intersection of co-benefits between green and social projects, a market of "sustainability bonds" developed to reflect changes in the use of proceeds bond markets.[48]

Sustainability-Linked Bonds

Sustainability-Linked Bonds (SLBs) are bonds for which the financial and/or structure characteristics vary depending on whether the issuer achieves self-identified ESG objectives. SLBs are distinct from GSS bonds in that there is no specific use of proceeds and rather are of "general purpose." Issuers explicitly commit to a series of sustainability outcomes within some time frame. These outcomes are measured through relevant and material KPIs and assessed against SPTs by external benchmarking and consistency with business strategy.[49] Examples of KPIs include water footprint and the number of workplace injuries; examples of SPTs include healthy workplace environments and low carbon emissions. Failure to meet outline objectives is "linked" to triggering discounted pricing on the loan until the next pricing adjustment date of the loan. Periodic reporting and punitive pricing serve as deterrents against issuers greenwashing their spending.[50] Oil and energy corporations tend to dominate SLBs for the

46. *Social Bond Principles*, ICMA. (2021). Jun., 2–4, https://www.icmagroup.org/assets/documents/Sustainable-finance/2022-updates/Social-Bond-Principles_June-2022v3-020822.pdf.

47. *Understanding Green, Social, and Sustainability Bonds*. PIMCO. (2021). https://www.pimco.com/en-us/resources/education/understanding-green-social-and-sustainability-bonds.

48. *Sustainability Bond Guidelines*. ICMA. (2021). Jun., 1–3. https://www.icmagroup.org/assets/documents/Sustainable-finance/2021-updates/Sustainability-Bond-Guidelines-June-2021-140621.pdf.

49. *Sustainability-Linked Bond Principles*, ICMA. (2020). Jun., 1–4. https://www.icmagroup.org/assets/documents/Regulatory/Green-Bonds/June-2020/Sustainability-Linked-Bond-Principles-June-2020-171120.pdf.

50. Katie McShane & Wesley Misson. ESG Loans—The Next Big Wave in Fund Finance. Cadwalader, (Mar. 19, 2021); "Sustainability-Linked Bonds—Making Sense of SLBs, KPIs and SPTs." Clifford Chance, (Jun. 2020.), https://www.cliffordchance.com/content/dam/cliffordchance/briefings/2020/06/Sustainability-Linked-Bonds-making-sense-of-SLBs-KPIs-and-SPTs.pdf.

flexibility in loan objectives (e.g., Italian energy infrastructure firm ENEL is the largest issuer of SLBs to date, having raised over 24 billion USD from SLBs).[51]

Recent legislation from the SEC has put pressure on ethical ESG reporting and labeling within large institutional firms. Since over $2.7 trillion in assets are invested in ESG-labeled funds, concerns are mounting over potential greenwashing and the lingering presence of oil giants like ExxonMobil in ESG funds.[52] Proposed changes by the SEC in 2022 include requiring companies to publicize detailed information about greenhouse gas emissions, firms to outline potential operation risks from climate change, and funds labeled "ESG" to invest at least 80 percent of assets according to the stated ESG strategy.[53] Examples of recent SEC crackdowns include BNY Mellon's settlement of 1.5 million USD over false claims that some mutual funds were subject to ESG quality review, an investigation into Deutsche Bank along with a police raid in the Frankfurt headquarters, and an investigation into Goldman Sachs' ESG mutual funds.[54]

Overall, ESG fixed income assets are quickly gaining international recognition. The next steps in the market include greater standardization of bonds and clearer balance of risks and rewards for investors. Standardization enables the scaling of sustainable portfolios to develop. As markets settle around certain internationally accepted standards, asset owners will be able to have stronger bond comparisons and access better risk mitigation. These steps will likely be facilitated by streamlining third-party sustainability fund ratings and ESG bond indices, such as Morningstar, S&P Green Project Bond Index, and so on. A clearer picture of rewards for both issuers and investors will also help incentivize more innovative uses of bond covenants and investment from funds.

---

51. Alessandro Canta. "Why Enel Turned to Sustainability-Linked Bonds." Environ Financ, (June 14, 2022). https://www.environmental-finance.com/content/analysis/why-enel-turned-to-sustainability-linked-bonds.html.

52. Catherine Boudreau. "The SEC Wants ESG Funds to Show Proof that They're Not Just Greenwashing to Draw in Investor Dollars." Business Insider, (May 25, 2022); Saijel Kishan & Natasha White, "A Basic Guide to ESG Investing and Why It Faces a Backlash: QuickTake." Bloomberg QuickTake, (Jul. 11, 2022).

53. Lydia Beyoud & Saijel Kishan. "SEC to Crack Down on Misleading ESG Claims with Fund Rules." *Bloomberg*, (May 25, 2022).

54. *Id.*; Christiaan Hetzner. "Deutsche Bank Raided by Authorities over ESG 'Greenwashing' Claims: 'We've Found Evidence that that Could Support Allegations of Prospectus Fraud,'" (May 31, 2022); Tim McDonnell. "The ESG Crackdown Is Coming for Goldman Sachs." Quartz, (Jun. 14, 2022).

CHAPTER 4

ESG in the Supply Chain and Sourcing Function

Ann Condon and Travis Miller

Our societies are built upon a complex network of supply chains that underlie our daily activities and enable our modern lives.[1] For most global manufacturing businesses, the environmental, social, and governance (ESG) risks extend far beyond the walls of the organization. There are rapidly evolving ways in which sourcing is under pressure from customers, investors, and regulators to take ESG concerns into account.

A definitional note before diving in: ESG, Corporate Social Responsibility (CSR), and sustainability are terms used to describe the non-financial risks of business activities. The best way to understand their differences is by understanding the driving forces behind these terms: ESG (the investor community), CSR (social and human rights activists), and Sustainability (climate and environmental groups). Over time, the subjects covered by these monikers have merged and largely overlap. From a company's perspective, ESG, CSR, and Sustainability are virtually interchangeable as the company must understand the major risks arising from their activities in all of these areas.

Overview

The Sourcing Function

We all source items ourselves, virtually every day. Whether through the internet or in a store, a merchant will offer an item for sale at a proposed price, which

1. See Jonathan Saul et al., *Global Supply Chains Buckle as Virus Variant and Disasters Strike*, REUTERS (July 26, 2021), https://www.reuters.com/business/global-supply-chains-buckle-virus-variant-disasters-strike-2021-07-23/.

we can accept, try to negotiate, or reject. Once a price is agreed, these virtually instant business-to-consumer (B2C) transactions are an example of classic sourcing "deals." Behind all of these B2C transactions is a complex web of business-to-business (B2B) transactions that bring that product or service to the point of sale. In most companies, the task of finding, screening, developing, and contracting with a network of suppliers is handled by the sourcing organization.

Prior to World War II many manufacturers were vertically integrated.[2] The role of sourcing was primarily to purchase commodities that the manufacturer would process to create components and end products. Most people think sourcing professionals are on the phone and web searching for the best price, quality, and delivery on commodities like oil or sand or #2 screws or many other conceptually simple items. It is still a main role of sourcing to manage the cost of products and to use competitive measures to reduce the cost of inputs. Cost deflation is one of sourcing's most important management metrics. Increasingly, sourcing is no longer a back-office function but, in most companies, is a strategic business partner and risk manager that works closely with marketing, manufacturing, and technology to develop supplier relationships that support the entire business.[3] The sourcing profession has grown in both complexity and breadth. Post WWII, specialization in manufacturing shifted work, usually to a number of geographically proximate suppliers, for specific components. A classic example is General Motors spinning off its significant parts manufacturing to Delphi.[4] These arrangements could be simple procurements or more complex processing. For example, many companies outsourced their plating and painting operations in the 1980s, as environmental regulation increased. Offshoring and outsourcing have been a hallmark of globalization for decades.

Global competition increased in the 1980s, putting more cost pressure on manufacturers. As a result, the offshoring trend accelerated as companies sought greater cost competitiveness by moving either their own processes or pushing their suppliers to move to lower cost countries. This greatly increased the risks to the brand company as aspects of the manufacturing were relocated to ever more complex "tiers" of suppliers both in their home country and globally. It also introduced a large element of opacity into the supply network. In some cases, the first- or second-tier supplier does not want to identify to their customer the next tiers of suppliers to maintain their own competitiveness. In addition, acquisition of some inputs (a good example is chemicals) is through complex networks of distributors and brokers.

Since the 1990s, the growth in digital technologies has increased the complexity of many of the products we buy. Test drive a new car and its dashboard looks like a computer. Much of this technology is developed by the makers of

---

2. See Daniel Gross, *Is Vertical Integration Making a Comeback?*, Strategy Business (Dec. 2, 2021) https://www.strategy-business.com/blog/Is-vertical-integration-making-a-comeback.

3. Christian Schuh et al., *Profit from the Source, Transforming Your Business by Putting Suppliers at the Core* Harv. Bus. Rev. (2022) (hereinafter, Profit from the Source).

4. See Robyn Meredith, *G.M. Is Set to Spin Off Parts Division*, N.Y. Times (May 25, 1999). https://www.nytimes.com/1999/05/25/business/gm-is-set-to-spin-off-parts-division.html.

semiconductors software and other technology inputs. The supplier may be more involved in the technology development of a component than the brand manufacturer's own technology teams. As we have learned through the automobile chip shortage of 2021/2022, the only people capable of manufacturing this technology may be a very few, far-flung suppliers.[5] These critical technology suppliers can have enormous leverage over their customers.[6]

While we will focus most of our attention on the acquisition of materials that are incorporated into the product (commonly referred to as direct materials), sourcing is also responsible for acquiring a whole suite of products and services that support the business. These "indirect materials" are those which are not incorporated in the product. For example, the acquisition of office supplies, travel, logistics, energy, and so on, may present significant ESG issues. However, they are more distant from the core business and can be harder to leverage. We will discuss strategies for how to prioritize attention below.

ESG Begins to Change Sourcing

In parallel with globalization, activists and union organizers began to highlight the pitfalls of moving significant manufacturing to low-cost countries, who often lacked the governmental and institutional frameworks to appropriately manage the relevant processes. In the late 1990s, apparel and electronic manufacturers came under intense scrutiny, especially for poor labor practices. The globalization of information flows through the internet brought these very troubling issues right into our living rooms. This kicked off the early efforts at developing guidelines, auditing, and other control programs. The fashion industry remains a high priority for many activists, especially due to the evolution of "fast fashion."[7]

As climate and environmental attention was paid to manufacturing, activists raised concerns about whether major companies were meeting their goals via actual reductions or via outsourcing. Pressure mounted to push environmental controls down into the supply chain. Fukushima, the Iceland volcanoes, the Thai floods, COVID, and Ukraine have graphically demonstrated how nature must be respected and how "just-in-time" manufacturing processes have made our supply chains fragile.

In the last five years, investor organizations have seen how these risks, along with weak business governance in the supply chain, can potentially undermine the investments they are managing on behalf of their clients. New generations of investors are also asking for more sustainable investment vehicles. These questions are routinely raised by investors with the companies they invest in. In parallel, a number of countries are enacting specific legislation that requires

5. The White House, Building Resilient Supply Chains, Revitalizing American Manufacturing, and Fostering Broad-Based Growth (100-Day Review Under EO 14017, Jun. 2021).

6. Christian Schuh et al. Profit from the Source: Transforming Your Business by Putting Suppliers at the Core 44 (2022).

7. See Vanessa Friedman, *New York Could Make History With a Fashion Sustainability Act*, N.Y. Times, Jan. 7, 2022, https://www.nytimes.com/2022/01/07/style/new-york-fashion-sustainability-act.html.

reports and/or disclosures by the companies that do business in their jurisdictions on their activities around the world. These disclosures range from the EU Non-financial Reporting Directive (NFRD)/Corporate Sustainability Reporting Directive (CSRD) to U.S. SEC Conflict Minerals Disclosures to the U.K. Modern Slavery Statements. Each adds to the supply chain due diligence footprint by requiring companies to publicly disclose how they identify and manage select ESG risks.

The result is that companies are increasingly under pressure to extend the values of their home country to other sovereign states and the independent companies that are their suppliers. This creates significant tension between the desire to "do the right thing" and to maintain legal independence. We will explore the specific challenges in more detail below. At this stage, the important thing to keep in mind is that addressing these issues requires a multidisciplinary team supporting the sourcing organization. Lawyers have a key role in helping companies shape their strategy. Lawyers are uniquely qualified at striking a balance between managing "the problem" and maintaining the legal independence of the suppliers. Sometimes helping to solve "the problem" is a better strategy. How you help a supplier solve the problem may require sophisticated communications to avoid stepping over the line into directly managing the supplier. You need a competent grasp of both the risks and response strategies to effectively manage significant ESG concerns.

The Risks

To manage these new expectations, whether from investors, customers, employees, the general public, or due to evolving legal expectations for transparency, a business should adopt a structured, coherent approach to evaluate supply chain risk that is integrated into your ESG strategy. The most used framework for preparing a non-financial disclosure or ESG report is the Global Reporting Initiative (GRI) framework.[8] The most common standard for auditing a non-financial report is the Sustainability Accounting Standards Board (SASB).[9] Most companies and their largest suppliers will have a degree of familiarity with the topics and approaches prescribed by these standards. At a minimum, they are a useful checklist for the topics you should consider in your risk assessment. The following table highlights key topics that can impact suppliers and align to the GRI framework.[10]

---

8. Global Reporting Initiative Resource Center, https://www.globalreporting.org/how-to-use-the-gri-standards/resource-center/.

9. SASB was recently merged with the IFRS Foundation, which established the first International Sustainability Standards Board (ISSB). SASB Standards are now under the oversight of the ISSB. See https://www.sasb.org/about/.

10. The numbers in the table features reference the applicable GRI standards for each topical area.

Environmental	Social	Governance
Climate Impact (GRI 302, 305, 308) ▶ GHG Emissions Reporting ▶ Reduction Targets ▶ Renewable Energy **Resource Use (GRI 303, 306, 308)** ▶ Water & Wastewater Management ▶ Waste & Hazardous Materials **Biodiversity (GRI 301, 304, 308)** ▶ Cotton ▶ Natural Rubber ▶ Forestry	**Labor Rights (GRI 401,403, 407, 408, 409)** ▶ Human Trafficking & Slavery ▶ Other Labor Rights ▶ Workplace Well-Being **Human Rights (GRI 414)** ▶ Health & Safety ▶ Safe Handling Measures **Diversity & Inclusion (GRI 204)** ▶ Ownership ▶ Workforce Demographics	**Organizational Commitment (GRI 205)** ▶ Business Ethics & Integrity ▶ Bribery & Corruption ▶ Business Conduct ▶ Antitrust ▶ Whistleblower **Resiliency (GRI 204)** ▶ Business Continuity & Planning **Data Protection & Privacy (GRI 418)** ▶ Data Protection ▶ Privacy

Governance

Organizational Commitment

Governance is the foundation for a supply chain compliance program. Selecting suppliers in the first place establishes the relationship and sets the tone for everything that follows. Ensuring the supplier is honest, has organizational capacity to manage compliance, will be capable of making the components or product to meet technology, delivery, and quality standards has long been part of sourcing's core agenda. None of the other activities of the supplier can be trusted if the supplier does not have a strong ethical approach to business.

Governance is the most well-developed ESG topic. Large companies spend millions of dollars annually on internal control programs that align with the Foreign Corrupt Practice Act (FCPA), whistleblower hotlines that align with the requirements of Sarbanes–Oxley, and strong staff training programs. To establish a sustainable supply chain ESG program that can be driven by qualitative and quantitative metrics, a manufacturing company should bring this same rigor to incorporating core ESG topics into its sourcing evaluations.

Resiliency

If COVID has proved anything, it is that just in time manufacturing techniques have made the supply chain fragile. That fragility can put not just the delivery of an individual product at risk, it can jeopardize your business and financial health and your customers. There may even be national security concerns.[11] A rapidly evolving ESG governance topic is resiliency or business continuity and planning. Supply chain resiliency requires both a global view of sole sourcing/redundancy and an individualized risk assessment associated with the geographic (external) and operational (internal) risks of a supplier's locations. The geographic (external) risks tend to be oriented around the political, environmental, and civil disturbance externalities that are most likely to impact the supplier site that is servicing the customer. The operational (internal) risks need to align to the policies any supplier has in place to mitigate site-specific risks that occur within the supplier's internal business operations that are servicing the customer. The business continuity plans a supplier implements will be specific to their operations. A customer seeking to incorporate resiliency into its governance program should review the supplier's business continuity plan and look for the following elements or understand the supplier's reasoning for not including them.

Sample Supplier Resiliency Evaluation Table

	Operational (Internal)	Geographic (External)
Cybersecurity	X	
Power Outage	X	X
Natural Disaster		X
Financial Distress/ Bankruptcy	X	
Water Scarcity		X
Illness	X	X
Civil Unrest/War		X
Worker Strike	X	
Port Closure		X
Machine Failures	X	
Second-Tier Supply Chain Disruption		X

The supplier business continuity plan should be evaluated to ensure that core risks have been considered adequately. An adequately addressed risk should include (1) responsible parties, (2) a detailed recovery plan in the event of a realized risk, (3) regular review/testing cycle with recorded updates, (4) crisis communication plans that include their customers, (5) safety plan that mitigates harm, (6) a strategy to continue operations if the site will have prolonged downtime, and (7) a mechanism to recover critical customer information and/or assets. A resiliency evaluation should prioritize suppliers that are critical to the organization's

11. See Bradley Martin, *Supply Chain Disruptions: The Risks and Consequences*, The RAND Blog (Nov. 15, 2021), https://www.rand.org/blog/2021/11/supply-chain-disruptions-the-risks-and-consequences.html.

continued operations. In the event that the evaluated/audited supplier business continuity plan does not adequately address risks, the customer should take its own steps to mitigate supplier risk. A few common practices for risk mitigation are vertical integration, supplier redundancy with split spend, inventory management, and insurance.[12]

Data Protection and Privacy

An emerging and rapidly evolving governance topic is data protection and privacy. Driven by regulations such as European Union General Data Protection Regulation (GDPR) to protect consumers, there are now cybersecurity standards that are required to manage the risk from cyberattacks. Effectively, this requires companies to develop a detailed inventory of the suppliers who manage and process data. These inventories are commonly referred to as software bills of materials (S-BoMs). The U.S. government has driven the creation, inventory, and management of S-BoMs via the requirement to comply with the National Institute of Standards and Technology (NIST) 800-171 that has been imposed on government supply chains via Federal Acquisition Regulation 252.204-7020.

A complex web of data protection and privacy laws are now in force that is anticipated to continue to increase in volume and complexity over the coming years. Accordingly, any company that is sourcing any activity that will result in a supplier coming into possession of or managing personal identifiable information (PII) or trade secrets should enter into contractual agreements. Generally, privacy and data protection agreements are called data protection agreements (DPAs), and trade secrets are protected through nondisclosure agreements (NDAs).

The best practice is to develop an inventory of suppliers who come into possession of a customer's data or an individual's PII data that a customer entrusts to them. Effective management requires a cross-functional data governance approach that can build out the S-BoM, track the information, gather compliance information from providers, and continuously monitor the providers. IT and security will need to be engaged to evaluate any software applications that are allowed access to sensitive business or personal information. This list of sub-processors of information will generally need to be disclosed to upstream customers. Policies related to the applicable laws and the associated contractual requirements will need to be flowed down to these sub-processors. Their security and data governance capability will also need to be evaluated to ensure that they are keeping up with industry standards and norms, for example, the NIST 800-171, ISO 27001, and SOC 2 compliance frameworks. Finally, an effective program should continuously monitor for breaches involving third party's sub-processors and perform at least annual reviews of programs to ensure the third parties remain compliant with the evolving regulatory and industry standards.

12. Profit from the Source.

Social

A history of labor abuses has been one of the strongest drivers for activism to improve supply chain management. As a result, this is the area with the most developed extrajudicial legal requirements, especially in the area of modern wage slavery. To align with the United Nations Global Compact and GRI standards, a supply chain social due diligence program should consider labor rights, human rights, and diversity and inclusion within supplier companies.

Modern Slavery

In the context of corporate ESG programs, the most troublesome labor issue is forced labor. The International Labour Organization (ILO) defines forced labor as "work that is performed involuntarily and under the menace of any penalty."[13] Tens of millions of people find themselves within this situation and the goal of tackling the underlying economic drivers led to the adoption of mandatory modern slavery due diligence laws, Withhold Release Orders (WROs), and sanctions against regions and parties responsible for modern slavery.[14]

To tackle these challenges, the adoption of reporting and transparency requirements is spreading around the world. The United Kingdom Modern Slavery Act, United States' Uyghur Forced Labor Prevention Act, and German Supply Chain Act all require companies doing business in the home country to, at a minimum, report on their programs to eliminate these risks. The legal requirements have some variability, which has prompted nongovernmental organizations, such as the Ethical Trading Initiative (ETI),[15] to develop guidance and standardization related to the contents of an effective Modern Slavery Disclosure.

In order to have something to report, the company needs a program and due diligence results that must be disclosed, typically on a company's website. While the exact requirements should align with the regulations your organization is subject to and you should seek the advice of competent counsel, the following ETI list of required fields provides a good framework of Modern Slavery Disclosures:

- Structure, business, and supply chains;
- Policies in relation to slavery and human trafficking;
- Identification of risks together with steps taken to prevent and manage that risk;
- Due diligence processes in relation to slavery and human trafficking in business and supply chains;
- Effectiveness in ensuring that slavery and human trafficking are not taking place in business or supply chains, measured against appropriate Key Performance Indicators; and
- Training and capacity building to identify and eliminate slavery and human trafficking.

---

13. See ILO Forced Labour Convention, 1930 (No. 29), https://www.ilo.org/global/topics/forced-labour/definition/lang--en/index.htm.

14. See Customs and Border Protection (CBP) Force Labor website: https://www.cbp.gov/trade/forced-labor/withhold-release-orders-and-findings.

15. See https://www.ethicaltrade.org/resources/modern-slavery-statements-evaluation-framework-pdf.

In instances where banned forced labor or sanctioned activities are identified, a company may be forced to discontinue business with an infringing supplier. Recently, there has been an increase in the number of Withhold Release Orders (WROs) and Findings by the United States Customs and Border Protection related to instances of goods produced by forced labor and imported into the United States.[16]

The web of international laws that mandate public disclosure of due diligence and risk product seizures has elevated the need for robust due diligence and actionable intelligence. To mitigate this risk and comply with the ever-increasing number of international antihuman trafficking and slavery laws, companies should look to industry standardized approaches to due diligence such as, the Social Responsibility Alliance (SRA), STRT (pronounced "Start") approach.[17] Collaborative initiatives allow companies to pool resources and benefit from insights derived from a group. Furthermore, they ease the burden placed on suppliers, by allowing them to prepare and disclose a single communication that can be distributed and satisfy multiple customers' needs for compliance information related to multiple regulatory requirements.

Once an approach has been adopted and communicated to suppliers, you will have a significant data management challenge: responses must be collected, reviewed, and risks identified. Competent internal or external resources will need to be dedicated to ongoing monitoring and mitigation of identified risks. A supplier that has been identified as presenting an elevated risk of either using forced or slave labor or benefiting from it must be investigated. General best practices for an investigation include an evaluation of the beneficial owners, second-tier supplier mapping, and sanctions/denied party screening. In addition, modern adverse media monitoring that tracks negative news stories and investigations related to the high-risk suppliers has emerged as a high value tool. If elevated risks are identified that require further confirmation, an on-site audit is a valuable tool to confirm or refute the suspicion. If investigation and monitoring activities establish a direct correlation to illegal sanctioned activities, the relationship with the supplier must be severed. If moderate or manageable risks are identified, remote ongoing monitoring could be a risk mitigation strategy, but the costs of that heightened scrutiny should be identified up front. Distinguishing risk level can be tricky, so this is an area where legal advice is often necessary.

Environment, Health, and Safety

Pressure on suppliers to adopt environmental, health, and safety strategies comes from a number of sources: the laws of the countries where the products are made, the laws of the countries where end products are sold, customers, and increasingly peer competitors and investors. These requirements are increasingly flowing down to suppliers as a core part of codes of conduct. See, for example, Responsible Business Initiative (RBI) Code of Conduct.[18]

16. See https://www.cbp.gov/trade/forced-labor/withhold-release-orders-and-findings.
17. See https://www.socialresponsibilityalliance.org/.
18. RBI website: https://www.responsiblebusiness.org/media/docs/RBACodeofConduct7.0_English.pdf.

Health and Safety

When we visualize a "sweatshop," most of the issues we think of are health and safety issues: poor lighting and ventilation, crowding, blocked exits, sloppy material and chemical handling, noise, etc. The catastrophes in the supply chain have often involved mass casualty events in buildings that should never have been used for manufacturing. Rana Plaza is a notorious example.[19] Keeping workers safe and healthy is a fundamental value in any ESG program.[20] Because of these tragic events, many of the available codes articulate detailed health and safety goals.

In virtually every country, the government has adopted basic health and safety laws. What may be missing are implementing regulations and enforcement. It may take significant educational efforts to convince suppliers that supplementing their local law with internationally utilized guidelines, such as the American Industrial Hygiene Association exposure standards,[21] is in their long-term interest. The field has evolved sufficiently that it should not be necessary to invent company-specific guidelines anymore, as it is challenging for suppliers to implement multiple disparate programs. Alignment to standardized norms that meet a broad and general framework required by multiple customers will normally move a supplier beyond local compliance to a greater extent than would any individual action.

Material Selection

Beginning in the 1990s, regulation of materials incorporated into products sold in the EU gave impetus to the strategy of controlling the exposure of the public to hazardous or toxic substances by banning specific materials in products sold in the country. Known as Restriction of Hazardous Substances (ROHS),[22] it was widely copied around the world. The EU also took the lead with modernizing its chemical regulation. Known as Registration, Evaluation, Authorisation and Restriction of Chemicals (REACH),[23] the regulation required, over time, that all chemicals be evaluated, categorized for toxicity, and prioritized for risk management measures. This strategy has been expanded with the adoption around the world of upgraded toxic materials regulation in, among others, the United States,[24] Canada, and Korea. Individual states and some smaller jurisdictions have also issued specific requirements impacting products, such as California's Prop 65.[25] Many other countries have followed the frameworks established by these leading countries in a proverbial race to the top. As a result, the volume of

19. See https://growensemble.com/rana-plaza/.

20. See https://www.ilo.org/global/topics/geip/WCMS_614394/lang--en/index.htm.

21. See https://www.aiha.org/taxonomy/exposure-assessment/occupational-exposure-limits.

22. European Union's Restriction of Hazardous Substances (RoHS), Directive 2011/65/EU (Jan. 2013), as amended.

23. See https://eur-lex.europa.eu/legal-content/EN/TXT/?uri=CELEX%3A02006R1907-20211001.

24. United States' Toxic Substances Control Act (TSCA), 15 U.S.C. ch. 53, subch. I §§ 2601–2629.

25. California's Safe Drinking Water and Toxic Enforcement Act of 1986 (Prop 65), CHAPTER 6.6. Safe Drinking Water and Toxic Enforcement Act of 1986 [25249.5–25249.14].

regulations dealing with product chemistry has increased rapidly. From a brand's perspective, each of these restrictions can effectively become a global requirement if they are selling into many jurisdictions.

These legal restrictions have been supplemented by major brands, often retailers, adopting their own restricted or declarable substance lists, especially for consumer products. Companies such as Apple[26] and other industry groups[27] have created shared declarable substance lists that are applied across diverse supply chains. These divergent lists can present significant technology challenges for the brand manufacturer, especially of sophisticated technology or industrial products. Controlling the introduction of these restricted materials by suppliers deep in the supply chain is incredibly challenging but necessary in order to maintain legal or contractual compliance. The presence of restricted substances and/or the failure to disclose declarable substances now represents one of the leading causes for product recalls, seizures, and product enforcement actions globally.[28]

Beyond material selection, the United States has adopted legislation to attempt to improve the lives of miners in the conflict regions of central Africa by imposing tracing on minerals sourced from the Congo.[29] This conflict minerals legislation has now been followed by legislation to prevent the importation of goods made using forced labor in the Uyghur region of China. The recently issued strategy[30] creates a rebuttable presumption that goods sourced from the region have been made with forced labor.[31]

Greenhouse Gas Emissions/Energy Use

Global companies began adopting greenhouse gas emission (GHG) targets in the 1990s. As climate activists became more sophisticated, they realized that many of the achievements in this area were made by shifting the GHG-intensive activities to suppliers, especially suppliers in developing countries.[32] Guidance by organizations such as CDP (formerly the Carbon Disclosure Project) began pushing brands to include their whole supply chain in their targets.[33] Typically referred to as Scope 3, these emissions require engagement with the supply chain. This has led to some very innovative programs, such as commitments by the major

---

26. See https://www.apple.com/environment/pdf/Apple_Regulated_Substances_Specification_March 2021.pdf.

27. International Aerospace Environmental Group (IAEG), Aerospace and Defence Declarable Substance List, https://www.iaeg.com/chemicalrpt/addsl/.

28. See, for example, Europe's Safety Gate: The EU Rapid Alert System for Dangerous Non-food Products, https://ec.europa.eu/safety-gate-alerts/screen/webReport (search for alerts with keywords "REACH" or "RoHS") and California Proposition 65's Annual Settlement Reports, https://oag.ca.gov/prop65/annual-settlement-reports.

29. United States' Dodd–Frank Act, Section 1502 (Conflict Minerals), Dodd–Frank Wall Street Reform and Consumer Protection Act, Pub. L. No. 111-203, 124 Stat., § 1502.

30. See https://www.dhs.gov/sites/default/files/2022-06/22_0617_fletf_uflpa-strategy.pdf.

31. Uyghur Forced Labor Prevention Act (UFLPA), Pub. L. 117-78 (2021).

32. See https://www.fastcompany.com/90698724/esg-investing-has-a-sustainability-blind-spot-supply-chains.

33. See https://www.cdp.net/en/research/global-reports/changing-the-chain.

technology companies for their data centers to obtain all of their energy from renewable sources. For example, Apple recently announced how its suppliers are implementing detailed renewable energy projects globally.[34]

This is probably the fastest evolving of all the ESG issues. It requires careful thought as understanding the supply chain can be overwhelming. Recognizing these challenges, the U.S. EPA has issued a high-level guide for engaging with suppliers, with recommendations based on experience to:

1. chose strategically which suppliers to engage with,
2. keep the data requests simple,
3. build trust,
4. provide training and capacity building, and
5. conduct pilot initiatives.[35]

In the last few years, many companies have adopted "net zero" goals. Net zero goals are expected to include the entire value chain, including customers and suppliers.[36] This is a huge challenge. Estimates are that about 25 percent of the investments will need to be made by small- to medium-sized enterprises.[37] This will require the kind of engagement and capacity building EPA identified. As an example, Unilever has laid out a very clear strategy for working with their suppliers toward their net zero goal.[38]

There are resources to help you begin. Major brands are beginning to collaborate on helping suppliers engage. For example, a number of companies have joined together with Guidehouse Consulting to form the Supplier Leadership on Climate Transition (Supplier LoCT) project, which aims to provide suppliers with the kind of expertise to reduce emissions that suppliers will need to actually execute clean energy projects.[39]

The Task Force for Climate-Related Financial Disclosures (TCFD) has a thoughtful tool for providing investors and other stakeholders with the most relevant information. In particular, the TCFD's recommendations require a company to disclose how it identifies, manages, and mitigates its major climate risks.[40] The TCFD also recommends companies use scenario analysis to look beyond the horizon.[41] For many companies, the most significant risks may be in their supply chain. CDP has aligned its questionnaires to reflect the TCFD's

34. See https://www.apple.com/newsroom/2022/04/apple-helps-suppliers-rapidly-accelerate-renewable-energy-use-around-the-world/.

35. See https://www.epa.gov/climateleadership/how-engage-suppliers.

36. See https://sciencebasedtargets.org/net-zero.

37. See https://www.weforum.org/agenda/2022/02/7-steps-for-delivering-net-zero-supply-chains/.

38. See https://www.unilever.com/planet-and-society/climate-action/partnering-with-suppliers-to-deliver-net-zero/.

39. See https://guidehouse.com/news/corporate-news/2021/guidehouse-mars-mccormick-pepsico-suppliers.

40. See https://www.fsb-tcfd.org/recommendations/#core-recommendations.

41. See https://www.fsb-tcfd.org/recommendations/#scenario-analysis.

recommendations.[42] The CDP supplier initiative also provides a platform for data gathering from suppliers.[43]

Water

Extreme weather, drought, and tsunami caused by earthquakes have made clear how our lives depend upon access to clean, potable water and how floods and drought can force migration, reshape the landscape, and interrupt our supply chains. As an example, in 2011, extreme flooding in Thailand interrupted computer and automobile part production for months.[44] Drought conditions in the western United States[45] and low river water levels in France[46] have caused power plants to have to reduce electricity output. Drought in California is forcing agricultural producers to innovate, and in some cases, abandon crops[47]and fires in Western Canada have impacted the cost and availability of building materials throughout North America.[48] In some regions, industrial uses of water are the first to be prioritized for reduction, giving households priority on available supply. These risks may be magnified in industries that need water for cooling, such as electricity production, and injection, such as fracking, or for electronic manufacturing processes that may require either significant amount of water for processing or compete with households for potable water.[49]

Closely linked to the climate challenge, understanding the business risk inherent in the use of water and proximity to it, are increasingly on stakeholders' agenda. CDP's water risk tool is used by investor groups to evaluate how well your company has evaluated its internal and supply chain risks.[50] Each of the risks identified above is likely somewhere in the supply chain; the issue for the brand is how to mitigate those risks (for example, with backup suppliers) and to help critical suppliers identify lower water use technologies.

Waste/Recycling/Circular Economy

Historically, brands sold a product and left it to the local authorities to arrange for waste management at the end of the useful life of the product. The EU took the lead by adopting waste take-back requirements in a number of sectors. This has largely evolved into a network of providers who, for a fee, will set up collection points and arrange for the recycling of the product and final disposal

42. See https://www.cdp.net/en/guidance/how-cdp-is-aligned-to-the-tcfd.
43. See https://www.cdp.net/en/supply-chain.
44. See https://www.reuters.com/article/us-thai-floods/thai-floods-batter-global-electronics-auto-supply-chains-idUSTRE79R0QR20111028.
45. See https://www.eia.gov/todayinenergy/detail.php?id=49676.
46. See https://www.rfi.fr/en/france/20200825-drought-provokes-shutdown-nuclear-reactors-northeast-france-belgium-ardennes-chooz-meuse.
47. See https://caclimatehub.ucdavis.edu/wp-content/uploads/sites/320/2016/03/factsheet3_crops.pdf.
48. See https://fortune.com/2021/07/02/british-columbia-fires-lumber-prices/.
49. See https://www.morganstanley.com/ideas/the-worlds-water-crisis-and-industries-at-risk.
50. See https://cdn.cdp.net/cdp-production/cms/reports/documents/000/005/577/original/CDP_Water_analysis_report_2020.pdf?1614687090.

of the residual waste. In other areas, the value of the material in the product and consumer pressure, especially in the electronics and appliances sectors, have encouraged companies to set up take-back avenues. This involves a kind of reverse logistics with suppliers taking most of the responsibility. This is increasingly attracting the attention of activists and investors, especially as it relates to materials that may be in short supply. For example, concerns regarding access to lithium and potential constraints on its use in batteries are seen as a challenge to our societal de-carbonization efforts.

All of this was made more complicated when major recycling practices with China were shut down in 2018.[51] Dealing with the 3R's (reduce, reuse, recycle) is also an expectation of a younger generation of consumers and may provide a competitive advantage when done well. Concerns about fast fashion are a prime example of how expectations evolve over time.

Biodiversity

Almost any industry can have impacts on nature's biodiversity, but some industrial sectors especially those involving the food supply are more impactful.[52] In some cases, the creation of large-scale agricultural plantations, often with a single cash crop, can create a monoculture that can have major impacts on the habitats on which biodiversity depends. Transportation can introduce invasive species that can crowd out natives. Building facilities near or on sensitive or protected habitats can endanger both habitats and species and present special concerns for those involved in the hospitality and material extraction industries. The apparel industry has been directly involved in species extinction for centuries. For example, cotton production accounts for 20 percent of worldwide pesticide use.[53] Many industries, such as construction, paper, and fabrics, use wood fibers. Some comes from certified sustainable forests, but depending upon the sector much does not. Initiatives such as the Forest Stewardship Council have started initiatives to address biodiversity issues in the apparel sector.[54]

Strategies

All of these issues can seem overwhelming. Some may have limited relevance for your business. Some will seem obvious. GHG emissions have long been a focus area for transportation and energy companies. Companies have focused

51. See https://e360.yale.edu/features/piling-up-how-chinas-ban-on-importing-waste-has-stalled-global-recycling.

52. See https://forest500.globalcanopy.org/.

53. See https://www.mckinsey.com/industries/retail/our-insights/biodiversity-the-next-frontier-in-sustainable-fashion#:~:text=The%20apparel%20industry%20is%20a,natural%20ecosystems%2C%20and%20waterway%20pollution.

54. See https://fsc.org/en/newsfeed/fashion-forever-green-pact-launched-to-promote-responsible-sourcing-of-renewable-fibre.

on the financial strength of their suppliers as a key risk management element for decades. But some may be newer and less obvious. The key to success is a multidisciplinary approach, working closely with sourcing, marketing, technology, legal, and human resources to identify the issues that must be addressed. The ESG pressures on sourcing have changed over the last twenty-five years and there are external resources such as the Responsible Mineral Initiative[55] that can be leveraged, for example, on tough issues such as conflict minerals. In some areas, it may make sense to leverage existing initiatives, such as those targeting indirect materials, where your company's purchases may not be significant enough to have much leverage over the supplier.

The key is to prioritize. The company may have thousands of suppliers, but perhaps only a few that could cause a major business interruption if they failed. Those may be the suppliers that get special scrutiny for physical risks, such as flooding, or for resilience screening. The company may be able to use life cycle analysis to identify the commodities that have the highest GHG content in their manufacture. These may be the right targets for discussions on their GHG strategies. Are there segments of the business that are at risk for use of migrant workers, for example, in construction or agriculture-based raw materials? Are there commodities that are only produced in countries with corruption issues? These issues may require next level attention.

Leverage external resources include nongovernmental organizations and activists. This can seem a bit scary, but many know their issues very well, can help the company narrow down to the issues that really matter, and can link your actions up with others. As an example, the Environmental Defense Fund has worked for years with Walmart.[56] Walmart is now working with CDP and HSBC on financing to help their suppliers to improve their ESG performance.[57]

Guidelines

Clarity of expectations is key with suppliers. Identify if your sector has already adopted guidelines or a code of conduct, such as that developed initially by the electronics sector and now embodied in the Responsible Business Initiative (RBI) Code of Conduct.[58] These guidelines may already be familiar to your supply base and can reduce conflict and confusion by the suppliers, who have sometimes felt barraged by competing standards. One advantage of these tools is that they already incorporate guidance developed by organizations such as the International Labor Organization (ILO)[59] or the Organization for Economic Co-operation and Development (OECD) Guidelines for Multi-National Enterprises.[60] Adopting

55. See https://www.responsiblebusiness.org/initiatives/rmi/.

56. See https://www.edf.org/partnerships/walmart#:~:text=Transforming%20the%20supply%20chain&text=EDF%20helped%20Walmart%20realize%20that,use%20and%20greenhouse%20gas%20emissions.

57. See https://corporate.walmart.com/newsroom/2021/12/08/walmart-creates-industry-first-by-introducing-science-based-targets-for-supply-chain-finance-program.

58. See https://www.responsiblebusiness.org/media/docs/RBACodeofConduct7.0_English.pdf.

59. See http://www.ilo.org/global/standards/lang--en/index.htm.

60. See https://www.oecd.org/investment/mne/1903291.pdf.

an industry standardized approach to governance offers the highest likelihood of successful implementation, because suppliers are more likely to be familiar with the requirements. Moreover, industry standardized declarations typically offer the highest economic benefit to adoption, because they provide a consistent dataset that aligns with multiple consistent customer requests. [61]

If the available tools do not fit your supply chain, you may need to create a more custom approach. If your company has one, start with your own company's code of conduct and customize it to address the critical issues identified in your risk assessment. If you need to start from scratch, there are now a significant number of consultants who can provide assistance. One lesson learned: there is a tendency to create very long, detailed, and cross-referenced codes. This can give a sense of comprehensiveness. However, supply chains are often far flung; the documents may need to be translated and supported by training. There is strength in simplicity and having expectations embedded in the code at an aspirational level can be very effective. As an example, the code could provide the supplier will "ensure all employees have a safe and healthy workplace" rather than trying to specify every aspect of safety (such as placement of fire extinguishers). These details can be introduced through reference to local legal requirements or generally applied industry guidelines if the local regulations need supplementation.

It is important to have legal involvement with drafting any code, requirement, or guideline to be enforced with the supply chain. Because suppliers are separate companies, your legal team will likely want to caveat the language. Similarly, any public statements about the compliance status of the supply chain should be carefully stated and reviewed. Marketing or communications may want to state: "all our suppliers . . ." But, despite best efforts, no compliance program, no matter how rigorous, can guarantee 100 percent success. We will talk more below about how to handle recalcitrant suppliers.

Once developed, introduction and enforcement of the guidelines can only be operationalized by the sourcing teams on the ground. This means those teams need to be educated themselves and have clarity on which aspects of the guidelines apply across the board, and which ones may be more targeted to higher risk activities. This may involve initial audits, training of suppliers, and a variety of tools to follow up on how well the supplier is executing against the expectations you have identified.

The Contract

Most significant sourcing arrangements involve some sort of contract. It may be as simple as a Uniform Commercial Code compliant purchase order, or be as involved as any merger and acquisition agreement, especially if a technology transfer is involved. Embedding your guidelines or code into all of the contractual tools is a key task that must be implemented with the legal team. The contract will also need to be specific on what information is required from the

61. See *Code of Conduct*, RBA Foundation, https://www.responsiblebusiness.org/code-of-conduct/.

supplier in terms of common data and reports. And, it should clearly provide your company with audit rights and an effective termination provision if the supplier fails to comply. Divorce is always hard and can be very painful if it could impact your company's ability to meet its own customer expectations. Setting out an escalating set of enforcement measures in major agreements may be one of your most useful tools to ensure effective ESG governance program adoption by the supplier.

Data and Technology Enablement

Complex manufacturing supply chains have many areas where risks can be hidden. Whether it is a newly restricted substance entering the supply chain at the earliest stages, or difficult-to-track multitier supplier relationships, any part can contain a host of risks that could impact regulatory compliance. Uncovering these risks requires supplier engagement and education, the ability to process large volumes of data, and streamlined management of the information to visualize and unlock meaningful insights. Generally, suppliers want to provide their customers with the information they need to verify their products can be purchased and used for intended markets. However, the cost of compliance and a fundamental lack of understanding of data requests can inhibit the supplier's ability to provide the required information. Manufacturers that invest in their suppliers, through regulatory training, supply chain education, or other means, will routinely receive more buy-in from suppliers and thus a more complete view of the supply chain.

Success is also intrinsically tied to streamlining data exchanges and reducing supplier friction. Collecting and managing detailed information about chemical substances, manufacturing processes, or country of origin information requires significant resources. Data exchange standards—such as the IPC 1752A, IPC 1754, CMRT, and others[62]—simplify the process, enabling faster communication, resulting in fewer errors, and offering more traceable processes. Companies seeking to deploy efficient supply chain due diligence engagement should start by identifying the standard bodies that are most representative of your organization's business operations and respective supply chains. Once identified, join the appropriate groups. They are generally staffed by volunteers and practitioners eager for support and equally eager to share their expertise in the area.

Technology enablement will add efficiency to programs by mapping information across product lines and business units. Collecting data is only half the battle for most complex durable goods companies and conglomerates. Information from component and materials suppliers must be accessible and visualized in ways that can be viewed and understood by teams from across an enterprise. When data are centralized in a single platform, diverse teams can benefit from data collection efforts. Engineering can design with compliance

62. See IPC Materials Data Exchange Homepage, https://www.ipc.org/materials-declaration-data-exchange-standards-homepage, and RMI Conflict Minerals Homepage, https://www.responsiblemineralsinitiative.org/reporting-templates/cmrt/.

in mind, compliance teams can efficiently produce necessary declarations, and procurement teams can have confidence their suppliers are upholding code of conduct standards. Creating a single source of truth will also minimize legal risk by ensuring that disparate data collected from cross-topical departments can be evaluated for veracity and consistency.

Audits

Audits have been the traditional way to evaluate suppliers, especially for labor, health and safety, and environmental risks. An on-site audit when the supplier is initially on-boarded is usually necessary to ensure technical capability, and the ESG issues should be addressed as part of that initial qualification assessment. Follow-on audits have a mixed history. They can be a good way to identify issues the supplier may need to prioritize, to ensure there has not been a change in management approach and to fix specific issues. At the same, they can be expensive, they reflect only a specific point in time, and no one, ever, has audited any activity into compliance (ongoing compliance requires adoption of a management system). Sadly, in some countries, the available third-party auditors have themselves been either corrupt or lack sufficient rigor in performing the audits. Frustration with the limitations of audits has led to experimentation in other quality control approaches.

The diverse array of concerns and the rapid evolution of emerging requirements, combined with travel restrictions and accessibility challenges due to COVID-driven environmental, health, and safety protocols, have further limited on-premises visits. To address these issues, supply chain compliance professionals have turned to tools such as adverse media screening, supplier mapping, sanctions watch-list screening, and social media aggregation to supplement direct surveys and questionnaires. These tools have historically been well leveraged by compliance officers for antibribery and anticorruption monitoring programs. Incorporating this technology into supply chain due diligence programs for ESG has proven to be an effective and novel approach to identify risk flags and to prioritize on-site ESG evaluations. Once information has been assimilated, specific focused direct questions, desktop reviews of supplier information, and on-site audits focused on specific topics of concern can provide significantly more effective than traditional scheduled on-site spot checks. While no solution is, respectively, free of risk, embracing technology can frequently mitigate risks by establishing more frequent touch points and continuous monitoring programs.

Data Verification

As ESG becomes more relevant to investors, the quality of the non-financial disclosures is a compliance issue. Non-financial disclosure audits are most commonly performed under the SASB framework.[63] To manage a non-financial audit, you need quantitative and qualitative data that support everything that is stated

63. See https://www.sasb.org/about/sasb-and-other-esg-frameworks/.

and any claims that are made. Both Europe, through the Non-financial reporting directive (NFRD), Directive 2014/95/EU, and the U.S. SEC, via Commissioner Lee's position on materiality,[64] have expressed a need for normalization and investor protections concerning non-financial disclosures. With this increased recognition of the impact that non-financial disclosures are having on investors, companies must expect increased scrutiny by auditors, investors, and regulatory authorities. To avoid claims of greenwashing, fraud, and material misrepresentation, it is imperative to maintain records on ESG analysis that support claims and meet the emerging standards tied to non-financial reporting. This extends to any statements made or data provided about your sourcing ESG program.

Tough Dilemmas

Historically, the assumption was the buyer had most of the power in supply chain relationships. If COVID has demonstrated anything, it is that some suppliers have far more power than their customers. We have seen some specific areas where these challenges arise.

Supplier Fails to Comply

Typically, supplier noncompliance arises mostly from lack of organizational capacity in the factory. The supplier may either not have resources to understand, for example, local permitting requirements, or the funds to make needed capital investments. Often, these suppliers can be supported with coaching, help finding local expertise and the tools and techniques discussed above.

Nevertheless, there are cases in which the supplier is simply recalcitrant. For example, access to specialty or rare materials may be limited to a few countries and suppliers. Switching to an alternative supplier may be impossible. As a result, in order to meet its own customer's expectations, the brand may be unable to enforce its standards.

Local Rules Are Inconsistent with Your Guidelines

This can be a significant issue with the social aspects of your program. For example, some countries limit the employment of women or minority groups. The government may prohibit the import of specific commodities that are produced locally, leaving local production dependent upon local suppliers.

Indirect Materials

Typically, the biggest costs involve the direct materials that are incorporated in the product. At the same time, the purchase of indirect materials can involve a

64. SEC Press Release: Living in a Material World: Myths and Misconceptions about "Materiality," Commissioner Allison Herren Lee, https://www.sec.gov/news/speech/lee-living-material-world-052421 (May 24, 2021).

large number of suppliers over whom the company has very little leverage. These purchases can be hyper-local, and the local teams may have very little choice or influence on the supplier's behavior. An example is the purchase of office paper or the site landscaper.

While these dilemmas may represent a small number of suppliers or an insignificant portion of the "buy," it is important to face them head on. It may require an exit plan if the supplier is recalcitrant. It may require engaging the local operational and business teams to work with local authorities to find special accommodations that can improve the situation even if they do not achieve 100 percent compliance with your ESG goals. Engagement with nongovernmental organizations can be very useful for educating them on the dilemmas and engaging their assistance in finding solutions. While your communications team might hate this idea, if there are gaps acknowledge publicly that it may be impossible to achieve 100 percent compliance with your program. You will get more credibility for acknowledging the difficulties and will reduce the risk of "greenwashing" or compliance misses given the linkage to financial reporting. Continuous improvement is still making things better even if the long-term goal cannot be achieved immediately.

Evolution and the Future

Many supply chain externalities are outside of the control of the organization, but the decision to work with a given supply chain partner is not. Recent trends of regulations targeting supply chain transparency and third-party risk are bringing this reality to the legal community. It is increasingly risky for a company to rely on the legal concept of the independence of the supplier as the main management tool. Ignoring activities that could fund exploitation or lead to forced labor, shifting environmental risks to third parties, or working with corrupt organizations are no longer business as usual. Companies are increasingly being held responsible, at least by their employees and investors, if not through legally enforceable government requirements, for the actions of those they choose to do business with to produce the products and services they profit from.

CHAPTER 5

ESG in Supply Chain Labor Practices

Sarah Carpenter

Introduction

To a large degree, U.S. corporations have built responsible labor and employment practices into their broader environmental, social, and governance (ESG) initiatives.[1] These efforts are a boon to employees—protecting workers better, promoting equality, and, in general, addressing the employer/employee power imbalance. Strong labor programs also mitigate risks to companies, such as consumer boycotts or shareholder actions resulting from poor labor practices. This change was brought, in part, by significant advancements in laws, regulations, standards, and litigation in multiple areas from workplace safety to labor–management relations, diversity to the right to organize.[2] However, as this chapter explores, a corporation's exposure to labor practice risks extends beyond its four walls and well into the supply chain. And, for most U.S. corporations, the supply chain is where the most egregious labor rights violations take place.

Forced labor, for instance, has been well documented across a variety of product supply chains, including those that create clothes, shoes, food, and electronics. Many of us may recall reading about forced labor in the disposable glove manufacturing sector in Malaysia during the COVID-19 pandemic.[3] The overwhelming majority of these victims were low-wage migrant workers from countries like Bangladesh, Nepal, and Myanmar. Employers and recruiters exploited these workers through debt-based coercion when they were unable to pay the onerous fees that were imposed on them during the recruitment process. Employers utilized additional practices indicative of forced labor, like excessive

1. See Alan Gutterman et al., In Labor and Supply Chain Practices for an excellent overview of US labor laws (Chapter 6), *The Lawyers Corporate Social Responsibility Deskbook* (ABA 2019).

2. A summary of U.S. labor laws and standards is available on the Department of Labor website: https://www.dol.gov/general/aboutdol/majorlaws.

3. CBP Issues Forced Labor Finding on Top Glove Corporation Bhd. (Mar. 29, 2021).

overtime, abusive working and living conditions, and retention of identity documents, to further exploit these workers.[4]

These stories and many like them give shape to alarming statistics on the prevalence of forced labor in the private economy. According to the International Labour Organization (ILO), private actors imposed forced labor on an estimated 17.3 million people in 2021,[5] with the manufacturing sector accounting for nearly one-fifth of all forced labor exploitation of adults, about 3 million people. These findings follow the upheaval wrought by the COVID-19 pandemic that caused mass unemployment for some workers, while heightening vulnerability to exploitation for others. Indeed, these estimates show that forced labor has increased significantly in the last five years. These risks are well known to many U.S. businesses. Indeed, according to a 2016 study by the Ethical Trading Initiative (ETI), 71 percent of surveyed companies believed there was a likelihood of modern slavery occurring at some stage in their supply chains.[6] If we then account for other types of labor abuses, like discrimination and union bans, we can see how supply chains mask a substantial modern slavery problem.

The supply chains of today were built for efficiency but not the transparency required to achieve the ambitious goals set out by new ESG regulations. For the last thirty years, U.S. manufacturers have sought to optimize profitability by outsourcing various stages of the production process. Often the stages that have been outsourced include some of the riskiest activities for workers. This chapter will provide companies with best practices to adapt their supply chains, assisting in building programs that provide meaningful action in the field of ESG labor and human rights protections.

Legal and Regulatory Requirements

In a free market society, legislators must walk the fine line between allowing a market—including the companies and consumers that comprise it—to operate independently of interference, and protecting people, the environment, or other entities that lack the market power to protect themselves. In regard to establishing safe labor practices through the supply chain, the U.S. government and others are evolving how they negotiate these two forces, which has resulted in a recent tightening of the laws surrounding labor standards in corporate supply chains and this is having serious financial implications for U.S. businesses.[7]

---

4. CBP Public Affairs. "CBP Modifies Forced Labor Finding on Top Glove Corporation Bhd." U.S. Customs and Border Protection, Sept. 9, 2021.

5. International Labour Organization. "Global Estimates of Modern Slavery: Forced Labour and Forced Marriage." Sept. 12, 2022, https://www.ilo.org/wcmsp5/groups/public/---ed_norm/---ipec/documents/publication/wcms_854733.pdf.

6. Quintan Lake et. al., *Corporate Approaches to Addressing Modern Slavery in Supply Chains*, Ethical Trading Initiative (2015), https://www.ethicaltrade.org/sites/default/files/shared_resources/corporate_approaches_to_addressing_modern_slavery.pdf.

7. See U.S. Department of State Business and Human Rights website: https://www.state.gov/key-topics-bureau-of-democracy-human-rights-and-labor/business-and-human-rights/.

A standard of conduct established by the United Nations Guiding Principles on Business and Human Rights (UNGPs) in 2011 anchors most of today's legal and regulatory requirements pertaining to labor standards in the supply chain. This standard of conduct stipulates that businesses have a responsibility to respect human rights and that due diligence is the means through which they meet this responsibility. States have and continue to use a range of different approaches to turn this soft standard into a hard requirement to increase its uptake by the private sector. This, in turn, reflects the duty of States under the UNGPs, which includes a duty to protect human rights by enforcing laws that are aimed at, or have the effect of, fostering business respect for human rights. These varying approaches are described below.

Procurement Requirements

States are using their enormous purchasing power to promote responsible business practices and reinforce their expectations of the private sector. Most States recognize that they have significant influence on the market and can motivate good practice by making due diligence a prerequisite for businesses to access and retain public contracts. Conversely, these same States recognize that they can sustain human rights abuses by failing to allow public procurement agents to consider sustainability when making purchasing decisions. The U.S. government, for instance, awards hundreds of billions of dollars annually to companies competing for a wide range of contracts related to government work, most notably in the defense sector. This market power gives the government an effective tool to influence desired behavior, such as reducing the risk of human trafficking in supply chains.

Since 2015, Subpart 22.17 of the Federal Acquisition Regulation (FAR) places several requirements on companies competing for government department contracts, including prohibiting:

- the use of forced labor,
- denying employee access to identity or immigration documents,
- the use of misleading or fraudulent recruitment practices,
- the charging of recruitment fees,
- failing to provide return transportation or pay for the cost of return transportation at the end of employment for certain employees, and
- providing or arranging housing that fails to meet the host country standards.[8]

8. U.S. Government. "Federal Acquisition Regulation; Ending Trafficking in Persons." Federal Register, Jan. 29, 2015, https://www.federalregister.gov/documents/2015/01/29/2015-01524/federal-acquisition-regulation-ending-trafficking-in-persons#:~:text=It%20provides%20for%20the%20use,to%20comply%20with%20the%20requirements.

These requirements extend to subcontractors via flowdowns and demand that contractors eliminate the risk of human trafficking in their operations and supply chains.[9]

As a policy tool, FAR Subpart 22.17 strengthened the U.S. government's policy of prohibiting government contractors, subcontractors, and agents from engaging in human trafficking. Severe forms of these prohibited activities are defined under Section 103 of the Trafficking Victims Protection Act of 2000 (TVPA).[10] They include the recruitment, harboring, transportation, provision, or obtaining of a person for labor or services through the use of force, fraud, or coercion for the purpose of subjection to involuntary servitude, peonage, debt bondage, or slavery. When it came into effect in March 2015, it codified trafficking-related prohibitions to federal contractors and their subcontractors and established requirements for general worker protection.

Noncompliance with FAR can have significant financial implications for companies. In declassified documents,[11] provided by the Department of Defense Inspector General's Office, a longtime defense contractor providing food services for a U.S. military base in Kuwait repeatedly failed to pay the required minimum wage according to Kuwaiti labor law, failed to provide individual employment agreements in English and Arabic, required employees to surrender passports after arriving in the country, failed to provide sanitary living conditions, and charged recruitment fees. After a series of warnings and remediation efforts by the U.S. government, the contractor was replaced with a competitor, losing a $22 million USD contract.

Disclosure Rules

States are also passing transparency rules to increase private sector uptake of the UNGPs responsible business standard. These rules are aimed at driving a race to the top by requiring companies to publicly disclose their due diligence practices. They are designed to give a company's stakeholders the information they need to act as de facto enforcement agents. By directing their spend elsewhere or holding Board members to account, these agents use a variety of tools to penalize businesses for failing to meet their expectations.

One of the most well-known human-rights-related disclosure rules in the United States is Section 1502 of the U.S. Dodd–Frank Consumer Protection and Wall Street Reform Act (Conflict Minerals). Conflict Minerals requires publicly traded U.S. companies to file an annual report via a Form SD that discloses the use of conflict minerals—tin, tungsten, tantalum, and gold (3TGs)—sourced

9. Andrew Mayock et al., Anti-Trafficking Risk Management Best Practices and Mitigation Considerations—Draft for Public Comment, Jul. 12, 2016, White House.

10. L. 106–386, §1, Oct. 28, 2000, 114 Stat. 1464.

11. Inspector General, U.S. Department of Defense, "Report No. DODIG-2019-088: Evaluation of DOD Efforts to Combat Trafficking in Persons in Kuwait." Jun. 11, 2019, https://media.defense.gov/2019/Jun/20/2002147915/-1/-1/1/DODIG-2019-088.PDF.

from the Democratic Republic of the Congo (DRC) and its adjoining countries. When they are used, issuers are required to submit a "Conflict Minerals Report" describing the measures taken to exercise due diligence, the facilities used to process the conflict minerals, the country of origin of the conflict minerals, among other details.

This kind of disclosure, which is also seen in the California Transparency in Supply Chains Act, the 2018 Australia Modern Slavery Act, and other regulations around the world, sidesteps the legal complexities of proving or disproving human rights violations in a supply chain by leveraging public scrutiny to influence behavior. And these disclosures often have implications for large U.S. multinationals given their broad scope, such as the U.K. Modern Slavery Act which requires companies with more than £36 million annual revenue to publish an annual modern slavery report when some or all its business is conducted in the United Kingdom.[12]

Failing to disclose a due diligence process that meets stakeholder expectations can have severe consequences for businesses. For example, in October 2016, KnowTheChain gave Monster Beverage, a California-based beverage company, a score of "0" in its Food & Beverage Benchmark Findings report, stating that it underperformed "across all thematic areas relative to its peers" related to forced labor disclosures.[13] It was one of twenty food and beverage companies benchmarked that year on themes of commitment and governance, traceability and risk assessment, purchasing practices, recruitment, worker voice, monitoring, and remedy. KnowTheChain updated the company's score to "4" in 2018 because it disclosed "a commitment to addressing forced labor as well as limited details on supplier audits and corrective action." However, it still noted that it "discloses significantly less information on its forced labor policies and practices than its peers."[14] A nonprofit organization called As You Sow filed a shareholder resolution on slavery in the supply chain for vote at the company's annual meeting. This resolution brought the issue before the company's shareholders and the board. This resolution asked the company to "issue a report containing the criteria and analytical methodology used to determine its conclusion of 'minimal risk' of slavery and human trafficking in its sugarcane supply chain." It was filed after As You Sow had an "unproductive dialogue" with the company and ended up garnering support from about 20 percent of its shareholders.[15] As You Sow also launched a campaign with Freedom United to back up its shareholder resolution.

12. U.K. Home Office. "Modern Slavery Act 2015." GOV.UK, Jun. 10, 2014, https://www.gov.uk/government/collections/modern-slavery-bill.

13. KnowTheChain. "Monster Beverage Corp.—2016 Food and Beverage." 2016, https://knowthechain.org/company/monster-beverage-corp-united-states/.

14. KnowTheChain. "Monster Beverage Corp.—2018 Food and Beverage." 2018, https://knowthechain.org/company/monster-beverage-corp-united-states/.

15. As You Sow. "Monster Beverage Shareholders Vote to Fix Slavery Problem." Jun. 8, 2018, https://www.asyousow.org/press-releases/2018/6/8/monster-beverage-shareholders-vote-to-fix-slavery-problem.

The petition, which urged the company to investigate slavery risk in its drinks, was signed by nearly 26,000 people around the world.[16]

In response, Monster Beverage built a more robust slavery and human trafficking program. It invested in supplier engagement, employee training, and training platforms for its suppliers. These efforts allowed it to avoid a second shareholder resolution and moved it from being a "laggard to leader on slavery in supply chain."[17]

Not all impacts of mandatory reporting laws are positive for victims of modern slavery, however. Indeed, the California Transparency in Supply Chains Act inadvertently may have made it harder to effect change in supply chains. Coming into force in 2012, the Act requires companies to publicly disclose to what extent "if any" it:

(1) engages in verification of product supply chains to evaluate and address risks of human trafficking and slavery; (2) conducts audits of suppliers; (3) requires direct supplies to certify that materials incorporated into the product comply with the laws regarding slavery and human trafficking of the countries in which they are doing business; (4) maintains accountability standards and procedures for employees or contractors that fail to meet company standards regarding slavery and human trafficking; and (5) provides employees and management training on slavery and human trafficking.[18]

The Act notably does not call for violations to be addressed, nor does it prescribe penalties for noncompliance. It excludes all corporations that do not identify as manufacturers or retail sellers on their tax returns and corporations with annual worldwide gross receipts of less than $100 million USD. It does not criminalize or create civil liability for actual engagement in forced labor. Rather it is "fundamentally a consumer protection statute, written to protect consumers from being duped into buying forced labor-produced products."[19]

As a result, the Act has been used as a "safe harbor" for companies that are being sued based on other consumer protection laws.

For example, in 2015, Nestlé USA, Inc., was sued by plaintiffs for violations of the California Unfair Competition Law, Legal Remedies Act, and False Advertising Law.[20] The plaintiffs alleged the company had violated consumer protection statutes by failing to inform consumers that "some proportion of its cat food products may include seafood which was sourced from forced labor."[21]

---

16. FreedomUnited. "Urge Monster to Investigate Slavery Risk in Its Drinks." FreedomUnited.org, May 2018, https://www.freedomunited.org/advocate/monster-slavery/.

17. As You Sow. "Monster Beverage Corporation—A Case Study in Shifting from Laggard to Leader on Slavery in Supply Chain." Jun. 4, 2019, https://www.asyousow.org/press-releases/monster-beverage-slavery-supply-chain.

18. Kamala D. Harris, "The California Transparency in Supply Chains Act—A Resource Guide." 2015, https://oag.ca.gov/sites/all/files/agweb/pdfs/sb657/resource-guide.pdf.

19. Emma Cusumano, "Is the California Transparency in Supply Chains Act Doing More Harm than Good?" Corporate Accountability Lab, Jul. 25, 2017, https://corpaccountabilitylab.org/calblog/2017/7/25/is-the-california-transparency-in-supply-chains-act-doing-more-harm-than-good.

20. California Unfair Competition Law, Cal. Bus. & Prof. Code § 17200 et seq, Legal Remedies Act, Cal. Civ. Code § 1750, et seq., and False Advertising Law, Cal. Bus. & Prof. Code § 17500, et seq.

21. Barber v. Nestlé USA, Inc., 154 F. Supp. 3d 954 (C.D. Cal. 2015).

Nestlé successfully argued that, since it met its reporting requirements as established by the California Transparency in Supply Chains Act, it was shielded from further requirements under the safe harbor doctrine. More specifically, Nestlé argued that because the California Legislature already considered the disclosures that large companies need to make to consumers, they are not obligated to make additional disclosures as sought by the plaintiffs. In 2016, the judge agreed to dismiss the lawsuit on the basis of the "safe harbor doctrine."[22]

Trade Controls and Sanctions

States are using import controls and sanctions to set standards for human rights. While disclosure rules are designed to help consumers make more ethical buying decisions, import controls are designed to stop products made with forced labor from entering the market in the first place. The United States has led the world in using import bans to protect labor rights. Section 307 of the Tariff Act of 1930 (19 U.S.C. § 1307) prohibits the importation of merchandise that has been mined, produced, or manufactured, wholly or in part, by forced labor. Although this law has been in force since 1930, it was rarely utilized as it contained a Consumptive Demand clause that exempted goods "not produced in such quantities in the United States as to meet the consumptive demands of the United States." When the clause was repealed under the Trade Facilitation and Trade Enforcement Act of 2015, enforcement took off.

If the Commissioner finds information that "reasonably but not conclusively" indicates that the goods have been made with forced labor, the U.S. Customs and Border Protection Agency (CBP) issues a Withhold Release Order (WRO). A WRO prevents the goods from entering the United States. The importer can then either re-export the goods or submit evidence demonstrating that the goods were not produced with forced labor to have them released. If the Commissioner has "conclusive" evidence that the goods were made with forced labor, they publish a formal finding in the Customs Bulletin and the Federal Register.

According to statistics released by CBP, the total value of cargo detained related to WROs in FY 2022 (as of June 30, 2022) was $357.8 million USD, compared to $218,000 USD for all of FY 2018.[23] These detentions have significant financial implications for businesses. As an example, Top Glove—the world's largest manufacturer of disposable rubber gloves—lost access to the U.S. market for fourteen months[24]—a period overlapping with the COVID-19 pandemic when demand soared for their products, after CBP issued a WRO in October 2021.

22. Keith Bishop & Allen Matkins, "Court Applies Safe Harbor Doctrine to CA Transparency in Supply Chains Act." JD Supra, Jan. 4, 2016, https://www.jdsupra.com/legalnews/court-applies-safe-harbor-doctrine-to-11190/.

23. U.S. Customs and Border Protection. "Trade Statistics." Sept. 16, 2022, https://www.cbp.gov/newsroom/stats/trade.

24. Top Glove. "US Allows Top Glove Imports after Company Pays Off Workers Debt Bondage." Feb. 12, 2022, https://www.topglove.com/single-news-en?id=716&title=us-allows-top-glove-imports-after-company-pays-off-workers-debt-bondage.

Supermax Corporation—another large manufacturer of disposable rubber gloves—saw revenues decrease 79 percent in Q2 2022 compared to the previous year's corresponding quarter.[25] These figures reflect the broad impact of a WRO, which usually extends beyond lost access to the U.S. market. In Supermax's case, the WRO was a contributing factor for the Government of Canada to terminate two health-sector-grade rubber glove supply contracts worth $222 million[26] and the Norwegian Wealth Fund putting them under observation.[27]

WROs cause problems for many U.S. businesses, because they have led to shortages of materials, components, and goods, which impacts their ability to fulfill customer contracts. For example, in a public comment submitted to the Department of Homeland Security, the U.S. solar industry disclosed that it had to cancel or delay nearly 33 percent of planned utility-grade solar projects set for 2021 after the U.S. government banned all silica-based products from a Chinese manufacturer due to forced labor allegations.[28]

Section 307 of the Tariff Act of 1930 served as a precursor for the Uyghur Forced Labor Prevention Act (UFLPA). The 2022 law created a rebuttable presumption that goods sourced from the Xinjiang Uyghur Autonomous Region (XUAR) of China are made with forced labor, and thus are inadmissible to the United States. According to a May 2022 letter from the top lawmakers at the Congressional-Executive Commission on China (CECC), the UFLPA raises the number of transactions subject to CBP review from less than 1 million to over 11.5 million. According to statistics released by CBP, the total value of cargo detained related to the UFLPA and WROs in August 2022 alone was $266.5 million USD,[29] compared to $486 million USD for all of FY 2021. The UFLPA is expected to disrupt a growing number of supply chains as CBP enhances its ability to prevent entry of goods at U.S. ports in violation of the UFLPA. It has secured funding for new tools, technology, and sixty-five positions.[30] At the time this book went to print, the White House had requested an additional $70 million USD to create another 300 full-time positions for forced labor enforcement,

25. "Supermax Revenue Plunges 79% Impacted by WRO and Lower ASPs." Business Today, May 25, 2022, https://www.businesstoday.com.my/2022/05/25/supermax-revenue-plunges-79-impacted-by-wro-and-lower-asps/.

26. Gavin Fridell, "Supermax Case May Signal Shift in Canada's Policy on Tackling Forced Labour." The Monitor, (Jan. 20, 2022), https://monitormag.ca/articles/supermax-case-may-signal-shift-in-canadas-policy-on-tackling-forced-labour.

27. *Decisions on Observation and Exclusion.* Norges Bank Investment Management. Jun. 15, 2022, https://www.nbim.no/en/the-fund/news-list/2022/decisions-on-observation-and-exclusion2/.

28. *Comment Submitted by American Clean Power Association.* American Clean Power Association. Regulations.gov, Mar. 11, 2022, https://www.regulations.gov/comment/DHS-2022-0001-0163.

29. U.S. Customs and Border Protection. "CBP Releases August 2022 Monthly Operational Update." Sept. 19, 2022, https://www.cbp.gov/newsroom/national-media-release/cbp-releases-august-2022-monthly-operational-update.

30. Homeland Security. "Strategy to Prevent the Importation of Good Mined, Produced, or Manufactured with Forced Labor in the People's Republic of China." Jun. 17, 2022, https://www.dhs.gov/sites/default/files/2022-06/22_0617_fletf_uflpa-strategy.pdf.

an amount that would increase its budget to a level that exceeds that of the Office of Foreign Assets Control (OFAC).[31]

The U.S. model of establishing import controls on goods made with forced labor was extended to the entire North American market with the United States–Mexico–Canada Agreement (USMCA). Other jurisdictions are considering similar legislation. For instance, the EU is working to ban the placing on the EU market of products made wholly or in part by forced labor. The ban would cover both domestic and imported products. It would allow the EU to stem the flow of goods made with forced labor that are being redirected to the EU because they are no longer allowed in the North American market. The proposed EU legislation would require businesses to destroy or render inoperable these goods so they cannot be exported to other jurisdictions.

The United States continues to use sanctions as a tool for addressing human rights issues. In April 2021, the United States sanctioned state-owned companies in Belarus under the Belarus Sanctions Regulations, citing human rights violations related to the detention of political prisoners in conjunction with the August 2020 Presidential elections. President Biden also issued an Executive Order in June 2021 prohibiting U.S. persons from investing in a list of Chinese companies that use surveillance technology to facilitate human rights abuses.

New Generation of Labor Rights Laws

Today, States are using and activating a new generation of labor rights laws to drive private sector uptake of the UNGPs responsible business standard. Some States have expressed a belief that disclosure rules have reached their limit and that mandatory provisions are now needed. For example, countries in Europe have enshrined mandatory human rights due diligence requirements into law. Countries with requirements include France, Germany, the Netherlands, Norway, and Switzerland. Other countries have similar bills in development and the EU, as a trading bloc, is working on a continent-wide approach to mandatory human rights due diligence.

This new generation of labor rights laws make it mandatory for businesses to undertake due diligence on specified commodities, sustainability topics, and areas of their business. Some are very prescriptive and detailed in what a legally compliant due diligence approach looks like. This contrasts the general nature of international standards and gets into the specifics of frequency, scope, and required activities. The German Act on Corporate Due Diligence Obligations in Supply Chains, or the Lieferkettensorgfaltspflichtengesetz (LkSG), is an excellent

31. Ana Swanson, *Companies Brace for Impact of New Forced Labor Law*. N.Y. Times, (Jun. 22, 2022), https://www.nytimes.com/2022/06/22/us/politics/xinjiang-uyghur-forced-labor-law.html.

example of how this new generation of labor rights laws operationalizes the due diligence standard. Under this Act, companies must:

1. Establish a risk management system to comply with their due diligence obligations. They must define in-house responsibility for risk management, and senior management must seek information about the work of this person or people at least once a year.
2. Perform risk analyses to identify human rights and environment-related risks in their operations and supply chain at least once per year. They must weigh and prioritize the identified risks according to the following criteria:
   a. the nature and extent of the company's activities;
   b. the company's ability to influence the party directly responsible for a risk or injury;
   c. the expected severity of the violation, the reversibility of the violation, and the probability of occurrence; and
   d. the nature of the causal contribution of the company to the risk or injury.
3. Establish preventive measures in their operations and supply chain. In particular, companies must establish contractual assurances with direct suppliers on human rights and environmental issues, implement procurement strategies that reduce risk, deliver training to employees, among other activities. The company must also issue a policy statement on its human rights strategy and this statement must be adopted by its senior management.
4. Take remedial action if they discover that a human rights or environment-related violation has occurred or is imminent. In the context of suppliers with whom it has a contractual relationship, the company must draw up a remediation plan that contains a concrete timeline. The company must continue the business relationship unless a specific set of criteria is met.
5. Establish an internal complaints procedure that enables people to report risks and violations. The company must ensure that the procedure is accessible, maintains confidentiality, and ensures that people can report issues without fear of retaliation.
6. Implement due diligence on sub-tier suppliers (called "indirect suppliers") when the company has substantiated knowledge that a human rights or environmental violation may be possible.
7. Continuously document their fulfillment of the due diligence obligation. They must keep this documentation for at least seven years, and they must prepare and publish on its website an annual report describing what it has done to fulfill its obligations.

This law, along with the UFLPA, requires companies to perform multitier supply chain due diligence to addressing labor rights risks in their supply chains. An indirect supplier is an entity that provides a good or service to a supplier of a manufacturer higher up the supply chain that is in scope of the LkSG. These suppliers are notoriously difficult to monitor, but actions executed by these groups have real labor rights impacts and, increasingly, represent a liability to companies.

Voluntary Standards, Norms, and Guidelines

To understand the legal and regulatory requirements pertaining to ESG in labor supply chain practices, we would have to go back to 2011 when the United Nations Human Rights Council endorsed the UNGPs. The UNGPs established an agreed standard of conduct for human rights. It set the standard that (1) states have a duty to protect human rights, (2) businesses have a responsibility to respect human rights, and (3) affected people must have access to remedy.

With respect to the second pillar, which is the obligation of businesses to respect human rights, the UNGPs further specify that due diligence is the means through which businesses meet this obligation. The principles, which are part of the greater framework, state the following:

- In order to identify, prevent, mitigate and account for how they address their adverse human rights impacts, business enterprises should carry out human rights due diligence. The process should include assessing actual and potential human rights impacts, integrating and acting upon the findings, tracking responses, and communicating how impacts are addressed. In order to gauge human rights risks, business enterprises should identify and assess any actual or potential adverse human rights impacts with which they may be involved either through their own activities or as a result of their business relationships.
- In order to prevent and mitigate adverse human rights impacts, business enterprises should integrate the findings from their impact assessments across relevant internal functions and processes, and take appropriate action.
- In order to verify whether adverse human rights impacts are being addressed, business enterprises should track the effectiveness of their response.

In order to account for how they address their human rights impacts, business enterprises should be prepared to communicate this externally, particularly when concerns are raised by or on behalf of affected stakeholders. Business enterprises whose operations or operating contexts pose risks of severe human rights impacts should report formally on how they address them.[32] The UNGPs establish wide-ranging principles that corporations are using as a framework for labor

32. United Nations Human Rights Office of the High Commissioner. "Guiding Principles on Business and Human Rights." 2011, https://www.ohchr.org/sites/default/files/Documents/Publications/GuidingPrinciplesBusinessHR_EN.pdf.

rights protections within their supply chain. It covers a broad set of rights given the potential for businesses to impact virtually the entire spectrum of internationally recognized human rights. More specifically, it specifies that "the responsibility of business enterprises to respect human rights refers to internationally recognized human rights—understood, at a minimum, as those expressed in the International Bill of Human Rights and the principles concerning fundamental rights set out in the International Labour Organization's Declaration on Fundamental Principles and Rights at Work."[33]

It is worth looking at the principles set out in the International Labour Organization's Declaration on Fundamental Principles and Rights at Work given their significance in the field of international law. All 187 ILO Member States, even if they have not ratified the fundamental conventions, have an obligation to respect, promote, and realize these principles. These fundamental principles and rights at work enable people to "claim freely and on the basis of equality of opportunity their fair share of the wealth which they have helped to generate, and to achieve fully their human potential."[34] They are "universal, inalienable and indivisible human rights and, at the same time, enabling conditions for decent work and sustainable economic growth. Mutually interdependent and reinforcing, they are the starting point for a virtuous circle of effective social dialogue, better incomes and conditions for workers, increased consumer demand, more and better jobs and social protection, rural development, rising enterprise productivity, and of formalizing the informal economy."[35] In short, they provide the foundation on which equitable and just societies are built and enable conditions for decent work and sustainable economic growth.

The ILO principles are as follows:

- *Freedom of association and the effective recognition of the right to collective bargaining.* This enables employers and workers to negotiate key aspects of their relationship and to promote the fair sharing of wealth they have helped to generate.
- *The elimination of all forms of forced or compulsory labor.* This ensures that workers will not be robbed of their dignity or their right to freely choose their own employment.
- *The effective abolition of child labor.* This refers to work that is "mentally, physically, socially or morally dangerous and harmful to children; and/or interferes with their schooling by: depriving them of the opportunity to attend school; obliging them to leave school prematurely; or requiring them to attempt to combine school attendance with excessively long and heavy work."[36]

33. *Ibid.*

34. International Labour Organization. "The Text of the Declaration and Its Follow-Up." 2022, https://www.ilo.org/declaration/thedeclaration/textdeclaration/lang--en/index.htm.

35. "Integrated Strategy on Fundamental Principles and Rights at Work 2017-2023." International Labour Organization, Feb. 2019, https://www.ilo.org/wcmsp5/groups/public/@ed_norm/@ipec/documents/publication/wcms_648801.pdf.

36. International Labour Organization. "IPEC." https://www.ilo.org/ipec/facts/lang--en/index.htm.

- *The elimination of discrimination in respect of employment and occupation.* This is a cross-cutting right and principle that aims to unlock the potential of the millions of people currently excluded or undervalued because of their age, religion, sexual orientation, sex, social and ethnic origins, political opinions, disability, or health status.
- *A safe and healthy working environment.* This right and principle protects workers against sickness, disease, and injury arising out of their employment.

The OECD Guidelines for Multinational Enterprises draw on and are aligned with the UNGPs. It is an important instrument that offers recommendations from governments to businesses on how to act responsibly. The Guidelines cover all areas of business responsibility, including labor rights, and promote observance of the standards and principles outlined in the ILO's Declaration on Fundamental Principles and Rights at Work. It notes that enterprises should, within the framework of applicable law, regulations, and prevailing labor relations and employment practices,

- respect the right of their employees to be represented by trade unions and other bona fide representatives of employees, and engage in constructive negotiations, either individually or through employers' associations, with such representatives with a view to reaching agreements on employment conditions;
- contribute to the effective abolition of child labor and the elimination of all forms of forced or compulsory labor;
- not discriminate against their employees with respect to employment or occupation on such grounds as race, color, sex, religion, political opinion, national extraction, or social origin, unless selectivity concerning employee characteristics furthers established governmental policies which specifically promote greater equality of employment opportunity or relates to the inherent requirements of a job;
- provide facilities to employee representatives as may be necessary to assist in the development of effective collective agreements;
- provide information to employee representatives, which is needed for meaningful negotiations on conditions of employment;
- provide information to employees and their representatives, which enables them to obtain a true and fair view of the performance of the entity or, where appropriate, the enterprise as a whole;
- promote consultation and cooperation between employers and employees and their representatives on matters of mutual concern;
- observe standards of employment and industrial relations not less favorable than those observed by comparable employers in the host country;
- take adequate steps to ensure occupational health and safety in their operations;
- in their operations, to the greatest extent practicable, employ local personnel and provide training with a view to improving skill levels, in cooperation with employee representatives and, where appropriate, relevant governmental authorities;

- in considering changes in their operations which would have major effects upon the livelihood of their employees, in particular in the case of the closure of an entity involving collective layoffs or dismissals, provide reasonable notice of such changes to representatives of their employees, and, where appropriate, to the relevant governmental authorities, and cooperate with the employee representatives and appropriate governmental authorities so as to mitigate adverse effects to the maximum extent practicable;
- in the context of bona fide negotiations with representatives of employees on conditions of employment, or while employees are exercising a right to organize, not threaten to transfer the whole or part of an operating unit from the country concerned nor transfer employees from the enterprises' component entities in other countries in order to influence unfairly those negotiations or to hinder the exercise of a right to organize; and
- enable authorized representatives of their employees to negotiate on collective bargaining or labor–management relation issues and allow the parties to consult on matters of mutual concern with representatives of management who are authorized to take decisions on these matters.[37]

The UNGPs are hailed for their "quiet radicalism" in how they established a "shared understanding of responsibility and a starting point for corporate accountability."[38] Due to their respective influence, they are often considered a "soft-law" due diligence obligation that are becoming "hard-law" requirements through their transposition into national laws as shown in the previous section of this chapter.

Governance and Compliance

As an emerging field, there are still a number of pitfalls in meeting governance and compliance standards related to ESG generally and specifically ESG in supply chain labor practices. To be effective in the face of these unique challenges, varied circumstances, and rapidly changing laws, companies should seek to focus efforts on establishing a good supply chain data management strategy and aligning programs with international due diligence standards. A labor governance program should consider the following leading practices.

Companies struggle to manage their supply chain impacts.[39] They are external to the enterprise, so the information needed to effectively manage supply

37. E. Christopher Johnson Jr. et al., *Labor and Supply Chain Practices in* The Lawyer's Corporate Social Responsibility Deskbook (Alan S. Gutterman et al. eds., 2019).

38. Francis West, "The Quiet Radicalism of the Responsibility to Respect." Shift, Jun. 15, 2021, https://shiftproject.org/ungps-radicalism/#:~:text=This%20is%20the%20quiet%20radicalism,quiet%20radicalism%20of%20the%20UNGPs.

39. Ashley Woods, "State of Compliance: Supply Chain Data Management Insights." Assent, Oct. 19, 2021, https://www.assent.com/blog/2021-state-of-compliance/ (a digital transformation typically includes the following aspects: removing data silos between departments, standardizing data collection processes, and automating repetitive processes).

chain risk is usually not readily accessible. Add on other factors like large supplier counts, a global supply base, and varying degrees of leverage and we can quickly see how supply chains present challenges. A growing number of companies are using technology to overcome these challenges. They are planning for a digital transformation whereby they are shifting processes from manual, reactive activities to automated, proactive tasks. It is a data-driven due diligence process that approaches the supply chain as a data source and optimizes how those data are collected, processed, and actioned.

Technology enables companies to manage risk at scale through automated procedures. It allows companies to better accommodate regional and national variations in their supplier engagement strategy through targeted tools and interventions. And, when companies share the same external system, it enables them to address these issues as a collective through data sharing and common requirements—leading to increased impact. Shifting to digital processes also alleviates resource costs. According to a study commissioned by the European Commission on due diligence requirements throughout the supply chain, "Costs related to the collection of information [. . .] are among the highest cost factors for companies. Emerging tracking and software solutions hold the potential to decrease companies' costs substantially [. . .] However, these technological advancements have not been taken into consideration by the vast majority of the respondents."[40] In helping bring costs down, technology enables a wider group of companies to prioritize due diligence.

Moreover, regulations now require a degree of data governance that would be difficult, maybe impossible, to meet without a shift to digital processes. The German Act on Corporate Due Diligence Obligations in Supply Chains or the LkSG, for instance, requires that companies have an auditable log of every activity, a long-term repository of information (at least seven years), and an up-to-date record of compliance that is readily available for examination by the competent authority. Given these requirements, electronic record keeping and retention has emerged as a critical element of labor ESG compliance.

Start with a Gap Assessment and Build from There

Although most U.S. companies are still working toward an appropriate ESG in supply chain labor practices program, many have elements in place in view of long-standing legal and market expectations. These elements may relate to specific high-risk commodities, such as 3TGs, or specific labor rights issues, such as slavery and human trafficking. They offer a good starting point for progress on broader supply chain labor practices, because their associated management systems and controls can be repurposed and used as a source of learning and inspiration for a broader program.

40. Francisca Torres-Cortés, et al., Study on Due Diligence Requirements through the Supply Chain: Final Report, Publications Office, 2020, https://data.europa.eu/doi/10.2838/39830.

Some of the key areas where companies will need to evolve their existing risk management approach to meet new requirements and market expectations include the following:

- Moving beyond slavery and human trafficking to address broader labor rights issues, which at minimum includes principles concerning fundamental rights set out in the International Labour Organization's Declaration on Fundamental Principles and Rights at Work.
- Moving beyond 3TGs to address a broader set of commodities where human rights abuses are well documented and known, such as mica, cobalt, and polysilicon. This includes broadening the perspective beyond specific regions, like the Democratic Republic of the Congo and its adjoining countries, to capture global sourcing risks.
- Moving beyond a reliance on commercial factors like spend and supplier criticality to consider a broader set of risk factors when prioritizing suppliers for further due diligence. While commercial factors matter because they can be a proxy for leverage, which is important to consider during a prioritizing exercise, they need to be complemented by other factors, like the severity of the violation, to align with the UNGPs and emerging legislation.
- Moving beyond a supplier-oriented approach to risk reduction to a shared approach that also considers how procurement strategies and purchasing practices contribute to risk in the supply chain. This includes short lead times and frequent changes in specifications, which can impact workers through excessive overtime, no toilet breaks, and short-term contracts.

Leverage Expertise on This Complex Topic

ESG labor practices within corporate supply chains is now a regulated topic, and the growing demand for professionals capable of running effective labor rights programs is evidence of this shift. Corporate compliance teams taking on managing a human rights due diligence program will likely need to adjust how they handle compliance issues. Product compliance, for example, largely deals with binary questions: Is this product compliant, yes or no? Teams collect and manage large data sets, discover the answer, and produce required documentation to get their products past regulators and into markets. Human rights compliance is completely different. It is not about being able to say definitively there are no violations in a supply chain—it is about creating a program that can identify and correct potential violations. While outcomes matter for human rights programs, the process is the real objective.[41]

With this key distinction in mind, companies need the right team running their program. Individuals who tend to excel in these roles are

41. Sarah Carpenter, "Supply Chain Jobs: Human Rights & Evolving Global Supply Chains." Supply and Demand Chain Executive, May 5, 2022, https://www.sdcexec.com/sustainability/article/22210731/assent-compliance-supply-chain-jobs-human-rights-evolving-global-supply-chains.

- Process-oriented individuals since they require the ability to design due diligence activities, communicate them throughout a supply chain, and track results.
- Effective change agents since they need to be able to disrupt the status quo while motivating others to collaborate for success.
- Innovative since they need to adapt their due diligence programs to a company's specific context. In other words, they need to be able to work without a defined blueprint.
- Learning-focused since they need to work toward continuously improving their impact as new research and findings emerge.
- Proficient concerning international human rights laws and guidance since their program needs to align with international standards to stand the test of time.

Keep Your Eye on the Bigger Picture

The regulatory and legal landscape for ESG labor practices in the supply chain is quickly expanding. The EU, in particular, is set to profoundly shape the compliance landscape for supply chain labor rights topics in the next three to five years. Major developments include the following:

- The proposed EU Directive on Corporate Sustainability Due Diligence would establish broad due diligence requirements on operations, subsidiaries, and across the value chain (upstream and downstream) of companies. This law will likely include corporate governance reforms, and cover human rights, the environment, and climate change. It would apply to U.S. companies active in the EU with a net turnover of €40 million EUR generated in the EU if they operate in high-impact sectors (e.g., textiles, agriculture, extraction of minerals). This threshold increases to €150 million EUR generated in the EU for companies operating in non-high-impact sectors. Companies would have to (1) integrate due diligence into company policies and update them annually, (2) identify actual/potential adverse impacts, (3) prevent potential impacts and end actual adverse impacts, (4) establish and maintain a complaints procedure, (5) review effectiveness of due diligence annually, and (6) publish annual report. The proposed EU Corporate Sustainability Reporting Directive (CSRD) would require nearly 50,000 companies to publish regular reports on the social and environmental impacts of their activities. It would amend the existing reporting requirements of the EU Non-financial Reporting Directive to capture the EU subsidiaries of non-EU companies as well as any non-EU company with transferable securities listed on an EU regulated market. It would also introduce a new third-party audit requirement of reported information, more detailed reporting requirements in alignment with the forthcoming EU sustainability reporting standard, and a new requirement that companies digitally "tag" the reported information so it is machine readable and feeds into an EU database.
- The proposed EU Regulation to ban products made with forced labor as described above.

Use Industry Standard Surveys to Gain Visibility into Supply Chains

Companies need meaningful data and engagement from suppliers, especially indirect suppliers deep in supply chains, which is challenging. Organizations have developed tools to assist industry in scoping for ESG-related risks. Such tools include the Slavery and Trafficking Risk Template (STRT), developed by the Social Responsibility Alliance, and the Conflict Minerals Reporting Template (CMRT), developed by the Responsible Minerals Initiative. These tools provide legitimacy to reports and streamline the data management efforts required to identify and correct human rights violations in the supply chain. They are built to be cascaded down supply chains for multitiered supply chain visibility into risks. In addition, they are maintained by multi-stakeholder groups that update and refine the templates to ensure they keep stride with the needs of industry. As new laws come into force and expectations expand, evolving tools such as these templates are crucial to helping companies understand and manage their legal obligations surrounding supply chain labor practices in ESG.

Summary and Key Takeaways

Labor issues in corporate supply chains are not new, but the social and legal response to them has undergone a dramatic transformation in recent years. As transparency increases, so do calls for accountability both within and outside of the corporation are driving lawmakers to take action. The growing body of legislation to protect human rights in supply chains, combined with previous regulation mandating public reports and growing ESG standards of supply chain accountability, creates a challenging landscape for corporations. With ESG in a nascent stage, rapidly changing, and often challenged, plotting a course to align supply chain labor practices with ESG standards is daunting. While ESG standards are largely unregulated and do not carry legal requirements, the trend of laws building on industry standards and guidelines has shown that aligning with such standards early is an effective way to ensure proactive compliance with planned human rights laws. By looking to publicly available guidelines and tools, companies can build supply chain labor practices that are resilient to legal changes and business challenges, saving time and money, mitigating business risk, and building better, safer, supply chains for all.

CHAPTER 6

Developing and Implementing Effective ESG Programs

David Hackett and Jamen Tyler

Introduction

In recent years, market and investor interest in company environmental, social, and governance (ESG)[1] performance has exploded, creating meaningful competitive opportunities—and risks—for companies. To meet that growing interest, companies face increasing pressure to disclose ever-expanding information about their ESG performance pursuant to varying and evolving ESG standards. Effective programs and disclosures can provide demonstrable market benefits ranging from easier access to capital to enhanced customer and market opportunities. Conversely, failure to meet ESG expectations results in meaningful negative market impacts, while providing inaccurate or misleading information can lead to embarrassment in the court of public opinion or challenging litigation. In the wake of public outcry and high-profile litigation arising from inaccurate external communications related to ESG efforts, companies must shift away from the historic view of ESG performance and communications as primarily risk-free marketing endeavors. While the still-emerging nature of regulatory standards or concrete mandates suggests that ESG programs and disclosures remain generally voluntary in name, companies that view ESG communication as more akin to advertising than financial disclosures do so at their peril. Responding advantageously to the burgeoning market appetite for ESG information, while minimizing risks associated with ESG-related disclosures and communications, requires the implementation of ESG programs well equipped to prioritize the

1. As discussed below, the term "ESG" encapsulates a wide array of environmental, social, and governance issues. For purposes of this chapter, the terms "ESG" and "ESG issues" refer to any and all such issues that a Company may seek to address.

ESG issues that matter, promote effective ESG performance, and deliver responsive and accurate information.

Accelerating Information Demand Risk and Opportunity

Unmistakably, the demand for ESG information has continued to grow rapidly both as to the volume and level of detail. Recent years have witnessed the continuous emergence of new ESG areas such as social justice, diversity and inclusion, racial equity, and biodiversity/nature adding to the response burden. At the same time, voluntary standard setters and the marketplace continue to press for more detailed, specific, and comprehensive information across the range of ESG reporting. Significantly, the demands no longer emanate solely from voluntary standard setters and nongovernmental organizations (NGOs), as investors, employees, shareholders, customers, and business partners all seek greater information for their use in making investment, purchasing, employment, and engagement decisions. Perhaps most importantly, governments increasingly are building from voluntary standards to promulgate extensive ESG disclosure requirements. While the SEC's proposed climate disclosure rule has captured major attention in the United States, U.S. companies have inadequately focused on the accelerating emergence of mandatory disclosures globally especially in the EU notwithstanding the derivative if not direct impact the EU requirements will have on U.S. companies.[2]

Furthermore, both voluntary and mandatory standards are pressing not only for ESG information about a company's own operations but increasingly also seek performance data related to its supply chain, compelling companies to assess the prospect of devoting potentially massive resources to extracting and vetting such information. Due to the magnitude and challenges of that undertaking, the strategy around ESG and the supply chain has become a critical dimension of ESG programs and reporting.

In response to the information demand, most companies issue an annual ESG report detailing their ESG objectives and performance.[3] However, overlapping and additional information is also furnished in other disclosures, such as customer surveys, investor requests, financial markets, rating agencies, public filings, and marketing materials. In particular, companies provide increasingly comprehensive information in relation to major voluntary standard setters, such as the Global Reporting Initiative (GRI), International Sustainability Standards Board (ISSB, the successor entity to Sustainability Accounting Standards Board

---

2. Most recently, the EU adopted, on Nov. 28, 2022, the Corporate and Sustainability Reporting Directive (CSRD), which extends and expands the EU Non-Financial Reporting Directive. The EU has also adopted the Sustainable Finance Disclosure Regulation (SFDR), which took effect on Mar. 10, 2021, and the EU Taxonomy Regulation, which becomes fully effective on Jan. 1, 2023. Furthermore, the European Financial Reporting Advisory Group (EFRAG) is consulting with GRI to develop and issue implementing standards related to the new CSRD.

3. These reports may carry different names (e.g., ESG, sustainability, corporate citizenship, or corporate social responsibility reports), but each reflects the company's effort to tell its ESG story and provide information to the marketplace. While the scope and nature may differ among them, the term "ESG report" in this chapter refers to a company's primary report addressing its ESG activities.

[SASB]), Carbon Disclosure Project (CDP), UN Global Compact Sustainability Development Goals (SDGs), Task Force on Climate-Related Financial Disclosure (TCFD), Assent, and EcoVadis.[4] While some of these submissions may be cross-referenced in the ESG report, each of them contains separate and extensive detailed information reviewed carefully by the recipients. For many companies, though, those additional disclosures may be prepared by internal groups well distant from those drafting and reviewing the ESG report. Furthermore, the growing and different disclosure requirements, not only in the EU but globally, have given rise to the prospect for multinationals of preparing multiple ESG reports. The full spectrum of reports and disclosures is tracked and reviewed carefully by financial analysts, rating agencies, NGOs, and the marketplace for their accuracy and consistency, creating real risks for any factual inconsistencies.

Not surprisingly, that greater scrutiny also brings with it growing risk. During the past several years, both in the United States and globally, plaintiffs have enjoyed growing success in challenging ESG performance and disclosures alleged to be false or misleading. In the United States, such claims have been pursued successfully under various consumer and securities fraud theories.[5] Generally, these actions contend that companies have made misleading statements about product attributes or provided false or misleading information regarding ESG performance. Significantly, in bringing such cases, plaintiffs no longer limit their review to ESG reports or public filings but are surveying ESG information originating from across the organization as presented in advertisements, management statements, press releases, marketing materials, submission of information to voluntary standard setters, investor briefings, and any other information in the public domain. Often those statements and communications are neither aligned nor consistent leading to material litigation risk related to misleading or inaccurate information. Those risks are only compounded by the growing governmental interest in reviewing ESG disclosures and the enactment of regulations governing ESG reporting.

Implications for ESG Programs

To respond efficiently and effectively to the evolving market opportunities and risks, companies will need to revisit and assess the suitability of their current ESG programs. In particular, the growing risk factors—especially related to investor and consumer reliance on the accuracy of ESG information and the growing governmental scrutiny of company ESG data and information—suggest that ESG programs embrace and reflect the framework that companies increasingly employ in compliance programs associated with regulatory requirements. Typically, those programs correspond to guidance from the U.S. Department of

4. There are further significant reporting frameworks on the horizon, including the Task Force on Nature-Related Financial Disclosure (TNFD).

5. See, for example, Hana V. Vizcarra, *The Reasonable Investor and Climate-Related Information: Changing Expectations for Financial Disclosures*, 50 ELR 10106, 1113-14 (2020); David Hackett, et al., *Growing ESG Risks: The Rise of Litigation*, 50 ELR 10849-10862 (2020).

Justice on the Evaluation of Corporate Compliance Programs, which outlines elements common to programs that effectively address and minimize compliance risks.[6] While these guidelines are based on well-defined, mandatory requirements, they provide a risk-reduction and program implementation framework that is equally applicable to the voluntary ESG context in which obligations are neither clear-cut nor uniformly prescribed. As discussed in depth below, elements such as board oversight, ESG-focused risk assessments, development and implementation of policies and procedures related to the ESG program and disclosures, and training on ESG program components and reporting requirements not only reduce risk of inaccurate ESG disclosures but also promote success of ESG efforts.

While taking a more expansive compliance program view potentially enhances ESG operational performance and mitigates disclosure risk, it does not address some impactful differences between ESG and compliance programs. In the compliance context, the obligations are clear as are the consequences for deficient performance. In the voluntary ESG context, the standards that apply are not prescribed; whether and which ESG issues to address resides solely within the company's discretion. Similarly, there are a plethora of potentially available standards relating to each individual issue (e.g., climate, water, human rights, energy, biodiversity) which can differ significantly as to their requirements and metrics, such that even after identifying the priority ESG areas, the company still must wrestle with determining the standard that it wishes to use. Virtually all companies have encountered challenges and difficulties in tracking effectively the emergence of new issues and standards to ensure they are focused on the ESG concerns that matter most to them. Those challenges underscore the need for an appropriate process to evaluate why ESG matters to them and to track and prioritize those corresponding issues that align with their business purpose and objectives. Absent foundational clarity about which issues matter and why, the resulting selection of priorities and the ESG compliance program—even if effectively implementing DOJ's guidelines—will not be positioned to maximize company purpose and value and will likely waste time and resources in extraneous efforts. Simply put, ESG programs must embody and advance critical business objectives or they will fail.

As a result, the development and implementation of an effective ESG program necessitates consideration of three fundamental questions:

1. Why are we addressing ESG—is it because of customer requirements, investor interest, market pressure, employee concern, competitive advantage, company values, or shareholder demands—and are we evaluating that consideration in the context of advancing the purpose of the enterprise?

6. See U.S. Department of Justice, Criminal Division, Evaluation of Corporate Compliance Programs, Updated Jun. 2020.

2. Based on our understanding of the rationale for addressing ESG, what ESG issues will we address and which of the varying potential voluntary standards applicable to those issues will we use?
3. How will we structure, implement, and manage our ESG programs to identify the appropriate issues and standards, satisfy the applicable performance requirements, and accurately report about them?

In the ESG context, the traditional scope of the compliance program needs to be expanded to take into account the means by which the first two questions will be addressed, including ensuring for clarity about the structure and processes governing responsibilities and roles for undertaking and determining those fundamental underpinnings. The success of an ESG program turns in major part around providing for the selection of the right ESG matters, advancing performance in an integrated manner, managing information across the organization to make certain it is aligned and accurate, and handling strategically ESG supply chain considerations. To do so, many companies rely extensively on ESG materiality assessments, viewing them as comparable to ESG risk assessments. However, as discussed below, while materiality assessments are useful, they do not serve as a substitute for ESG risk assessments and are not necessarily designed to ensure that the right issues are being addressed by the right people with the right resources in the right way. Repositioning ESG programs to mirror more directly fundamental aspects of traditional compliance programs along with revisiting ESG risk assessment considerations presents a useful pathway for delivery of more effective ESG programs.

ESG Corporate Compliance Program Elements

Tone at the Top—Governance and Management Structure

As with more traditional regulatory compliance, ESG program management relies on both a clear commitment from senior leadership and an effective governance and management structure. Top-down endorsement and oversight of ESG issues and disclosures can help impress the importance of ESG performance on personnel at all levels. Consistent and regular communication from leadership about ESG matters and their significance to the advancement of the company's business objectives helps establish an environment enabling ESG programs to flourish. As part of creating that affirmative ESG culture, it is also important to clearly empower and encourage personnel to implement ESG goals and communicate any concerns or issues directly with senior leadership.

Board and Committee Roles, Responsibilities, and Accountability

A successful ESG governance structure requires effective oversight and engagement by the board and other senior leadership. Ultimately, that undertaking embodies addressing ESG issues reflective of traditional board oversight, such as strategy, risk, compliance, and long-term operational sustainability. As such, the board has responsibility for monitoring ESG-related risks and the achievement of stated ESG goals as well as ensuring ESG impacts are integrated into strategic decision-making. Accordingly, the board should carefully oversee decisions regarding why the company is pursuing ESG, what the company's ESG goals are, and the means by which the company intends to achieve them (i.e., which issues to focus on and what success should look like). Finally, the board must ensure that adequate ESG policies, programs, systems, and procedures are in place to support fulfillment of those goals and should monitor the implementation and effectiveness of the ESG program.

While it is the responsibility of management to design and implement an ESG program, the board's oversight duties call for it to engage sufficiently with the ESG program to be positioned to evaluate meaningfully the effectiveness of the program. As a starting point, the board must be sufficiently informed and involved to ensure that the program is aligned with the company's strategy, purpose, and objectives. Related to that assessment, the board needs to be satisfied that the Company has employed appropriate processes bringing together the relevant personnel from across the organization to enable the entity to make a reasonable judgment about the ESG areas to prioritize, the applicable standards to select, and the commitments to make. Furthermore, as with any other major compliance risk, the board should understand and feel confident that a viable structure exists to manage the program, evaluate performance, and achieve objectives. The board also must be assured that the Company has an appropriate process to gather, manage, and integrate ESG-related information throughout the organization not just within the ESG group or the ESG report. In effect, the board is called upon to exercise responsibilities commonly undertaken with regard to compliance programs with the added complexity associated with additionally reviewing the underlying business rationale for addressing ESG and the adequacy of the determinations around which ESG issues, standards, and commitments to embrace.

To enable the board to discharge those responsibilities, companies should consider either creating an ESG Committee on the board or explicitly including ESG oversight in the remit of an existing committee. To date, companies have more commonly chosen to extend the responsibility for oversight to an existing committee, with the designation of the committee varying significantly across companies so as to fit best within their overall oversight structure. Regardless of its location, it is important to have specific clarity about the role and expectations to ensure that the committee is both empowered and accountable for oversight of ESG. Among those responsibilities, the designated committee needs to engage directly with management and senior ESG leadership to be positioned to assess the competence of the responsible personnel, the adequacy of the available resources, and the effectiveness of the program. That undertaking needs to be pursued with the same vigor and seriousness associated with oversight of regulatory compliance.

The relevant board committee should have oversight and authority of the Company's ESG programs and disclosures, as well as oversight of the Company's key management ESG personnel responsible for managing and implementing the program. In that respect, the board committee needs to have direct lines of communication with personnel responsible for implementing ESG programs and disclosures, such as Chief Sustainability Officers (CSOs), legal departments, auditing personnel, and other management with major ESG authority. In that many companies have moved toward having ESG management committees; the board needs to have clear expectations and procedures for engaging regularly with that management committee.

At a minimum, the board should be provided with an annual performance update and include review of the progress in its agenda. The board committee responsible for ESG should obtain more regular updates and review ESG performance and developments at its regular committee meetings. For presentations to the board and the board committee, ESG management should be encouraged to move beyond high-level and strategic slides to provide more detailed spreadsheets reflecting specific tasks, personnel responsibilities, and target dates. Importantly, the board should focus in particular on receiving and reviewing annual ESG risk assessment aimed at prioritizing and explaining the priorities and resulting material strategy modifications related to the constantly changing ESG environment. Whether that ESG risk assessment is undertaken as a standalone assessment, part of an annual Enterprise Risk Management (ERM) review, or as some other part of enterprise risk consideration, given the state of play in the ESG world, it is critical to reassess regularly the significant ESG risks and opportunities for the Company and make certain that the ESG strategy and plan reflects those realities. Importantly, the oversight review needs to probe the existence and adequacy of standards and controls around ESG information gathering and reporting. In light of the growing litigation risk for alleged dissemination of misleading information, the board needs to test the sufficiency of standards, controls, and processes to ensure that ESG information across the enterprise is integrated, consistent, and defensible. Finally, the board carries the responsibility as well for reviewing the strategy and program, as well as ensuring that there are sufficient resources to fulfill those plans and commitments.

Given the relatively recent development of the ESG field, it is not surprising that few boards have board members with deep expertise related to ESG programs and matters. To that end, may boards have expressed uneasiness about the sufficiency of their understanding to perform optimally their oversight responsibilities. In response to that concern, many have turned to outside consultants, law firms, and other experts to provide training or assistance to elevate their ESG knowledge through various presentations, materials, and education programs. Furthermore, a number of boards have retained those third parties to undertake evaluation of the ESG programs to lend specific additional support and perspective to board review of those programs.

ESG Leadership and Management

In response to the growing significance of ESG, increasingly companies have formed ESG management committees comprised of senior management and executive leadership members who are then responsible for leading and overseeing the Company's ESG strategy and performance. While the specific functional areas forming the committee (i.e., CEO, CFO, General Counsel, COO, marketing, audit, procurement, supply chain) will vary depending on the Company's business needs and priorities, the clear trend is to create such committees and populate them with senior management empowered to make decisions. A cross-functional management group facilitates inclusion of critical perspectives from departments responsible for or impacted by ESG, and enhances implementation of ESG strategy, policies, programs, and performance. Often one of the committee members is designated as the lead with the CSO and comparable personnel reporting to them.

Although that ESG management committee will make major decisions about strategy, structure, priorities, and budgeting, typically an ESG group or department is established to operate the program on a day-to-day basis with the designation of a clear lead ESG manager. Frequently, that lead manager is denominated as the CSO and has the structural status equivalent to other senior management leaders. While the ESG teams led by the CSO are growing in size, because of the distributed nature of ESG within companies, many of the key ESG functions and performers are housed outside the ESG or sustainability group, necessitating clarity around roles and responsibilities as well as coordination across functional lines.

Fundamentally, the ESG group is responsible for managing the process to identify ESG priorities, select applicable standards and commitments, oversee ESG risk assessments, develop performance plans with defined responsibilities, monitor performance, gather ESG information, draft ESG reports, and prepare budgets. The CSO must work closely with leaders throughout the Company who have a role related to ESG objectives and ensure that there is alignment and coordination among them. ESG groups in international companies universally find it difficult to stay abreast of global ESG developments and emerging standards that potentially may affect them. Many groups look to outside consultants, accounting and law firms, trade associations, key standard setters, and various business associations (e.g., U.S. Council on International Business, World Business Council for Sustainable Development, UN Global Compact) to help with this challenge. However it is done, the importance and the difficulty of the undertaking merit careful and thoughtful consideration to develop a clear and specific plan.

The ESG management committee needs to ensure that the CSO and ESG functional team have sufficient authority, resources, and access within the company to enable effective performance. This consideration should include developing and compelling compliance with ESG policies, procedures, and requirements for implementing, tracking, and communicating ESG initiatives. It is imperative that the ESG group and ultimately the management committee have access to all ESG-related information throughout the Company to provide meaningful assessment of progress and the delivery of accurate information to the marketplace.

Notwithstanding the effectiveness of mandates from the ESG management committee, the CSO needs to establish relationships and regular communications with counterparts in the core functional areas connected to ESG to communicate regularly regarding developments affecting performance and objectives.

Risk Assessments

Risk Assessments and Materiality Assessments

Balancing the increasing demand for ESG-related information with the potential legal and reputational risks created by disseminating this information has increasingly troubled ESG staff, senior management, and legal and compliance personnel. Underlying those concerns are the questions of what issues to address in their activities and disclosures and what information they should—and can—include in their ESG disclosures. Environmental sustainability and more broadly ESG encompass a broad and rapidly changing array of issues. Sustainability alone contemplates issues such as climate change, water use, deforestation, biodiversity, waste, and use of chemicals/plastics. ESG's incorporation of social and governance issues further expands potential activities and disclosures to such areas as diversity and inclusion, human rights, modern slavery and fair labor practices, board diversity, executive compensation, social equity, racial justice, and ethical decision-making. The sheer volume and changing nature of potential issues presents meaningful challenges for companies.

Increasingly, to address that challenge, many companies have undertaken materiality reviews intended to identify those ESG issues of greatest moment. Whether undertaken internally or externally through outside consultants, those assessments often involve some variation of a stakeholder engagement process. In that undertaking, various stakeholders (e.g., investors, shareholders, employees) are surveyed or interviewed as to the issues that matter to them. Often that materiality assessment includes consideration of the issues selected by competitors and those denominated as important for that industry by varying standard setters (e.g., SASB [now ISSB], GRI, industry). From that review, companies often determine the priority ESG issues and select an accompanying voluntary standard by which to base their performance and reporting. As discussed above, with the proliferation of issues and standards globally, identifying the priority ESG issues has become increasingly challenging.

The ESG materiality assessments represent an important aspect of an effective ESG program. However, many companies view the materiality assessment as fulfilling ESG programmatic risk assessments and fail to undertake the following critical evaluations:

- First, with respect to the ESG materiality assessment itself, if, as often is the case, it is performed in isolation from why ESG matters to the Company and its business purpose, there can be an overweighting of individual stakeholder priorities, leading to misguided company issue selection and misalignment with corporate strategy. To avoid that result, it is important to have clarity about the business priorities and objectives—the why we are doing this—either preceding or integrated into the ESG materiality assessment. Often to do so entails broadening the ESG materiality assessment team to ensure for participation from across the Company and management engagement to ensure for alignment.

- Second, while materiality assessments have become more common around issue selection, they often do not include risk assessments or reviews around which voluntary standard to select and/or which voluntary target to set. There are multiple reporting frameworks and numerous individual issue voluntary standards. What those standards require and their performance implications for a company can vary significantly. Yet too few companies model or assess what compliance with a specific standard may entail and the company's ability to meet it. Before committing to a specific standard, it should be well understood what performance means and the comparative benefits and risks versus competing voluntary schemes.
- Third, while companies increasingly periodically revisit their materiality assessment, far fewer undertake a risk assessment related to actual performance. Yes data is gathered and annually disclosed, but there often is not an evaluation of the costs, risks, and challenges of ongoing and future performance obligations.
- Fourth, in many ways, ESG and the supply chain has become the central battleground for ESG. Increasingly, standard setters and the markets are driving companies to obtain and disclose information about ESG in their supply chains. To do so potentially involves massive time, complexity and expense, and—unless done well—presents a material risk of disclosing inaccurate information. It is critical that ESG supply chain risk assessments be undertaken to understand the realities and implications of committing to and meeting supply chain voluntary standards. Whether the supply chain assessment is addressed as part of the ESG materiality assessment or separately by the company's supply chain (or procurement) group, all impacted groups need to be involved in examining the risks and implementation practicalities related to standards and commitments that require disclosure of ESG supply chain performance data.

In short, while companies should be commended for undertaking materiality assessments, for too many entities that has subsumed performing other important undertakings, such as (1) ensuring that selected priority ESG issues are aligned with business purpose and objectives, (2) understanding with specificity the requirements and consequent operational implications for selecting a specific standard, and (3) reviewing regularly the ongoing and future implementation implications of meeting selected voluntary standard requirements and commitments. To address those potential shortcomings, consideration should be given to undertaking broader ESG risk assessments.

ESG Risk Assessments

ESG issues can arise in any number of areas of a company's business, and companies must understand both what their ESG risks are and how to prioritize resources to address them. Most companies already undertake regular risk assessments, and many have mature ERM programs. Where possible, these can and should be leveraged in undertaking ESG risk assessments. Companies should incorporate ESG risk reviews in their regular ERM process, similar to how companies integrate compliance risks.

The goal of the ESG risk assessment, like the goal of risk assessment more generally, should be to provide the company a picture of obligations and expectations related to ESG issues and disclosures and to identify areas where a company is at a high risk for failing to meet them. The lack of regulatory guidance certainly complicates the ESG risk assessment process. There is no set definition of ESG risks, and material risks will depend on the nature of a particular company's business model, product or service lines, operational structure, locations, values, and other considerations. However, as noted above, a number of ESG standards have been developed by entities such as GRI and ISSB. These include industry-specific standards and standards around issues these organizations have determined to be financially material to investors. Companies can assess their operations against these standards as one potential reference point to identify areas of ESG risks within their operations and develop programs to remediate those risks.

In addition to a review of the standards set out in a company's chosen ESG framework, the risk assessment should identify risks related to ESG disclosure. This should include identifying areas in the company's operations that may limit gathering or communication of ESG data, business units that may be unable or unwilling to meet the company's stated ESG goals or commitments, or other potential issues the CSO or others may face in preventing disclosure-related legal or reputational harm. The assessment may review, for example, whether ESG data is available throughout its global operations and, if not, whether making statements without the data from particular geographies or business units may result in a material misstatement of the company's ESG risks or achievements. By understanding these risks and limitations, the company may be better equipped to understand where it can, and where it should not, make concrete, specific, and/or verifiable statements in its disclosures and what risks may be involved in doing so.

Once a company has conducted an initial ESG risk assessment and developed an ESG compliance program, it should regularly review risks in its operations, including through periodic risk assessments and ongoing monitoring. Risk assessments should be conducted at the same time every year and be conducted by a consistent group, such as a company's internal audit department or ERM team. Such annual risk assessments act as a strong preventive measure if they are performed before something goes wrong. In addition, they allow for benchmarking and assessment of program effectiveness over time, which in turn can help compliance officials improve and enhance program elements.

Between periodic reviews, companies should continue to monitor ESG risks, including changes in market demands, regulatory requirements, industry risks, and investor expectations. Since ESG issues often implicate reputational risks, ongoing reviews should include monitoring of social media, news, and other indicators of public opinion. Moreover, companies should continually evaluate internal data to identify potential gaps between disclosures and practice, as well as potential new risk areas in their operations. Such ongoing risk assessments can help companies curb ESG issues before they can lead to investigations, litigation, or reputational harm.

Program, Policies, Procedures

Compliance program generally includes three levels of standards and controls: (1) Code of Conduct that expresses the company's values, ethics, and expectations; (2) standards and policies that build on the Code of Conduct and articulate Code-based policies; and (3) procedures developed to confirm those policies are implemented, followed, and enforced. Companies, including the board and ESG committee, CSO, and other ESG compliance personnel, should establish all three elements to address ESG risks and ensure ESG disclosures/announcements are accurate.

Codes of Conduct should incorporate language that communicates the company's commitment to both addressing ESG risks and ensuring transparency and truthfulness in reporting these ESG issues to external stakeholders. They should also serve to express expectations regarding compliance with ESG policies and procedures. In doing so, the Code can help establish, at a high level, a culture in which ESG issues, including risks related to ESG disclosures, are taken seriously. This in turn can help promote adoption of and compliance with ESG-related policies and procedures as well as transparency when issues arise.

Building off the general expectations set in the Code of Conduct, companies can develop policies and procedures that lay out the practical aspects of implementing their ESG program. This should include policies and procedures designed to accomplish ESG goals, such as policies specifying requirements for energy usage in operations or setting minimum standards for work conditions in the company's global operations. With respect to disclosure-related risks, companies should implement a rigorous process for communicating ESG information internally, reviewing data to ensure accuracy and completeness, and ultimately preparing and reviewing ESG disclosures. This should include procedures for evaluating reliability of data, implementing controls over ESG-related data, and addressing information gaps.

In most companies, ESG-related data, like other compliance-related information, is spread out over a diverse array of roles, business units, and geographies. This means that processes and procedures for collecting, reviewing, and assessing ESG information need to involve individuals beyond those directly responsible for ESG compliance. This may include, for example, members of a company's legal, investor relations, finance, risk, compliance, and human resources teams. It may also require gathering information from procurement, data security, or other operational elements. The CSO (or equivalent) must consider all stakeholders in the company and think critically about how to leverage existing policies and procedures when developing ESG policies, procedures, and controls.

Given investors' growing reliance on ESG disclosures in making investment decisions, companies may be expected to provide more detailed and objective data regarding their ESG risks and related programs. Indeed, such reliance has led some commentators to suggest that courts going forward may be more willing to find specific information regarding ESG risks and programs "material" under U.S. federal securities laws, thus requiring their disclosure in SEC filings.[7] As discussed above, doing so increases the risk of both legal action and reputational harm if information provided in the disclosures is found to be inaccurate. In such circumstances, companies should consider adopting controls over ESG data similar to those imposed on financial information. In addition, companies may need to consider engaging third parties to review and audit data, similar to audits of financial information.

Companies will also need to determine who has ultimate authority over public disclosures, including decisions regarding what information to include and how to present ESG information (e.g., in SEC filings, on company websites). This role may shift depending on the nature of the disclosure. For example, the CSO or investor relations team may have ultimate authority over sustainability statements published on a company website, while the legal team responsible for SEC compliance may have ownership over ESG information contained in proxy statements or other SEC filings.

Training

Another pillar of a strong compliance program is properly training company officers, employees, and third parties on relevant laws, regulations, corporate policies, procedures, and prohibited conduct. Ensuring that training effectively communicates the company's ESG risks and program depends on several key elements, including what topics training covers, who a company trains, how the training is conducted, and how often training occurs.

Ensuring the effectiveness of an ESG program requires training the right people. Companies should prioritize audiences in areas that are critical to implementation of the program and mitigation of ESG risks. With respect to disclosure-related risks, training should focus on individuals and business units that are responsible for collecting, documenting, and sharing ESG-related data as well as those responsible for implementing ESG-related policies and procedures. Compliance personnel should also focus training efforts on individuals or business units identified as posing a heightened ESG-related risk, including risks related to collecting and communicating ESG data.

In the context of ESG disclosure compliance, training should educate the audience on the importance of ESG disclosures, the legal and reputational risks associated with making them, and the importance of following policies and procedures designed to mitigate those risks. All training should encourage the audience to raise concerns and issues through the company's whistleblower hotline or other communication channels.

Specific training should be conducted on the company's data collection policies and procedures. These training should emphasize the importance of

7. See, for example, Hana V. Vizcarra, *The Reasonable Investor and Climate-Related Information: Changing Expectations for Financial Disclosures*, 50 ELR 10106, 1113-14 (2020).

transparency, accuracy, and completeness. Depending on the framework or standards adopted to evaluate ESG risks, a company may also consider requiring individuals to complete certification courses or standard-specific training. Doing so can help these individuals better identify potential gaps or inaccuracies in ESG data before it is made public.

Live, in-person training is generally preferred when presenting compliance concepts to those with key roles in the ESG data collection and disclosure process and to those that might present a risk for inaccurate, incomplete, or unreliable information. Such individuals may include those in offshore facilities over which the CSO and ESG teams have limited oversight or in business units that face operational or financial pressures to ignore ESG issues and risks. Such live training, particularly when conducted by the CSO or other high-ranking officer, helps emphasize the importance of compliance with company policies and procedures. It also allows for immediate feedback from employees that would be much less likely to occur during a webinar or other remote training. Lastly, during live training, employees are more likely to make casual mention of a potentially risky practice, giving compliance personnel the opportunity to address it before it becomes a larger problem.

Compliance personnel should always pay attention to employees' responses during training. Questions and comments can provide insight into potential ESG issues, impediments to achieving ESG goals or commitments, or limitations in ESG data collection. For example, during training, employees might ask specific questions about what information is relevant to ESG disclosures, and whether "ballparking" or "estimating" figures is sufficient. Likewise, employees may mention practices that could call reliability of data into questions, such as failing to account for certain types of waste or water or energy usage.

Training content must be developed in a way that ensures individuals understand and retain information presented. This is particularly important when developing training related to gathering and communicating information to be included in ESG disclosures. Processes and procedures for collecting data and other ESG information must be applied consistently across facilities, geographies, business units, and other company segments. This means that individuals responsible for implementing and/or overseeing them must receive training that provides uniform description of responsibilities, requirements, and expectations. At the same time, training often involves individuals across geographies, business units, roles and compliance responsibilities. As such, training may need to be tailored to ensure that it is communicated in a way that is understandable and relevant to the particular audience. CSOs and ESG staff should carefully consider how they prepare and present training on these issues to ensure that they are at once internally consistent and effective for each audience.

Auditing, Monitoring, and Remediation

A critical component of managing and mitigating risks related to ESG disclosures and related issues is ongoing evaluation of the company's ESG compliance program, including whether employees comply with ESG policies and procedures, whether the company is achieving stated goals and commitments, and whether on-the-ground activities continue to reflect information provided in ESG disclosures. In particular, companies must be able to monitor, audit, and respond quickly to allegations of misconduct, such as falsifying or misrepresenting ESG data or information, failing to implement ESG risk mitigation measures, or undertaking activities contrary to stated ESG commitments and objectives.

As used here, monitoring refers to reviewing and detecting compliance programs in real time and then reacting quickly to remediate them. A primary goal of monitoring is to identify and address gaps in the ESG program—whether related to actual ESG performance or the collection and dissemination of ESG information—on a regular and consistent basis. Companies should establish a regular monitoring system to spot issues and address them. This should include a communication and escalation process to ensure the board and other senior leadership is aware of potential ESG risks, gaps in ESG data, and other issues that may implicate the company's accomplishment of ESG-related goals or the accuracy or completeness of ESG disclosures.

It should also include a set of protocols, checks, and controls to detect and remediate ESG compliance problems on an ongoing basis. The ESG compliance team should regularly communicate with individuals responsible for overseeing ESG program implementation and data collection to evaluate whether there have been any setbacks, delays, or irregularities in data gathering. Managers should be required to keep tabs on activity in the operations they oversee that might conflict with information in the company's public ESG disclosures. In addition, the board, ESG committee, and ESG team should meet or communicate as often as every month to discuss issues as they arise.

Auditing is a more limited review that targets a specific business component, region, or market sector during a particular time frame in order to uncover and/or evaluate specific risks. Auditing and monitoring are related functions that typically operate in tandem, with monitoring activities sometimes leading to audits. For instance, if the ESG team learns that a facility uses water from a source that is not included in its water usage records, an audit may be necessary to review that facility's water usage and tracking practices. That audit may then lead to a review of such practices throughout the company's global operations.

Companies should establish procedures and protocols to ensure that ESG-related investigations and audits are conducted effectively and consistently. These can typically leverage existing investigation procedures developed in the more general ethics and compliance space. Such protocols may include standards for conducting interviews and on-site visits, data review, and sample testing, and document and record reviews, as well as guidance on preparing reports, determining whether to engage outside counsel, evaluating remediation plans, and escalating findings to senior leadership and/or the board. While existing investigation procedures may require such investigations to be conducted by legal, compliance, internal audit, or other functions, the CSO and ESG compliance personnel should work closely with the investigation and audit team to develop a review plan; assist in review of relevant documents, interviews, and information gathering; and preparing investigation or audit findings and reports.

Companies must quickly remediate problems identified as a result of ongoing monitoring and/or audits. This may include reviewing and revising ESG goals and commitments, plans or programs for implementing those goals, and protocols for gathering and communicating information and data about the company's ESG risks, strategies, and activities. Following the previous example, if a company finds that it has underreported water use as a result of numerous facilities using water supplies that are not included in usage data, the company must not only determine whether and how to disclose this information, it must also create a plan for correcting this issue going forward. It is not enough to just gather information and identify compliance problems through monitoring and auditing. To fulfill this essential element of compliance, companies also have to respond and fix the problems.

Special Supply Chain Considerations

The extension of ESG requirements to the supply chain has materially complicated fundamental decisions and performance around the ESG program, as does the frequent reliance on information and data provided by third-party suppliers. The sheer volume of suppliers for many companies, coupled with the greater difficulty in effectively gathering information outside the company's control, presents substantial burdens and challenges for companies. Critically, the reliance on that information if it is inaccurate can give rise to material risks either in litigation or the court of public opinion. Indeed, several consumer protection cases alleging misrepresentation of ESG information in company statements have been based on third-party activity.

As companies develop ESG compliance programs, they should also ensure that their company integrates ESG considerations into their supply chain management programs. Generally speaking, third-party ESG programs should reflect the elements described above. As an initial matter, companies should evaluate how to manage risks and who should be responsible for doing so. Where possible, it may be useful to leverage existing internal compliance processes and structures. For example, a company's procurement department may have responsibility for overseeing third-party compliance with applicable regulatory standards and company policies. In such cases, it may be appropriate for procurement to also oversee third-party compliance with ESG-related policies and procedures developed by the CSO and ESG compliance personnel. Regardless of who implements such programs on a day-to-day basis, however, both the CSO and the board should retain oversight and decision-making authority.

The costs associated with compliance strategies (such as auditing) for all suppliers to achieve the desired performance and provide accurate information can be prohibitive. As such, an ESG program should take a risk-based approach to third-party suppliers and consider adopting various strategies that have been used to address other supply chain issues such as product quality. For example, supplier contracts may include provisions requiring third parties to comply with the company's ESG policies, procedures, and controls, including those implementing ESG goals and commitments. Companies may also consider creating a supplier code of conduct that defines the company's expectations, including around ESG issues such as resource conservation, human rights, and accurate reporting of ESG data and information that the company may request.

The CSO and ESG compliance team, with oversight from the board and relevant committees, should identify which strategies should apply to third-party suppliers based on the particular risk profile of the company and its supply chain. Building from due diligence practices developed to address Dodd–Frank conflict mineral reporting, companies can group suppliers into different categories based on their risk profile and employ different implementation measures depending on the category. Those suppliers deemed as high risk (by virtue of defined risk factors such as geography and importance of supplier) should receive greater attention and more substantial engagement and requirements. In the ESG context, companies may, among other contractual provisions, require high-risk suppliers to receive training on ESG issues and company expectations or include additional contractual provisions related to accuracy of ESG information disclosures.

Due diligence is an important control in any compliance program and should incorporate ESG considerations. This may include review of relevant business practices, such as treatment of laborers, energy consumption, and environmental degradation. It should also include review of reputational issues related to ESG practices. Where information about the supplier's business practices will be incorporated into the company's ESG reporting, the company should also review data collection and communication practices to evaluate reliability of such information. By conducting due diligence before hiring and onboarding third-party suppliers, a company can evaluate the risk that a third party poses relative to ESG issues. Where a supplier's risk cannot be sufficiently mitigated by contractual obligations or other controls, the company can avoid exposure to potential risks by simply not hiring them. Finally, ongoing monitoring, auditing, and review is a critical component of supply chain management, including with respect to ESG-related considerations.

To minimize the supply chain challenges, it is apparent that companies need to undertake ESG supply chain risk assessments. Those assessments need to look at selected, and especially potential, standards and evaluate the implementation implications, costs, and risks. In addition, if the company adopts ESG standards that include supply chain mandates, it is important to regularly assess the performance risks and adjust the implementation plan accordingly.

Supply chains should also be reviewed as part of the company's enterprise-wide ESG risk assessment. This should include evaluation of potential ESG issues arising out of conduct by individual suppliers as well as those stemming from the company's ESG risk management program. In particular, companies should evaluate whether they engage suppliers in industries or geographies that may present heightened risk for ESG-related issues like environmental degradation, human rights abuses, or similar. These assessments should also review potential risks related to data availability and reliability—or lack thereof. Results of the risk assessment should be communicated to the CSO, board, and others with oversight and decision-making authority and used to develop and refine related third-party programs.

Reporting and Disclosure

Unmistakably, perceived litigation and market risk around deficient disclosure along with accelerating prospects for governmental disclosure regulation in countries around the world has triggered vastly greater board and senior management attention on ESG. It has also stimulated substantial restructuring of information gathering practices and responsibilities within many companies. Financial and audit functions, and especially legal, have assumed far greater roles related to ESG disclosures. That involvement is transforming practices and structures to move programs toward the approaches and controls commonly required for financial disclosures. Increasingly, legal departments are scrutinizing disclosures and testing the sufficiency of the practices that generated specific data and information ultimately contained in the ESG report. Given the market interest in ESG information and the potential risks associated with inaccurate or misleading information, the standards and controls around reporting and disclosure should be as rigorous and obligatory as those for financial disclosure.

Even the traditional controls and processes associated with financial reporting may need to be enhanced to address some unique aspects of the ESG reporting process. While there are commonly accepted accounting and auditing processes around financial reporting which are generally well understood and implemented by responsible staff in the financial reporting process, that is not the case with ESG reporting. Because of the uncertainty about methodologies for generating information and performing calculations pursuant to various standards, perhaps not surprisingly many companies have found that responsible personnel have used differing approaches and assumptions in generating data and calculations about ESG performance. Accordingly, for those companies operating in multiple locations, it is important to train responsible personnel on the desired practices and the use of common methodologies to ensure accurate and consistent data and information is reported upward within the organization.

In addition, while considerable progress has been made in recognizing and advancing the utility of clear standards and controls around information to be presented in the ESG report, that same rigor is not necessarily governing the creation and sourcing of information conveyed in statements, press releases, responses to investor and customer questions, and voluntary standard submissions. Particularly concerning are the submissions to the major standard setters (e.g., GRI, CDP, ISSB) in which companies provide extensive detailed information. Yet often those submissions are not subject to the same standards and controls as the ESG report. This divergence of practice can dangerously produce significantly different information about company ESG performance on the same ESG topics across various disclosures and responses. As a result, companies will need to consider expanding the enhanced oversight and management of information underlying the ESG report and public filings to all communications throughout the company regarding ESG commitments and performance, especially those made to major voluntary standard setters.

Furthermore, these difficulties will only be accentuated by the growing number of divergent country-specific ESG disclosure requirements which understandably will cause many multinationals to produce multiple and somewhat different ESG reports for disclosure. For decentralized companies in particular, it will be especially important to have effective coordination and oversight vehicles to provide consistent and aligned individual country ESG reports.

Conclusion

As the market significance and impact of ESG has grown, so too has the importance of effective ESG programs. At its best, ESG programs help advance the business opportunities and the purpose of the enterprise. For many companies though, to do so requires an enhancement of the ESG program, imbuing it with the seriousness of compliance programs and connecting it directly to the core business strategy of the company. Grounding the program on business purpose is critical for navigating the ever-changing ESG world to choose the right priorities, make the right commitments, achieve the best results, and communicate that success convincingly to the marketplace.

CHAPTER 7

Product ESG

Travis Miller

The term "globalization" has only become commonplace over the last few decades, because of the rapid expansion of outsourcing and the economic advantage of producing products in less developed nations.[1] These major changes were driven to a large extent by an increase in the cost of production resulting from increases in regulation and wages in developed economies.[2] The consequence of this phenomenon has been the displacement of the traditional Western manufacturing base to countries with a lower cost of labor and per unit production.[3] This trend has also resulted in traditional environmental regulation, focused on the manufacturing process, to be found wanting by many major economies—prompting the establishment of new regulatory regimes focused on product stewardship.[4] These regulations shift the burden of compliance onto the supply chain and the importer of finished goods. Consequently, companies seeking to import products into regulated markets must maintain complex databases evidencing compliance with the environmental laws that impact the products that will enter such markets.

The diverse physical locations of parts and assembly services required to produce goods often means that the components required to produce products traverse the globe several times before a product is assembled.[5] These global supply chains established critical shipping lanes, ports, a need for logistics expertise,

1. Roland Robertson. *Globalization: Social Theory and Global Culture* (1992). (Globalization is the compression of the world and the intensification of the consciousness of the world as a whole).

2. See Fred Hoerger et al. *The Cumulative Impact of Health, Environmental, and Safety Concerns on the Chemical Industry during the Seventies*, 46 Duke L. & Contemp. Probs. L. Rev. 60, 62–3, 93. (1983).

3. See Dion Wiggins and Diane Morello, *Outsourcing Backlash: Globalization in the Knowledge Economy* Gartner (2003). http://www.gartner.com/id=405776.

4. Nicole C. Kibert, *Extended Producer Responsibility: A Tool for Achieving Sustainable Development*, 19 J Land Use 2, 503, 510–11 (Spring 2004).

5. *Building Resilient Supply Chains, Revitalizing American Manufacturing, and Fostering Broad-Based Growth*, 100 Day Review Under Executive Order 14017, The White House (Jun. 2021), https://www.whitehouse.gov/wp-content/uploads/2021/06/100-day-supply-chain-review-report.pdf.

and service providers who specialized in moving products and materials across and through multiple jurisdictions. Shipping, air freight, rail, and truck transportation have also boomed, as goods traveled longer distances, requiring many modes of transportation to arrive at the customer's desired location. The principal advantages of these systems have been the effective and efficient production of products, increased access to lower cost goods, and profitability.[6] However, the safety of the products and impact on the environment have required innovation aligned with the ESG movement and regulatory controls.

Regulations rarely occur in real time, as they tend to follow innovation by business. Once the business processes have been established, industry standards typically align around best practices and seek to deter undesirable and unethical actions. In time, this pattern and/or the resulting cases that highlight the consequences of failing to abide by industry norms will lead to defined laws. The laws, in turn, will establish rules that businesses and their suppliers are expected to abide by. This pattern of regulatory evolution was coined the "race to the top," meaning that once a best practice or undesirable activity was identified and regulated, others would all adapt to incorporate the new best practice. Historically, this trend has also led to traditional environmental and commerce regulation, focused on the manufacturing process or point source regulations on facilities. Unfortunately, point source laws were found to be insufficient by many major economies, as cases and problems began to emerge around supply chain actors or the finished products entering a country. To close this gap, regulators began to establish a new series of laws that regulated the sale of products into the country that was receiving the goods.

Product regulations establish legal obligations that demand rapid changes and coordinated efforts from suppliers, contract manufacturers, distributors, logistics providers, customers, and solution providers.[7] As a result, a growing need has emerged to have internal and external expertise dedicated to product compliance within most businesses. Product-based regulation has also become a core enforcement area, with product compliance regulations now generating more enforcement actions in the European Union than any other regulatory regime.[8] To mitigate risk, companies have leveraged industry standards to shift the burden of compliance onto the supply chain and the importer of finished goods through warranties, contracts, and/or certifications of compliance.[9] To accomplish this burden shifting, complex databases that can track, evaluate, and disclose due diligence records must be maintained and accessible by key personnel. These databases establish chains of custody and support the identification

---

6. Travis Miller, *Know Thy Product: The Global Expansion of Product Stewardship Laws' Impact on Environmental Law*, Geo. Int'l Env. Law Rev. (May 8, 2015).

7. Travis Miller, *Guide to Supply Chain Compliance Laws and Regulations* (2021).

8. European Commission: Safety Gate, https://ec.europa.eu/safety-gate-alerts/screen/webReport (last visited Aug. 2, 2022).

9. International Electrotechnical Commission (IEC) 63000:2016/AMD1:2022 (Amendment 1—Technical documentation for the assessment of electrical and electronic products with respect to the restriction of hazardous substances).

of where supply chain breakdowns are occurring through systematic record keeping.

To fully understand and appreciate the complexity of a product's manufacturing in a globalized economy, it is helpful to understand the actors. The following description offers a high-level overview of the key actors in modern manufacturing and the central role they play in the delivery of a product to an end customer.

- *Extractives:* The extractives sector comprises the businesses that take raw materials; the examples include timber, oil, coal, gold, iron, copper, and other minerals from the earth. The industrial processes for extracting minerals include timber harvest, drilling and pumping, quarrying, and mining.
- *Processing:* Once extractives have been obtained in sufficient quantities; they are transported to hubs known as mills, smelters, and/or refineries. These hubs take the raw materials and turn them into usable products for the industry to manufacture goods.
- *Suppliers:* Create materials and products that are needed by other businesses. Supplier's products will be incorporated into other companies' products, or they may perform a specialized service or finishing activity that is required to complete a product.
- *Contract Manufacturers:* Perform assembly work and are hired by original equipment manufacturers (OEMs) to scale the manufacturing of OEM designed goods and products.
- Original Equipment Manufacturer (*OEMs):* Branded owners of manufactured goods that are sold to end users and consumers.
- *Original Design Manufacturers (ODMs):* Predesigned or Commercial-off-the-Shelf (CotS) manufacturers of goods that are purchased, as is from a manufacturer.
- *Organization:* This will be the general, all-purpose word used throughout the book to describe the reader's company, its subsidiaries, and affiliates.
- *Distributors:* Third parties who purchase, warehouse, and sell large volumes of OEM products and service parts that are used by end users and consumers. Distributors frequently position themselves as a single entity that can support the acquisition of key components or parts from multiple OEMs and can take advantage of purchasing volume to offer competitive prices and services to customers.
- *Logistics Providers:* Provide a service of moving a product or material from one location to another and often will take on the role of clearing customs. Logistics providers can be global in scope or specialized in a specific region or country that might have atypical or specialized customs clearance requirements.
- *Solution Providers:* Software firms and/or consultancies that provide guidance and develop workflows or processes that support compliance, trade paperwork acquisition, and tracking of goods shipments from the various parties in the supply chain.

- *Regulators and Customs Authorities:* Developers of the legal framework and parties charged with enforcing compliance with the laws impacting supply chain compliance.
- *End-Users, Consumers, or Customers:* The end purchaser of a fully assembled device that intends to use the device for its intended purpose.
- *Waste Operators:* The parties who are responsible for recovering and disposing of or recycling a finished device, scrap, or discarded parts that are no longer fit for the intended purpose.

Understanding Product Compliance Regulations

The origin of the new environmental movement can be traced to the concept of product stewardship and the initial packaging regulations[10] that began in the EU. As with most environmental laws, this new extended producer responsibility (EPR) law and those that would follow were reactionary. EPR originated from a growing concern about the capacity of European countries to handle the quantity of imported waste packaging materials. It was forecasted that the waste stream caused by primary, secondary, and tertiary packaging would rapidly overwhelm the capacity of the union if unchecked and unfunded recycling programs lagged far behind those of the United States. The EU took action by drafting and deploying the packaging directives, followed by the regulation of battery waste,[11] and the regulation of waste electrical and electronic equipment (WEEE).[12]

These regulatory schemes applied a mandatory fee to the import of waste that was "placed on the market," meaning the item had reached its final destination and would eventually become waste. In this context, the importer of record was the business or individual who held the title when the product was sold to a retailer or end user. This concept of placing the financial burden on a business in advance of waste being generated is referred to as the "polluter pays principle." The polluter pays principle is intended to serve as a financial deterrent and serves as the guiding light for product compliance laws. The passage of these EPR rules fundamentally changed environmental regulation by establishing a legally mandated recycling fee for manufacturers, distributors, and importers of record under a nexus of reasonably foreseeable harm, rather than the actual harm itself. The EPR laws also established a precedent that set a path toward a series of increasingly burdensome supply chain compliance regulations that have reshaped corporate supply chain operations and programs globally. These obligations initiated a proverbial race to the top,[13] where various jurisdictions and legal regimes developed supply chain regulations that attempted to keep up or surpass the burden.

10. Council Directive, 94/62/EC, 1994, O.J. (L 365), 10 (EC).
11. Council Directive, 2013/56/EU, 2013, O.J. (L 329), 5-9 (EU).
12. Council Directive, 2012/19/EU, 2012, O.J. (L 197), 38-1 (EU).
13. Mallory Elise Flowers et al., in *The LEED: Racing to the Top in Environmental Self-Regulation*, WILEY BUS. STRATEGY & ENVT. (2020).

Product compliance regulations focused on the fact that knowledge of materials or qualities of a product are a requirement of market access requirements. Product regulations impact a product's ability to enter into a given market and/or come in the form of taxation/fees, restrictions on material composition, and related disclosure/registration obligations. When conducting a market surveillance assessment for product compliance laws, an engineering team should be engaged. The engineering team will have critical knowledge of the components and how the product is assembled, and why certain materials selections were made. The supply chain compliance team will also need to be cognizant of the supply chain and financial implications associated with bringing a product to market. Product compliance regulations are very data heavy. Each component and often individual articles[14] or materials within a product will have to undergo evaluation and require certification by the manufacturer of the component. The product compliance team is responsible for managing this assessment and ensuring that the quality of the data achieves the necessary regulatory obligations.

The EPR regulations proved that supplier legislation could impact upstream producer's behavior. After this practice was normalized, the EU regulatory authorities expanded the legal obligations tied to product import by expanding the concept of product stewardship to include substance restrictions and product certification mandates.[15] To address the near impossibility of establishing an enforcement body that knew about all products entering a market, the EU shifted the burden of demonstrating compliance to the producer and/or importer of the product.[16] This burden shifting forced manufacturers and importers of record to extend supplier due diligence programs into the business functions of product lifecycle management (PLM), engineering, and design.

These product compliance regulations became a critical topic in both international trade and environmental law, as an increasing number of nations began to implement similar regulations. The resulting patchwork quilt of regulations created an untenable position for global manufacturers. Competing data needs, priorities, and lists of required/restricted substances have broken down the manufacturer's vision of a single product that can be sold globally. To address this new reality, the industry reacted by implementing standards to exchange highly detailed substance-level compliance data. To facilitate this, industry bodies established legally binding material content data exchange standards to provide two essential functions:

1. Provide a mechanism to transfer compliance data throughout the supply chain.
2. Offer legally binding template agreements and declarations for a supplier to certify compliance with the law(s).

---

14. ECHA REACH Website, https://echa.europa.eu/regulations/reach/candidate-list-substances-in-articles (last visited Aug. 2, 2022).

15. E.U. Comm'n, (2016/C 272/01) (Blue Guide).

16. See E.U. Comm'n, New Legislative Framework website, https://single-market-economy.ec.europa.eu/single-market/goods/new-legislative-framework_en#:~:text=To%20improve%20the%20internal%20market, the%20quality%20of%20conformity%20assessments.

As a consequence of these product compliance laws, organizations seeking to produce products that were sellable in a given market had to ensure both made and purchased components meet these industry-standard requirements. Compliance with product compliance laws generally requires detailed due diligence into the materials present in and used in the manufacture of goods. The finished products also required testing and adherence to a series of safety standards that were developed to ensure the product was compliant with local expectations for the product's use.[17] In order to gain permission to sell a product into a given market, companies must develop robust technical files detailing the steps and actions taken to prove supply chain compliance. This documentation must be tracked and refreshed, as the laws change. Due to outsourcing, the frequency of component/material changes, and the need for continuous due diligence, most product compliance-related business risks now exist with vendors.

There are many types of product compliance regulations that are likely to impact a product. To understand these regulations, it is helpful to understand the types of regulations that will be at play when managing and putting together a product compliance program. The following presents a noncomprehensive list of the types of product compliance regulations that an organization is most likely to encounter during a product compliance materiality assessment.

- *Battery Regulations:* Battery regulations are issued to prevent the release of hazardous substances into the environment, reduce waste, and ensure the recycling of valuable raw materials. Battery regulations impact manufacturers, importers, and sellers of batteries, as well as products that contain batteries. Regulations in this area may restrict the use of hazardous materials in batteries, require producers to take back and recycle waste batteries, establish marking and labeling requirements, and require that batteries in products be easily removable for disposal. Related regulations may cover energy efficiency for battery chargers.
- *Chemical Transparency Regulations:* Chemical disclosure regulations are enacted to necessitate that chemical disclosures are made to citizens if the chemical is listed or has a certain property or attribute. These "right-to-know laws" obligate organizations to inform consumers if certain hazardous chemicals are present in products or their packaging. Frequently, the administrator of the regulation will be responsible for publishing a list of chemicals known to the state to cause a specific harm, including, but not limited to, cancer, birth defects, or other reproductive harm. The regulation imposes controls on the chemicals on this list to ensure consumers can make informed choices about the products they purchase, and to enable residents or workers to take whatever action they deem appropriate to protect themselves from exposures to these harmful chemicals.

17. See, for example, IEC 63000:2016/AMD1:2022 Standard (Amendment 1—Technical documentation for the assessment of electrical and electronic products with respect to the restriction of hazardous substances).

- *Chemical Management Regulations:* Chemical management regulations impact the actual sale of chemicals, mixtures, or raw materials. Chemical management regulations will obligate the organization to notify, and perform risk assessments and registration of chemicals in order to increase the information on toxicological and ecotoxicological properties of existing and new chemicals. Disclosures will often include classification (as carcinogenic, mutagenic, or toxic for reproduction) and labeling of chemicals in order to inform the user about the properties of the chemicals and to give advice for their safe use and disposal. Multiple organizations that produce or import the same chemical will often have a shared responsibility of gathering and presenting an open exchange of information about the substance. These organizations may gather in collectives or interest groups to share information and make consistent submissions, while sharing and offsetting the direct cost of the analysis. In certain instances, the regulation may call for a phasing out of the production and use of the chemical, as well as the waste management programs.
- *Eco-design Regulations:* Eco-design regulations regulate the design and use phase of a product by ensuring that products are manufactured to specific environmental technical criteria in order to minimize the environmental impact of the product throughout its life cycle. These specific criteria generally focus on power consumption and power management of a product. This can include setting maximum limits on power levels in off and standby modes and power management requirements, such as automatically switching into standby after the shortest possible period of time.
- *Ecolabeling Regulations:* Ecolabeling regulations involve the environmental certification and labeling that can be done on a mandatory or voluntary basis. Ecolabels ensure consumers can make informed purchasing choices allowing them to opt for products that are proven to be environmentally preferable overall to other products in the same category. Ecolabels can also be used as an indicator to regulatory authorities that compliance efforts have been made, vetted, and found to be in adherence to a standard.
- *Electromagnetic Compatibility (EMC) Legislation:* EMC laws are intended to ensure that electrical and electronic equipment does not generate, or is not affected by, electromagnetic disturbance. Such legislation limits electromagnetic emissions from equipment in order to ensure that, when used as intended, such equipment does not disturb radio and telecommunication, as well as other equipment. It also governs the immunity of such equipment to interference and seeks to ensure that this equipment is not disturbed by radio emissions, when used as intended.
- *Waste Electrical and Electronic Equipment (WEEE):* WEEE or electronic waste legislation aims to protect the environment and human health by ensuring that WEEE is properly managed. It includes requirements for the collection, storage, sorting, transport, treatment, preparation for reuse, recycling, and disposal of WEEE.

- *Food Contact Materials (FCMs):* Regulations for FCMs and articles typically require FCMs, products that come into contact with food, and articles that are contained in food contact products to comply with good manufacturing practices (GMPs), and also require them to comply with restrictions or prohibitions on specific substances. FCM regulations are intended to ensure that, under normal or foreseeable conditions of use, the substances will not transfer harmful chemical constituents to food in quantities which could endanger human health, bring about an unacceptable change in the composition of the food, or bring about a deterioration in the organoleptic properties of the food. FCM regulations may also require certain labeling and traceability requirements for products that come into contact with food.
- *Packaging Regulations:* Packaging and packaging waste management regulations seek to provide a high level of environmental protection concerning the materials used in packaging and fund recycling programs. They encourage the minimization and reuse of packaging, and the reduction of landfill disposal of packaging waste. In many instances, they will specify reporting in standardized formats tied to the sales of goods that will support the packaging waste recycling sector.
- *General Product Safety Directives (GPSD):* GPSD laws aim to ensure that products placed on the market are safe. A GPSD serves as a backstop and applies to all products entering a market in the absence of other legislation, national standards, recommendations, or codes of practice relating to the safety of products. Testing laboratories are frequently used to assess compliance with GPSD regulations related to specific product types.
- *Life Cycle Assessment (LCA):* LCA is the systematic analysis of the potential environmental impacts of products or services during their entire life cycle.

From an executive perspective, compliance with product regulations translates to the ability to sell a product into a given market.[18] Accordingly, it is important to be able to identify the regulations of key concern within the markets where the organization is seeking to do business. Once identified, the supply chain compliance team will need to track, manage, and disclose any necessary information to comply. In each region, different regulations, directives, and laws will require different levels of attention and will be prone to differing levels of maturity and enforcement. To facilitate this understanding, this section will highlight the core product compliance regulations that will impact a company when the business seeks to sell a product into a given market.

18. See, for example, European Commission. Safety Gate: The EU Rapid Alert System for Dangerous Non-food Products, https://ec.europa.eu/safety-gate-alerts/screen/webReport, and California Office of Attorney General Prop. 65 enforcement website, https://oag.ca.gov/prop65.

The Americas

North American and South American supply chain regulations are significantly more fragmented than the European, the Middle Eastern, and African (EMEA) requirements, as there is rarely a uniform country or region-wide approach to product compliance. A consequence of this lack of uniform policy has resulted in countries, states, and/or territories implementing disparate policies that must be considered by manufacturers seeking to enter into these markets. As a general practice, testing houses, laboratories, and the industry or market-specific counsel/consultancies are highly leveraged to determine which regulations are impactful and how compliance should be managed. Consequently, it is difficult to develop a one-size-fits-all approach to the Americas, because, while the United States dominates policy and regulatory enforcement in the region, it has lagged in implementing supply chain product compliance laws. As a result, other markets and individual states/territories within the Americas region have developed a patchwork quilt of their own policies and programs.

When evaluating the U.S. product compliance regimes, a manufacturer and/or importer must consider not only broad nationwide requirements, see the Consumer Product Safety Commission,[19] but also the specific locations of critical economic importance. This reality is well illustrated by the state-specific requirements that are present in the State of California. For example, California's Safe Drinking Water and Toxic Enforcement Act of 1986 (Proposition 65) is an international driver of supply chain product compliance due diligence. However, California's Proposition 65 is an outlier. More commonly, U.S. states have taken to regulating individual sectors or product types.[20] Latin America has tended to study and take steps toward alignment with the European model of product regulations that includes registration of products, fee-paying obligations, and some initial steps toward materials regulations.[21] However, most Latin American supply chain centric regulations of products remain in draft form or are in the early implementation phase and are significantly underfunded from an enforcement perspective. Latin America regional expertise is generally required to ensure that your client's specific target markets remain free from market restricting regulation—regional expertise is generally required.

Canada has traditionally implemented a blend of European and U.S. modeled policies that have been motivated by free trade agreements and market access requirements that its domestic organizations face. For example, Canada

19. CPSC website, https://www.cpsc.gov/Regulations-Laws--Standards.

20. See, for example, Washington Children's Product Safety Act, https://ecology.wa.gov/Waste-Toxics/Reducing-toxic-chemicals/Childrens-Safe-Products-Act; California's Restriction of Hazardous Substances, https://dtsc.ca.gov/restrictions-on-the-use-of-certain-hazardous-substances-rohs-in-electronic-devices/; or the Texas Waste Electrical and Electronic Equipment Law, https://www.tceq.texas.gov/assistance/industry/e-recycling/e-recycling-regs.html.

21. See Latin American Environmental Regulatory Tracker: Sept. 16–Oct. 15, 2018, https://www.natlawreview.com/article/latin-american-environmental-regulatory-tracker-september-16-october-15-2018.

has implemented a robust set of provincial and territorial WEEE regulations.[22] However, materials regulations have tended to more closely align with the United States' safety regulations and chemical control regime.[23]

Europe, Middle East, and Africa (EMEA)

For the last decade, the EU has been at the forefront of product compliance regulations. By complying with the general EU regulations, a company generally can develop a robust compliance program that can support EMEA compliance. To bring a product to market in the EU, a company must perform a Conformitè Europëenne Mark (CE Mark) assessment.[24] A CE Mark assessment requires a manufacturer to evaluate each product in a structured process that walks through a conformity assessment analysis that is well described by the European Commission on the Internal Market, Industry, Entrepreneurship, and SMEs (small and medium-sized enterprises) website.[25]

The European Commission publishes a highly leveraged resource known as the "Blue Guide" on the implementation of EU product rules, 2016.[26] This resource should be read in conjunction with Regulation (EU) 2019/1020 of the European Parliament and of the Council, of June 20, 2019, on market surveillance and compliance of products and amending Directive 2004/42/EC and Regulations (EC) No. 765/2008 and (EU) No. 305/2011.

While the CE Marking directives are obligatory requirements, they are not representative of the full scope of market access requirements that a manufacturing company must consider when seeking to enter into the EU. Specifically, a manufacturer and/or importers must also consider European-country-specific fee-paying requirements, such as the packaging directive,[27] battery directive,[28] and the WEEE directive.[29] Each of these regulations obligates a manufacturer to register with in-country schemes, register products, and fund recycling/take-back programs. Consequently, a manufacturer must pay special attention to the cost structure and develop internal information technology (IT) systems that

---

22. See OECD Promoting Sustainable Materials Management through Extended Producer Responsibility: Canadian Waste Electrical and Electronic Equipment (WEEE) Case Study, https://www.oecd.org/environment/waste/Canadian%20WEEE%20EPR%20Case%20Study%20-%2012June2014.FINAL.pdf.

23. See Canadian Environmental Protection Act, https://www.canada.ca/en/environment-climate-change/services/canadian-environmental-protection-act-registry/related-documents.html.

24. See EU CE Mark website: https://europa.eu/youreurope/business/product-requirements/labels-markings/ce-marking/index_en.htm.

25. Internal Market, Industry, Entrepreneurship and SMEs, CE Marking website, https://ec.europa.eu/growth/single-market/ce-marking_en.

26. Blue Guide website, https://eur-lex.europa.eu/legal-content/EN/TXT/?uri=uriserv:OJ.C_.2016.272.01.0001.01.ENG.

27. Directive 94/62/EC, 1994, O.J. (L 365), 10 (EC).

28. Directive 2006/66/EC of the European Parliament and of the Council, Sept. 6, 2006, on waste batteries and accumulators and repealing directive: Directive 91/157/EEC.

29. Directive 2012/19/EU.

incorporate specific bills of materials (BoMs) to allow them to itemize and pay these fees.

Lateral disclosure laws surrounding the use and disclosure of hazardous materials also require special attention when assessing whether a product can be imported into the European Economic Area. While these regulations tend to be product and industry vertical specific, there are a few that are widespread and require specific attention. For example, the EU Registration, Evaluation, Authorisation and Restriction of Chemicals (REACH)[30]; Persistent Organic Pollutants (POPs) Regulation (EU)[31]; and Biocidal Products Regulation (BPR)[32] are all broad and general applicability. Moreover, each follows a standardized restricted or declarable substance threshold detection methodology that involves supplier inquiry that is described by the technical standard EN IEC 63000:2018.

AsiaPac

From a product compliance standpoint, Asia and the Australian subcontinent has been in a transition process over the last several years. As Europe was originally developing and deploying a robust product compliance regulatory regime, the AsiaPac region was driven to adopt voluntary initiatives aimed at aligning industry standards and norms around European requirements. The Joint Article Management Promotion (JAMP) consortium and Japan Green Procurement Survey Standardization Initiative (JGPSSI) efforts from Japan were good representations of the work product driven by this approach. However, more recently, the laws have been passed and adopted that have modernized and resulted in the implementation of a series of new product compliance-driven regulatory controls.[33]

Each of the four core economies in the region has adopted varying product compliance laws that align with core concerns. China has focused on restrictions of materials by leveraging China's Restriction of Hazardous Substances (RoHS) and requiring labeling and safe use on electronics. Korea has invested in developing a chemicals database modeled after the EU REACH regulation.[34] Australia has developed a waste management taxation and a take-back system, as part of the country's product safety laws.[35] Japan has continued its voluntary compliance approach that has followed the JAMP as the industry association has developed the ChemSHERPA tool.[36]

---

30. EC 1907/2006.
31. EC 2019/1021.
32. Regulation (EU) 528/2012.
33. See, for example, China's Administrative Measure on the Control of Pollution Caused by Electronic Information Products (China RoHS).
34. The Act on Registration and Evaluation of Chemicals, https://www.ncbi.nlm.nih.gov/pmc/articles/PMC5336359/.
35. See Austrian Product Safety Website: https://www.accc.gov.au/business/treating-customers-fairly/product-safety.
36. See ChemSHERPA website: https://chemsherpa.net/.

As a whole, the AsiaPac region has a robust series of mandatory regulatory regimes that rival the EU's product compliance scheme. However, lax enforcement and the lack of normalized policy around the region have created a reality where most organizations are highly sensitive to investing time and resources into developing a defensible AsiaPac due diligence program. The consequence is that enforcement sweeps in the region tend to demonstrate a high level of noncompliance. This reality perpetuates throughout the region as smaller economies will tend to adopt product compliance standards modeled after the larger neighboring regional players. Accordingly, shipments should be closely monitored against local product compliance laws, and a network of regional and local counsel is advisable to support audits, investigations, and product holds that may arise if proper due diligence is not fully implemented within either your company or suppliers to our company.

Practical Tips for Auditing a Product Compliance Program

Scoping a product compliance audit should relate to purchased products from suppliers or, if internal, products that are intended for shipment into a regulated jurisdiction. As there are a significant number of product compliance regulations, your audit should also be narrowly tailored toward a specific jurisdiction. Triggering a new audit and undergoing the process described below, for each jurisdiction and/or regulatory requirement, is often untenable for organizations operating in multiple jurisdictions. Companies should look to implement processes and systems that allow them to collect/validate/manage data for various requirements simultaneously, and leverage that data as needed to meet more specific jurisdictional requirements. When evaluating your internal company or an external supplier for product compliance, you need to be able to access the database that houses part and product compliance information and the technical files for the products in the scope of the audit. These two core document types should contain core data attributes that are necessary to demonstrate a valid product compliance program. These attributes are as follows:

- General description of the product;
- Documents for materials, parts, and/or subassemblies;
- Information showing the relationship between the documents and the corresponding materials, parts, and/or subassemblies in the product; and
- A list of harmonized standards and/or other technical specifications that have been used to establish the technical documents and which are mentioned by the available documentation.

Once the appropriate electronic and hard copy technical files are available, you will need to take a sample product BoM and/or a random sample of component parts. Product compliance programs will require documentation and a chain of custody that evidences how materials and components compliance status was determined. The provided files should include a certification of conformity (CoC) or contractual assurances, engineering analysis statements, and/or analytical testing reports that demonstrate each supplied item meets the specific requirements of the regulation(s). These documents will need to be kept on file and accessible to customers, auditors, and other parties that might be entitled to review the technical and compliance information related to the product.

While each evidence type has value, the highest value document is a CoC from the OEM of a part. A CoC is essentially a warranty from the manufacturer assuring that all purchased components with a specified manufacturer part number (MPN) meet those requirements. When reviewing the evidence trail for a CoC, the following attributes for any document should be present.

- The CoC should be on company letterhead or indicate the manufacturer that is making the declaration.
- The legislation the CoC is making a compliance statement for should be referenced and cited appropriately within the document.
- The CoC should reference any unique MPNs that are covered by the declaration.
- The compliance status (compliant or not) along with any claimed exclusions from the scope of the regulation/directive or technical exemptions for the product or part being evaluated should be contained in the CoC.
- If the product is not in compliance, due to the presence of either a restricted or declarable substance, then, at a minimum, the substance should be referenced by both chemical name and Chemical Abstract Service (CAS) number.
- The CoC should contain a signature block that features the signature and title of an authorized representative with authority to bind the company to the warranty statement and familiarity with the subject matter.
- The CoC needs to be date stamped to demonstrate that the compliance claim is current and up to date with the latest version of the regulation the CoC is claiming conformance with.

Internal claims of conformance will need to have a basis and/or explanation for the decision included in internal documentation. It is not enough for a technical file to make an unsubstantiated claim of conformance. There should be information concerning the product, part, material, or raw chemical that reveals its chemical composition to a degree that justifies the claim. While there is not a definitive list of all documentation formats that will demonstrate internal due diligence, there are a few common formats that are frequently leveraged by industry. These formats include full material content declarations (a full breakdown of the materials used to produce a product), ASTM International standards or grades of raw materials, and chemical safety data sheets. These supporting collateral documents will have to be reviewed by technically competent staff if they are to be used to demonstrate that they align to the part or material being evaluated. In addition to this supporting documentation, there should also be a certifier from within the company who has both authority and technical expertise sufficient to allow them to make the claim of compliance.

The final industry-standard norm for making a claim of part or materials compliance is a third-party analytical test of the component. There are a large number of independent third-party laboratories that can conduct these analytical tests. The test will need to align with the current standards that have been designated by the European authorities (see previously mentioned "Blue Guide"). The cost of these tests will vary by the number of regulations, substance lists, and demand to conduct the tests at the time the test is ordered. The tests are conducted on a random sample of a specific product, part, or material. Consequently, while the test is deemed a valid approach to demonstrating compliance, it is considered more limited than a blanket declaration from the OEM, due to the limitation of only being applicable to the given sample. When evaluating an analytical test report, it is also important to evaluate whether the test report is a counterfeit. Many of the large and reputable third-party laboratories will have a free report verification service. Report verification and confirmation that a product, part, or material was the actual evaluated item are important steps in a compliance audit that features analytical test reports.

Product Compliance Disclosures to Customers

A product compliance disclosure to a customer will require the organization to roll up the compliance status related to each component part and/or material used in the finished product. These statuses are linked to the documentation and evidence from the organization's suppliers. The compliance status is intended to reveal the presence or absence of a restricted or declarable substance. Customers will likely request information in multiple formats and/or through multiple systems. The organization will have to make key decisions regarding whether it will comply with and communicate in the customer's format, adopt its own standardized format for declaration, or elect to not make a declaration. If the decision is made to make a declaration, then the option of the format will likely be binary. If the decision to comply with the customer request is met, then the only outstanding decision to make is whether to communicate back in the customer's format or in an industry-standardized format.

Meeting any customer requirement will mean that the company will need to invest resources to research, aggregate, and prepare the responses. This will mean that the organization will inevitably meet customer requirements that it does not have information to address. To meet these requirements, the organization will need a process to quickly ingest the request, transform it into a compliance request to its own suppliers, and disseminate the request to the appropriate contacts within its own supply chain. The corresponding close working relationship with the suppliers will need to be maintained and require significant transparency and cooperation to be successful. Upon receipt, the data will need to be ingested, validated, rolled up against the product, formatted for the customer, and communicated to the customer in a timely fashion.

Communicating in a standard format will meet resistance from customers, who will often have established a system and process for ingesting supplier responses in their own request format. As a result, the customer will have to adapt the data into a format or implement a special process to input the data into their own system of record. The advantage of this process to the organization is that the size of the department will not need to be as large and processing the request will not be as resource heavy. However, the organization will need to have a well-reasoned, industry-standard-based position to be able to articulate. This position will serve as the baseline for ongoing discussions with the supply chain counterpart on the customer side. These documents will serve as evidence and will likely be recorded and archived in the customer's supply chain compliance system of record. Accordingly, there will need to be evidence and a linkage between the organization's declaration and the requirements of the customer's compliance needs. If this connection is not met and does not align with the needs of the customer, then it will be rejected for a myriad of potential reasons.

What Constitutes Noncompliance with a Product Compliance Law?

Noncompliance with product compliance law(s) means that a company has (1) produced and imported a product that does not meet safety standards, (2) not implemented a program that will allow it to detect and disclose a declarable substance, and/or (3) missed the identification of and/or failed to disclose a restricted substance. In each of these cases, the auditor will likely have either performed a spot check on data for an imported good or will have conducted a detailed audit against a company's system of records. Adequate documentation that follows the process prescribed by the regulation and/or guidance available surrounding the regulation can offer a due diligence defense or a presumption of conformity in certain jurisdictions. Conversely, noncompliance can bear significant enforcement consequences and costs culminating with fines, penalties, product recall, and criminal prosecution. Accordingly, regardless of the position the organization takes, it needs to have confidence in its approach.

Unsafe product determinations are generally binary in nature. If a product does not have the required independent third-party laboratory test or internal test documentation, it is noncompliant. Unsafe products are not allowed to operate within a market and are not sellable. A paperwork audit will often be conducted at customs during inspections or by authorities during on-premises investigations. If a company cannot provide technical documentation demonstrating that the product meets the safety standards of the jurisdiction, it will likely be seized and/or recalled. Many customs authorities will not have specific knowledge related to every product safety standard. In addition, many customs authorities will not know the precise application of an imported device, so they will not necessarily be able to conduct a comprehensive evaluation at the time of import. Accordingly, it is entirely possible that a noncompliant product might clear customs and arrive at its final destination. The manufacturer and importer of record are then most likely to face liability either when the product is registered with the local department(s) responsible for permitting the installation of the device or during an on-site audit of the warehouse, manufacturing facility, or retailer. In the event of an injury, the manufacturer and/or importer of a noncompliant product will likely bear a very high standard of proof, culminating with strict liability for importing and selling unsafe products. On-site inspections of devices are almost inevitable if a person is harmed during the use of the device.

Paperwork noncompliance that does not demonstrate a company has implemented a process-based approach to substance detection and disclosure is the most common form of identified noncompliance. The inability to produce product registration documentation or present technical documentation for a product on request is prima facie evidence of noncompliance. The customs authority or inspector will likely request a registration number or access to the paperwork that demonstrates that the technical standard for detecting a declarable substance and/or the safety standards for a product have been met. If the company does not have this information readily available, the product will likely be held at customs until the paperwork is available, the importer of record will be required to test a sample of the product at an approved laboratory, or the detainment will result in a recall. If a product makes it into a market, but also contains a declarable substance that has not been declared, a request for information to the OEM or importer of record can still be made. These requests might come from either a customer or a regulatory authority. If the request for information falls within a regulatory mandated records retention period, the failure to provide documentation may constitute prima facie evidence of noncompliance and could result in product recall, legal claims, and/or other fines and penalties.

Importing a product that is or contains a restricted substance or material, without approval or authorization by a valid technical exemption claim is illegal. Customs authorities will frequently use systems of record that flag products known to contain restricted substances. If a shipment's importation documentation is flagged, the importer will be expected to provide detailed information concerning the materials within the product. The product might also be spot checked within a warehouse using substance detection tools, for example, Portable XRF Analyzer System. The importer might also be required to send a sample of the product to an approved testing laboratory and pay for analysis to prove compliance. Importers lacking documentation that are found to have imported a restricted material will face potential civil and criminal liability. Costs associated with testing, prosecution, product recall, fines, harm to customers, and criminal prosecution of the business or individuals should be anticipated if restricted substances are intentionally imported and sold. Detection of noncompliance has become progressively more sophisticated and likely, as tools, processes, and technologies have matured alongside the regulations.

Enforcement

Noncompliance with product compliance laws has been among the top reasons for product recalls globally for the last decade. In Europe, noncompliance with product compliance laws that mandate the disclosure of substances of very high concern has driven major regulatory reforms.[37] Yet, even given the volume of product compliance enforcement, there has been a general finding that enforcement needs to increase and companies have had a high degree of noncompliance.[38] The following provides a digest and highlights a few key cases that identified key supply chain compliance issues with product compliance laws that are instructive in developing an internal program.

In 2019, Continental AG and Robert Bosch GmbH discovered that they had been leveraging a Chinese supplier who had been providing them with automotive parts that exceeded the permissible amount of lead in components. The Chinese supplier had been communicating through an industry-wide shared centralized database called the International Material Data System (IMDS). The declarations had not been vetted independently by the companies until 2019, when a materials audit revealed the noncompliance. Both companies performed voluntary self-disclosures and implemented recall and replacement programs to correct the noncompliance in the electronics. Reliance on database solutions without independent due diligence and verification can generate risk. Moreover, REACH and RoHS enforcement has been escalating over recent years and now represents a leading cause of enforcement and expense related to European product recall.[39]

On June 5, 2019, California's acrylamide and coffee saga came to a close. For years, Proposition 65 litigation had ensued with the plaintiff's counsel filing suit against food businesses that had failed to warn consumers of the presence of a Proposition 65 known carcinogen, acrylamide, in their products.[40] Acrylamide is a by-product of the coffee bean roasting process and, in fact, many baking/cooking processes. (Note: similar failure to notice lawsuits were filed against Starbucks, Frito-Lay, General Mills, Kellogg, Utz Quality Foods, and more.[41]) The final judgment after hundreds of thousands of dollars in legal fees was that there was no scientific evidence that could be traced to prove that acrylamide in coffee causes cancer in a substantial way. However, the expense to defend Proposition 65 lawsuits has developed a boutique plaintiff's counsel industry resulting in tens of millions of dollars in settlements annually.[42] Consequently, it is prudent to develop a Proposition 65 due diligence, substance identification, and disclosure/labeling program to avoid the most significant fines and penalties.

37. See, for example, European Union Rapid Exchange (RAPEX) website: https://ec.europa.eu/consumers/consumers_safety/safety_products/rapex/alerts/?event=viewProduct&reference=A12/0157/19&lng=en and United States Consumer Product Safety Commission Product Recalls website: https://www.cpsc.gov/Recalls.

38. See, for example, ECHA REACH-EN-FORCE FORUM, https://echa.europa.eu/about-us/who-we-are/enforcement-forum/forum-enforcement-projects.

39. See Chemsec website that shows the cost of REACH through 2019 has worked out to approximately 3 billion Euros, https://chemsec.org/industry-predicted-the-costs-of-reach-they-were-wrong/.

40. OEHHA Proposition 65 list website, https://oehha.ca.gov/proposition-65/proposition-65-list.

41. See the curious case of acrylamide: Kendall Powell, California's Prop. 65 Explained, https://knowablemagazine.org/article/health-disease/2018/curious-case-acrylamide-californias-prop-65-explained.

42. See Office of Attorney General Prop. 65 Plaintiff's Settlement pages, https://oag.ca.gov/prop65/report/judgments-by-plaintiffs?year%5Bvalue%5D%5Byear%5D=2018.

Product Compliance Checklist

Product compliance laws are primarily a precursor to obtaining market access to countries that have implemented a product compliance program. When building a product compliance program, a company must perform a materiality assessment to determine whether the investment required for a compliance program and the associated costs will be met with a sufficient return on investment (ROI). Failing to perform, this assessment can yield an unfortunate result. Specifically, an organization may commit to sales of a product, only to learn that the product is not fit for sale and that significant redesign is required or that the orders will have to be canceled. To calculate the ROI associated with implementing a product compliance market access program, guide your team to evaluate the cost of the compliance program against the projected revenue from the sales of the product into a given market and/or the expected revenue that will result from an expansion of the total addressable market derived from sales of the product in question.

The following provides a checklist of steps that are taken to perform a materiality assessment concerning what markets and correspondingly what product compliance regulations should be in the scope of your compliance program:

- Check with sales and logistics to determine what markets your products are currently being sold in. (Take care to look at internet sales, which can trigger product compliance requirements, but are often overlooked.)
- Obtain sales and profitability data related to the volume of sales that are in a given region and/or country.
- Work with engineering (your organization may also have a dedicated regulatory, product ecology, or product compliance function that can also perform this function) to develop an understanding of the current process for building a compliant technical file and which regulations are considered.
- Review any communication templates that the supply chain team is using to collect product compliance information from suppliers and map the workflow related to how that supplier information is assessed and archived.
- Audit the IT system that is leveraged to document compliance data received by suppliers. Validate that the system that is maintaining current records is date stamping records and displays appropriate visual indicators showing compliance status described by the on-file data is accurate.
- Conduct a gap assessment to identify any critical product compliance regulations that are not currently in place. Perform a gap assessment at a regular cadence and/or join industry- standard associations to maintain awareness of key impactful regulations of concern and to forecast custom requests that will align to industry-standard documentation requests.
- Close any gaps identified through this process and enhance systems to accommodate for new compliance issues that are not currently being adequately addressed.

CHAPTER 8

ESG Marketing

Sarah Gudernatch Smith and Shyla John

Highlighted by Edelman's twenty-second Annual Trust Barometer, societal leadership is now a core function of business. As corporations learn more about the environmental, social, and governance (ESG) criteria their stakeholders care most about and review the differences between ESG and sustainability/corporate social responsibility (CSR), disclosure and marketing practices have increased significantly and begun to change. Sustainability and CSR reporting has been a common practice for more than a decade targeting multiple stakeholder audiences: employees, prospective employees, consumers, regulators, investors, and more. However, today ESG and Sustainability/CSR communications extend well beyond this to a diversified and ever-changing portfolio of integrated communications and marketing initiatives. In this chapter, we look at the current trends in ESG Communications and Marketing.

Trend 1: Investor-Focused ESG Disclosure

When we first began drafting Sustainability/CSR Reports in the early 2000s, a common first step was to interview internal and key external stakeholders to determine the report content. While subject-matter experts continue to play a critical role in contributing to both Sustainability/CSR Reports and ESG Reports, the questions asked to these subject-matter experts today are different from the questions asked ten years ago.

While some questions, "What were the major initiatives and accomplishments in your area of work this fiscal year?" carry over from year to year, new questions such as "Is your cybersecurity system ISO-certified?" or "Who oversees human capital management?" are added each year. These questions are in response to investors' continued push for decision-useful ESG disclosure and corporations continued evolution to provide investor-focused disclosure.

Why Corporations Create Investor-Focused ESG Disclosure

Access to Capital

Investors control access to capital and the cost of capital. Despite the political climate, the investment community has increasingly noted the link between ESG risks and financial risks and have pushed corporations to disclose ESG information that is material to the company. While the reasoning behind investors' interest in ESG is not the focus of this chapter, one only has to look at Bank of America's Global Research team, which recently estimated that more than $600 billion of market cap for S&P 500 companies have been lost to "ESG controversies."[1]

As another example, the S&P reduced credit ratings on ExxonMobil, Chevron, and ConocoPhillips in February 2021, in part citing the "growing risk from the energy transition due to climate change and carbon/GHG emissions," while other leading credit rating agencies have also integrated ESG factors into their credit analyses.[2]

There are numerous studies that speak to increasing investor interest in ESG. According to the most recent 2020 Global Sustainable Investment Review, conducted biennially by the Global Sustainable Investment Alliance, global sustainable investment has grown to $35.3 trillion, a growth of 15 percent in two years.[3] The PwC 2021 Global Investor Survey, which reaches 325 global investors, found that 79 percent of respondents said the way a company manages ESG risks and opportunities is an important factor in their investment decision making.[4] In the same survey, 49 percent of respondents expressed willingness to divest from companies that are not taking sufficient action on ESG issues.[5] The Principles for Responsible Investment (PRI), a United Nations–supported organization, began in 2006 to encourage investors to use responsible investment to enhance returns and better manage risks. The PRI has grown consistently and, as of June 2022, included 5,000 signatories representing $121 trillion of assets under management.[6]

In addition to access to capital, companies disclose their ESG initiatives and performance data due to the *cost of capital.* According to a Morgan Stanley Capital International (MSCI) study, companies with high ESG scores, on average, experienced lower costs of capital compared to companies with poor ESG scores in both developed and emerging markets during a four-year study period. In the MSCI World Index, the average cost of capital of the highest ESG scored quintile was 6.16 percent, compared to 6.55 percent for the lowest ESG scored quintile.[7]

---

1. See Interview with Savita Subramanian, *ESG Viewpoints: Bofa Securities,* RepRisk (Sept. 2020), https://www.reprisk.com/media/pages/static/2906052835-1663140334/esg-viewpoint-bofa-securities.pdf.

2. See Gail Glazerman, *ESG and Access to Captial,* MORNINGSTAR (Oct. 8, 2021), https://www.morningstar.in/posts/65105/esg-access-capital.aspx.

3. See http://www.gsi-alliance.org/wp-content/uploads/2021/08/GSIR-20201.pdf.

4. See Press Release, PwC, PwC's Global Investor Survey 2022 (on file with PwC).

5. *Ibid.*

6. See 2021-2022 Annual Report, PRI with United Nations Global Compact (2022), https://dwtyzx6upklss.cloudfront.net/Uploads/b/f/m/pri_annual_report_2022_689047.pdf.

7. See Ashish Lodh, *ESG and the Cost of Capital,* MSCI (Feb. 25, 2020) https://www.msci.com/www/blog-posts/esg-and-the-cost-of-capital/01726513589.

Shareholder Resolutions

In addition to access to and the cost of capital, corporations are proactively disclosing additional ESG information to avoid shareholder resolutions and other unfavorable voting outcomes during proxy season. From the PwC 2021 Global Investor Survey, 59 percent of respondents said a lack of action on ESG issues makes it likely they would vote against an executive pay agreement, while fully a third say they have already taken this action.[8]

In the 2021 proxy season, we saw Engine No. 1, an activist investor, install three directors on the board of ExxonMobil with the goal to push the company to reduce its carbon footprint. In this instance, institutional investors BlackRock, Vanguard, and State Street voted in support of Engine No. 1's board directors and against ExxonMobil leadership.[9]

A 2022 proxy season study by Harvard Law School Forum on Corporate Governance found that, as of May 2022, 924 shareholder proposals were filed, with 520 of them involving ESG topics, an increase of 20 percent from 2021.[10] The same study found that of the 286 proposals voted on at that time, 30 related to environmental matters, 107 involved social issues, and 149 related to governance issues.[11] At the time of the study, six environmental proposals, ten social proposals, and twenty-eight governance proposals had passed.[12] As the study notes, the submissions of environmental proposals increased 39 percent between 2021 and 2022.[13]

While passage rates of these resolutions were low (environmental proposals had a 20 percent passage rate; social proposals had a 9.3 percent passage rate; and governance proposals had an 18.8 percent passage rate), ESG proponents considered it a successful season. As Pillsbury Law puts it, "Beyond an increase in the sheer quantity of ESG shareholder proposals, the significance of the ESG demands made during the 2022 proxy season rose, revealing more targeted and action-oriented proposals. For example, in 2022 shareholder proposals on diversity in the workplace newly go beyond asking for EEO-1 data disclosure, instead asking for information on companies' diversity programs and outcomes."[14]

Examples of ESG-focused shareholder resolutions that passed in the 2022 proxy season include the following:

- Microsoft shareholders approved a proposal with 77.97 percent of votes asking the board to publish a report on the effectiveness of its workplace sexual harassment policies, even though the board recommended a "no" vote.[15]

---

8. See *Id* at note 4.

9. See Matt Phillips, *Exxon's Board Defeat Signals the Rise of Social-Good Activists,* N.Y. Times (June 9, 2021), https://www.nytimes.com/2021/06/09/business/exxon-mobil-engine-no1-activist.html.

10. HannahOrowitz et al., *An Early Look at the 2022 Proxy Season,* Harv. L. Sch. Forum on Corp. Gov. (June 2, 2022), https://corpgov.law.harvard.edu/2022/06/07/an-early-look-at-the-2022-proxy-season/.

11. *Ibid.*

12. *Ibid.*

13. *Ibid.*

14. See Stacie D. Yee et al., *ESG Over the 2022 Proxy Season,* Pillsbury Law (2022), https://www.pillsburylaw.com/print/content/1026603/esg-2022-proxy-season.pdf.

15. See Jordan Novet, *Microsoft Shareholders Vote for the Company to Publish Sexual-Harassment Report, in Rare Win for Activists,* CNBC (Nov. 30, 2021), https://www.cnbc.com/2021/11/30/microsoft-shareholders-vote-for-sexual-harassment-report.html.

- Lowe's shareholders approved a proposal with a 58 percent majority brought forth by sustainability-focused investment management firm Arjuna Capital, asking the company to transparently report on racial and gender pay gaps. The Lowe's Board of Directors opposed this proposal.[16]
- On the environmental side, 91 percent of Boeing shareholders supported a resolution filed by As You Sow, a shareholder advocacy nonprofit, asking the company to align its greenhouse gas emissions with the global Paris Agreement's net zero by 2050 goal. In this instance, the Board supported the proposal.[17]

Passage rates are also not the only measure of success. According to a Ceres study, while in the 2022 proxy season investors filed a record 215 climate-related shareholder resolutions, shareholders negotiated agreements on 103 of these, with companies committing to take actions sought in exchange for withdrawal.[18]

How Corporations Create Investor-Focused ESG Disclosure: Frameworks and ESG Raters

In our experience, corporations often receive direct inquiries from their investors asking to provide additional disclosure around ESG topics. In addition to these direct requests, corporations look to reporting frameworks and ESG raters to proactively disclose information on key topic areas ahead of investor requests and shareholder resolutions.

Frameworks

While investors have increasingly pushed for ESG disclosure, they have also pushed for standardization of ESG disclosure to better compare company performance. Although the Global Reporting Initiative (GRI) remains the most commonly used reporting framework, key investor-focused reporting frameworks include the Sustainability Accounting Standards Board (SASB) Standards and the Task Force on Climate-Related Financial Disclosures (TCFD).

- *GRI:* Founded in 1997, the GRI Standards strive to create a common language for organizations—large or small, private or public—to report on their sustainability impacts in a consistent and credible way. The GRI Standards consider the broad needs of all key stakeholder groups and are the most widely adopted sustainability reporting standards. As of

16. See Ben Maiden, *Lowe's Shareholders Vote for Pay-Gap Report*, CorporateSecretary (June 6, 2022), https://www.corporatesecretary.com/articles/esg/33040/lowe%E2%80%99s-shareholders-vote-pay-gap-report.

17. See Press Release, 91% of Boeing Shareholders Support Net-Zero Climate Report (May 3, 2022) (on file with As You Sow). https://www.asyousow.org/press-releases/2022/5/3/boeing-shareholders-support-net-zero-climate-report.

18. See Press Release, 2022 Proxy Season Begins Record Numbers Climate Resolutions (2022) (on file with Ceres). https://www.ceres.org/news-center/press-releases/2022-proxy-season-begins-record-numbers-climate-resolutions-and.

January 2022, 10,000 companies had published a GRI report and 70 percent of Fortune 500 companies use or refer to the GRI Standards.[19]

- *SASB:* Investors increasingly want to know how ESG topics impact corporate value creation. SASB was founded in 2011 with a goal to help businesses and investors develop a common language about the financial impacts of sustainability. The SASB Standards are a set of seventy-seven industry-specific standards designed to identify the ESG issues most relevant to financial performance. As of August 2022, the SASB Standards are now part of the IFRS (International Financial Reporting Standards) Foundation and under the oversight of the International Sustainability Standards Board. Of note for corporations, Blackrock requested that the companies they invest in publish a disclosure in line with industry-specific SASB guidelines by year-end 2020.[20]
- *TCFD:* The Financial Stability Board created the TCFD to develop a disclosure framework that supported investors, lenders, and insurance underwriters in assessing and pricing specific risks related to climate change. The TCFD framework, released in 2017, provides detailed guidance on environmental risk and data disclosures and is structured around four disclosure areas: governance, strategy, risk management, and metrics and targets. Of note for corporations, Blackrock requested that the companies they invest in publish a disclosure in line with TCFD by year-end 2020.[21]
- *Other disclosure frameworks:* There are numerous other ESG disclosure reporting frameworks.

The World Economic Forum released its Stakeholder Capitalism Metrics in 2021, which draw from existing voluntary standards, in an aim to simplify and standardize non-financial reporting.[22] There are also industry-specific frameworks, such as the *Sustainability reporting guidance for the oil and gas industry*, published by Ipieca, the American Petroleum Institute, and the International Association of Oil & Gas Producers.[23] New frameworks are introduced regularly, such as the Taskforce for Nature-Related Financial Disclosure (TNFD), which recently completed its pilot phase.[24]

ESG Rater Requests

In addition to following reporting frameworks, corporations utilize the indicators asked by ESG rating agencies, including those from MSCI, ISS (Institutional Shareholder Services), and Sustainalytics, among others, to determine report

19. See https://www.globalreporting.org/media/ervdeb02/gri-perspective-business-case-for-environment-and-society.pdf.

20. See Larry Fink, *A Fundamental Reshaping of Finance,* Blackrock (2020), https://www.blackrock.com/us/individual/larry-fink-ceo-letter.

21. See *id.*

22. See https://www.weforum.org/stakeholdercapitalism.

23. See https://www.ipieca.org/our-work/sustainability/performance-reporting/sustainability-reporting-guidance/.

24. See https://www.fsb-tcfd.org/.

content. For corporations that sell to other businesses, EcoVadis is a commonly used rating.

- *MSCI:* MSCI's ESG rating is released annually and rates companies from AAA (best) to CCC (worst). MSCI's methodology is based on a company's exposure to ESG risks and how well they manage financially relevant ESG risks relative to peers.
- *ISS:* ISS also provides data designed to identify ESG risks and opportunities. ISS's ESG corporate rating is issued annually and rates companies from A+ (best) to D- (worst). The scoring is based on a two-dimensional matrix of Social and Governance rating and Environmental rating. ISS also produces a monthly ISS QualityScore, which rates companies between 1 (best) and 10 (worst) in ESG pillars.
- *Sustainalytics:* Sustainalytics provides an annual ESG Risk Rating that takes into account the company's exposure to industry-specific material ESG risks (ESG Risk Exposure) and how well the company is managing these risks (ESG Risk Management). The ESG Risk Ratings are categorized across five risk levels: negligible (0–10), low (10–20), medium (20–30), high (30–40), and severe (40+).
- *EcoVadis:* An EcoVadis sustainability assessment is used by many business-to-business (B2B) companies to satisfy their customers' requests for sustainability information. EcoVadis ratings allow companies that are suppliers to other companies to fill out a single assessment regarding their ESG initiatives and performance. Companies are then rated in five performance levels: outstanding (score 85–100), advanced (score 65–84), good (score 45–64), partial (score 25–44), and insufficient (score 0–24).

Spotlight: Emerging ESG Topic Areas

In response to proxy season proposals, direct investor inquiries, reporting frameworks, and ESG rater requests, in our experience, corporations have been asked to consider disclosure around the following emerging ESG topics: employee mental health, accessibility of products and services, accessibility as it relates to employees and prospective employees, sustainable manufacturing, supply chain transparency, supplier diversity, ethical advertising, whistle-blowing, political contributions, geopolitical challenges, CEO pay ratio, cybersecurity, pay equity, Scope 3 emissions reduction, and net zero emissions.

Trend 2: Regulations Are Changing ESG Disclosure

As of December 2022, there are currently no mandatory ESG disclosures at the federal level in the United States. In 2002, the Sarbanes–Oxley Act was passed, which legally obligates companies to disclose any risks, including ESG risks, in the company's form 10-K filed annually with the U.S. Securities and Exchange

Commission (SEC). In March 2022, the SEC proposed a rule on climate disclosure, which would require a registrant to disclose its governance of climate-related risks, how any climate-related risks have a material impact on business, a company's Scope 1 and Scope 2 greenhouse gas emissions, and a company's Scope 3 greenhouse gas emissions if material or if a target has been set, among other requirements.[25]

While this proposed regulation is relatively new in the United States, global reporting requirements have existed for many years. According to a World Business Council on Sustainable Development 2018 report, the number of sustainable reporting requirements increased more than tenfold from 1992 to 2017, with more than 1,000 reporting requirements for sustainability information existing across the globe at the time of publication.[26]

In November 2022, the European Parliament adopted the new Corporate Sustainability Reporting Directive (CSRD).[27] The CSRD introduces more detailed environment, human rights, and social reporting requirements and approximately 50,000 companies will be covered by the new rules, an increase from the 11,700 European companies currently required to disclose on ESG topics.[28]

In the United Kingdom, reporting requirements exist for many companies, including energy use and greenhouse gases for large businesses,[29] disclosure on targets and the representation of women and ethnic minorities on boards and executive management teams,[30] and human trafficking after the 2015 Modern Slavery Act was passed.[31] The top 1,000 companies, by market capitalization, listed on India's local stock exchange must produce a Business Responsibility and Sustainability Report beginning in FY 2023.[32] And, in Canada, the Office of the Superintendent of Financial Institutions will require federally regulated financial institutions to publish climate disclosures aligned with the TCFD framework beginning in 2024.[33]

Spotlight: Legal Tension between Investor Demand and Regulatory Requirements

As described above, in the past decade, many investors have increased the amount of ESG information they request from the companies they invest in. Although disclosing certain information may satisfy investors, companies that disclose

25. See https://www.sec.gov/news/press-release/2022-46.

26. See *ESG Reporting Trends,* The Reporting Exchange (Feb. 2018), http://docs.wbcsd.org/2018/02/Reporting_Exchange_Report_ESG_reporting_trends_2017.pdf.

27. See https://www.europarl.europa.eu/news/en/press-room/20221107IPR49611/sustainable-economy-parliament-adopts-new-reporting-rules-for-multinationals.

28. *Ibid.*

29. See https://www.gov.uk/guidance/measuring-and-reporting-environmental-impacts-guidance-for-businesses.

30. See Financial Conduct Authority Policy Statement (April 2022), https://www.fca.org.uk/publication/policy/ps22-3.pdf.

31. See https://www.legislation.gov.uk/ukpga/2015/30/contents/enacted.

32. See https://www.sebi.gov.in/sebi_data/commondocs/may-2021/Business%20responsibility%20and%20sustainability%20reporting%20by%20listed%20entitiesAnnexure1_p.PDF.

33. See https://www.esgtoday.com/canada-introduces-mandatory-climate-disclosures-for-banks-insurance-companies-beginning-2024/.

certain ESG information may open themselves up to legal risk. As an example, in 2020, an Oracle shareholder sued the company for claiming a commitment to diversity and claiming that diversity starts at the top while having a largely white staff with no black or Asian board members.[34] While Oracle later won dismissal of the lawsuit, as did Facebook and The Gap, Inc., in similar diversity suits, declaring these diversity commitments did open the company up to legal risk.[35]

As another example, investors typically push companies to disclose their priority ESG topics, also referred to as "material issues" as decided through a "materiality assessment" in the ESG space. According to the U.S. Supreme Court, the materiality requirement is satisfied when there is "a substantial likelihood that the disclosure of the omitted fact would have been viewed by the reasonable investor as having significantly altered the 'total mix' of information made available."[36] A quick Internet search will show you that many companies overlook this legal definition, instead using "material issues" as a synonym for "priority topics" in ESG/Sustainability/CSR reports. In our experience, as ESG/Sustainability/CSR Reports move closer to potential regulation in the United States and as they move into the realm of documents used for discovery in lawsuits, legal guidance has been to remove any reference to "material" and "materiality."

Trend 3: Employees Push for ESG Action

The corporate world has shifted to recognize that happy and thriving employees are a key ingredient to a sustainable and successful company. However, what drives employee happiness and satisfaction has changed. Recognizing the sheer number of hours we devote to our workplaces, employees today are seeking meaningful purpose at work and, even more so, looking for the workplace to help feed and shape personal purpose.

McKinsey research shows 70 percent of people define their purpose through work.[37] And this has only increased since the pandemic. Nearly two-thirds of U.S.-based employees surveyed said that COVID-19 has caused them to reflect on their purpose in life with the importance of societal impact as a factor to considering a new job or staying with a current job increasing 66 percent since the pandemic. According to Carol Cone's Purpose under Pressure study,[38] 86 percent believe having "meaning" in their work is more important to them than ever; 91 percent of employees say their company's purpose makes them feel like they are in the right place amid challenges such as the pandemic and economic risk; and 84 percent will only work at purpose-driven companies/brands.

There is also the future pipeline to consider. By 2029, the Millennial and Gen-Z generations will make up 72 percent of the world's workforce, compared

34. See https://news.bloomberglaw.com/esg/oracle-wins-dismissal-of-shareholders-board-diversity-suit.
35. *Ibid.*
36. See https://www.gibsondunn.com/u-s-supreme-court-decides-scope-of-materiality-under-federal-securities-laws/.
37. See McKinsey, "Help Your Employees Find Purpose—or Watch Them Leave," Apr. 2021.
38. Carol Cone is a twenty-five plus year pioneer and long-standing ESG and social impact thought leader.

to 52 percent in 2019.[39] These generations place greater importance on environmental and social concerns than their predecessors do—and will expect more from employers on these issues.

Furthermore, research shows that meaningful work most impacts employees' happiness at work—beating out being well paid, autonomy at work, and having opportunities to advance.[40] Research by author and social impact thought leader Bea Boccalandro shows 13 percent higher job satisfaction, on average, in employees whose work experience incorporated social purpose than in those whose work did not.

The other side of purpose and meaning at work is values alignment. Employees today want to work for companies that align to their values. According to Edelman's twenty-second annual Trust Barometer, 60 percent of people will choose a place to work based on their beliefs and values. They also want to know their company is doing the work it should be: 60 percent of employees want their CEO to speak out on controversial issues they care about, and 59 percent of employees say the more socially and environmentally responsible their company becomes, the more motivated and loyal they become.[41]

Authentic and Engaging Employee Communications

When organizations face ESG-related challenges, engaged employees will be innovators and problem-solvers on the front line.[42]

Ensuring employees are aware, informed, and engaged remains a key driver of success and one that separates the ESG and sustainability/CSR leaders. Carol Cone emphasizes that a key principle to building a business that operates for and with society is to *put employees at the center*, and her research shows that helping employees understand how corporate purpose aligns with individual values (51 percent) is the top recommendation for how companies can strengthen ESG moving forward.

Additionally, it shows "while Purpose is understood—and highly valued—at the senior executive levels of business, it fails to have the same effect at other levels within organizations." There is a significant difference in how functions see the value and their accountability for ESG with 70 percent in human resources agreeing their work contributes to their company's purpose and only 36 percent of marketers and 32 percent of strategists strongly agreeing.

Here lies the opportunity and challenge—how to effectively communicate a company is going beyond its bottom line; that its approach to ESG is meaningful, tangible, authentic, and strategic; and where its employees fit into this. Doing this requires thoughtful and targeted employee communications *both internally and externally.*

---

39. Mercer, "ESG as a Workforce Strategy."
40. CNBC|Momentive Workforce Happiness Index, May 2022.
41. BBMG, 2021 (via Carol Cone on Purpose).
42. Ed O'Boyle and Andrew Robertson, *Beware of Junk Employee Engagement Metrics for ESG Reporting*, Gallup (May 2, 2022), https://www.gallup.com/workplace/392219/beware-junk-employee-engagement-metrics-esg-reporting.aspx.

Internal Communications

Internally, companies are using a multitude of platforms and channels to build ESG awareness and engagement, including

- Intranet (announcements, blog articles, newsletters);
- internal social media platforms;
- internal meetings (all-company/all hands, functional, leadership, ESG steering committees, employee resource groups, and more);
- email (all-company, leadership, functional, manager);
- regional and global ESG road shows;
- new hire onboarding (e.g., training, presentations);
- employee resource groups;
- regional and local community impact champions; and
- purpose-driven engagement campaigns.

Spotlight: Increasing Role of the CEO in Communicating ESG

The CEO is becoming a more engaged and critical piece to authentic and effective ESG employee communications. To trust that ESG and purpose are real, employees want to hear from their CEO. Employers are now seen as the most trustworthy source of information—above governments and media[43]—and the CEO ultimately has the strongest credibility with employees, especially those that do not understand their connection to the company's ESG efforts; 60 percent of employees want their CEO to speak out on controversial issues they care about, and 80 percent expect CEOs to be a part of their company's conversations around public policy and social impact.

There are various channels CEOs use to communicate to employees, including the annual ESG report CEO letter, company videos, brand campaigns, all hands meetings, and more. For example, Unilever was recently recognized for its internal communications campaign, Unmute, where CEO Alan Jope and #MeToo movement founder Tarana Burke joined a virtual Town Hall for the entire company.

Spotlight: Connecting Purpose to the Every Day

It is widely believed and shown that ESG is most successful when it is directly tied to a company's core business. Employees also connect to corporate purpose when they understand their role, how it relates to what they do, and how they—or can—contribute. ESG employee communications are increasingly focused on telling this story through a variety of ways:

- emphasizing the business case for ESG in the employee narrative;
- increasing communication around employee opportunities such as skills-based volunteering and giving;
- developing tailored employee ESG communications by function;

43. Edelman Trust Barometer, 2022.

- embedding ESG throughout functional training ranging from sales to product development;
- leveraging touchpoints with managers at all levels to further discuss ESG and training managers to be ESG ambassadors for their team through authentic communication;
- building strong relationships with functional teams to uncover collaborative opportunities (e.g., investor relations, human resources, product, compliance); and
- developing employee engagement campaigns around key ESG priorities.

For example, VMware is making this connection for employees by assessing each product line for its ability to "spark innovation that creates lasting change." CEMEX's workforce experience objectives include making an impact above and beyond the company. Cisco's various social impact initiatives including Networking Academy, crisis response, and its annual Global Problem Solver Challenge help employees see the potential of the company's technology for good. Employee engagement campaigns throughout the year help shift employee awareness and behavior around sustainability. Often centered around key dates such as MLK Day, Earth Day, Pride month, Giving Tuesday, a global day or week of service, and more, campaigns promote office environmental sustainability, sustainable transportation, home office sustainability, sustainable living, volunteering and giving, and more. For example, HP's three-week EcoChallenge included participation from over 1,000 employees, across eighty-five teams and forty-four countries, and the month-long Earth Month campaign saw over 1,600 employees pledging to take action or change habits to be more sustainable. Gen holds a virtual Pride parade led by employee resource group N-PRIDE, and Cox Enterprises' Chairman Challenge, running since 2012, encourages employees to measure and reduce their carbon footprint.

External Communications

A key external vehicle for reporting to all stakeholders, including employees, continues to be the company's website and annual ESG report. However, it is important to note that the ESG report is typically detailed and extensive, serving more as a resource for companies to slice and dice stories and content to their employees throughout the year. External employee storytelling draws on this across a variety of channels.

- *Social media:* The use of social media for ESG communications has continued to increase, including in targeting employees. Social media analytics enable companies to target their employees where and when it is most effective. Many companies now have a dedicated ESG or CSR blog, Twitter/IG feed, while also integrating into corporate social media channels. They also leverage paid social media partnerships to further share their ESG message with employees.
- *Purpose-focused brand campaigns* are also a prime vehicle for engaging employees, connecting ESG to the core business and helping connect ESG to the everyday work of employees (see the following section for examples).

- *Traditional and ESG media* serve as another credible voice for sharing a company's ESG story with employees. While employees are not always the primary target audience, external media placements demonstrate credibility, make employees proud, and meet employees in places company communications can't otherwise. ESG communications and media services (CSRWire, 3BL Media), CSR media (Sustainable Brands, GreenBiz), and ESG-focused traditional media (across all major publications, including *Reuters*, *The New York Times*, *The Washington Post*, *The Guardian*, *Forbes*, *Fortune*, *Time*, and more) offer a multitude of opportunities.
- *Events and conferences:* Lastly, company events and conferences also reach employees with the ESG message and help connect to the company's purpose and core business. ESG integration can range from the CEO keynote to ESG booths to event-related purpose campaigns and initiatives. For example, in past years at Cisco's largest external event, Cisco Live, the CEO keynote highlights the company's vision to power an inclusive future for all.

Spotlight: Targeted ESG Communications

In ESG marketing and communications today, we create yearlong communication calendars that focus on getting the same ESG information out to different stakeholders in targeted ways. As an example, ESG Reports are helpful to investors and ESG analysts looking for a single source document of all ESG information, however, are typically too long, dense, and not very interesting to employees or consumers. To the same point, a social media post or short video highlighting an environmental initiative may be interesting to consumers or employees, however, will not provide enough detail for investors and analysts. Even when information is of interest to multiple stakeholders, the presentation of this information should be tailored to each audience. As an example, the diverse representation of the workforce and leadership development programs may be important to both employees and investors. While investors may prefer getting this information in an ESG issue brief, that same information should be provided to employees in an All-Hands slide, via bullet points in an all-company email from the Chief Executive Officer, or in a visual graphic on Slack or the company's Intranet to make it easier for employees to digest.

Trend 4: Consumers Push for Brand Purpose

The momentum and demand for ESG transparency continues to customers. Seventy-six percent of consumers state they will discontinue relations with companies that treat employees, communities, and the environment poorly[44]; 63 percent of global consumers prefer to buy from companies that stand for a

44. PwC Consumer Intelligence Survey, 2021.

purpose that reflects their values and beliefs[45]; 58 percent buy or advocate for brands based on their beliefs and values[46]; and 78 percent of U.S. consumers will purchase products and services from companies that act sustainably—an increase of 9 percent since 2021.[47]

> Overall, when a brand is Purposeful, it connects with consumers on an emotional level, while a brand that is functional connects with consumers on a rational level. We feel Purpose automatically, but have to think through function rationally—which means Purpose becomes more deeply embedded into our psyche and, ultimately, our decisions . . . strong programs, policies and initiatives are only half the battle for Purpose-driven companies. Brands must actively communicate their Purpose too—and embed it into their brand ethos at myriad touchpoints.[48]

Porter Novelli's latest reputation research shows that messaging alone must be backed by action. Half (51 percent) of consumers said they will stop or reduce purchasing from companies that do not deliver on social and environmental promises; 84 percent believe companies should demonstrate how they are following through on their promises to people, the planet, or society; and 74 percent believe they should have a point of view on environmental sustainability.

How Are Companies Communicating Purpose and ESG to Their customers?

Through B2B Sales Conversations

B2B customers also care about ESG impacts. According to research by Fleishman-Hillard on the importance of ESG in B2B sales[49]:

- 50 percent of businesses that are seeking new suppliers say that improving their ESG performance is the top reason,
- 76 percent of B2B decision makers think companies should do more to communicate ESG commitments publicly,
- 73 percent want organizations to provide clearer and more transparent ESG Reports,
- 71 percent B2B buyers also expect other organizations to review ESG priorities regularly, and
- 64 percent believe that organizations failing to do so are missing out on profitable business opportunities.

45. RepTrack 2021 (via Carol Cone on Purpose).

46. Edelman Trust Barometer, 2022.

47. Sustainable Brands Socio-Cultural Research, 2022 (annual research that surveys 3,000 U.S. consumers to measure their intentions toward adopting sustainable lifestyles).

48. Porter Novelli. (2021). *Purpose Perception: Implicit Association Study*, https://www.porternovelli.com/wp-content/uploads/2021/02/Porter-Novelli-Purpose-Perception-Implicit-Association-Study.pdf.

49. Fleishman-Hillard, "The Impact of ESG on the B2B Buying Process," 2022.

B2B companies are starting to incorporate ESG into sales training and providing toolkits for sales conversations. For example, this last fiscal year (FY 2022), Cisco launched Sustainability Central, an internal site that includes resources for sales teams on sustainability.

Additionally, as B2B purchasing preferences increasingly shift online, company websites, including ESG sections and ESG Reports, are also a key channel (also see Spotlight below).

Through Their Products

One of the most authentic ways companies communicate their commitment to ESG to customers is through their products. Fast Company's World Changing Ideas Awards shares top product-related innovations solving the world's biggest challenges such as IBM's 2-nanometer chip has the potential to reduce energy consumption by 75 percent[50] and Cushon offering the world's first net zero pension plan. Ben & Jerry's has advocacy inspired flavors related to Black Lives Matter (Pecan Resist) and Change the Whirled (social justice and equity). Crayola has created a "Colors of the World" line celebrating diversity. Degree launched Degree Inclusive, the world's first adaptive deodorant. Stripe launched Stripe Climate, allowing any Internet business to direct a portion of their revenue to carbon renewal without any Stripe processing fees. VMware customer use cases provide examples direct from customers on how their products help customers build brighter futures from expanded access to education, improved community policing, accelerated lifesaving medical treatment, and reduced carbon footprints. Momentive, formerly SurveyMonkey, offers Workplace Equity IQ, to help companies measure DEI and develop impactful programs. And in addition to Patagonia's world-leading product sustainability, the company's home page features an "activism" tab right alongside the "shop" tab.

Through Purpose-Driven Marketing and Advertising Campaigns

As consumer consciousness is increasing, brands are looking to connect with customers on a personal level. They are turning to purpose-driven marketing and advertising campaigns as a vehicle to do this: it humanizes brand purpose, it can be targeted for the diverse set of audiences a brand may speak to—from sustainability pioneers to everyday customers, and its reach can be tracked and measured.

Purpose-driven marketing was a top trend in Deloitte's 2022 Global Marketing Study. The world's largest celebration of advertising and marketing work, the Cannes Lions, features many purpose-driven winners and in 2023 will add DE&I and Sustainability and Impact to its award categories.[51]

The examples in this space are extensive, but notables include Hellmann's Make Taste Not Waste campaign that reached over 200 million people across the world, and the following year featured a 2022 Super Bowl Ad addressing

50. Fast Company, "World Changing Ideas," May 2022.

51. The awards already feature purpose-driven categories such as the SDG Lions, Grand Prix for Good, and Lions for Change.

food waste. P&G's Whisper campaign highlighted and supported vital menstrual education for young females in India. Cisco's Bridge to Possible campaign highlighted compelling customer stories demonstrating the positive impact of its products on the environment and society.

Spotlight: The Rise of the Web in ESG Reporting

According to research by L'Oréal USA in partnership with Morning Consult, more than half of U.S. consumers surveyed[52] (54 percent) expect a company's website to feature ESG or sustainability/CSR information. As companies look to provide clear, transparent, authentic, and timely ESG information to a multitude of internal and external stakeholders (including the two mentioned in this chapter), companies have begun to build a reporting and/or ESG destination on their website. The "one-stop shop" makes it easier for stakeholders to find what they need and for companies to respond to the numerous requests and needs around ESG. Typically, these include top ESG stories and news, key performance highlights, strategy overview, progress against key performance indicators (KPIs) and goals, ESG data, external recognition, and the full annual ESG report. For example, Cisco offers an ESG Reporting Hub, and HP's Sustainable Impact website is an interactive resource for everything ESG.

Through Bold Commitments

There is a lot of noise, positive and negative, for customers to digest today, and a lot of ESG information as well. Breaking through this with a clear message on company values and priorities can be challenging. Another way companies are communicating their ESG priorities to customers—and all stakeholders—is through bold commitments and goals. For example, in September, Patagonia announced they were "going purpose" with all funds that are not reinvested in the business directed at fighting climate change. Unilever has announced its vision to be the global leader in sustainable business and make sustainable living commonplace. Momentive (formerly SurveyMonkey) wants to be tech's most inclusive workplace. IKEA is committed to becoming climate positive by 2030.

Spotlight: Corporate Activism and Marketing: How and When Should Companies Respond?

There is also the challenge of activism. School shootings, gun violence, social equity and justice, a women's right to choose, LGBTQ+ rights, climate change, and more are all issues companies are taking a stand on. They know their customers are looking to them; however, it is complicated to navigate. According to Porter Novelli research,[53] 44 percent of consumers will stop or reduce purchasing from companies that speak out on a political topic that opposes their

52. 2,000 U.S. consumers surveyed.
53. Porter Novelli, Purpose Priorities Report, 2022.

own views; 78 percent of consumers believe companies should have a point of view on environmental sustainability; however, only 39 percent believe companies should comment on *political* topics in the news. A recent *Forbes* article also highlights the complicated trends on how much the public wants companies to speak out.

Companies are looking to their Public Policy and Advocacy teams, senior executives, boards, and employees to decide how and when, and to prepare for the next. For example, Momentive (formerly SurveyMonkey) recently published a blog discussing the issues rubric they use and sharing a survey template to help companies begin assessing their corporate response to events. Ben & Jerry's, well known as historic activists, leverages an internal activism team to help guide the company's responses.

Purpose-Driven Marketing Gets Complicated: Driving Impact beyond Clicks and Sales

What companies are looking to achieve with ESG and sustainability/CSR communications and marketing (whether internal or external) gets complicated. It is not simply driving clicks, conversions, or sales—it is educating, engaging, building awareness, shifting mind-sets, changing behaviors. And many times, this behavior, or value, shift does not relate to purchasing a product or service; in fact, it can mean quite the opposite. For example, many brands have launched campaigns against Black Friday such as Freitag's S.W.A.P., Poshmark's Secondhand Sunday, Patagonia's famous "Don't Buy This Jacket," and REI shutting its doors on the day for nearly a decade. Leading global brands, a part of Sustainable Brands' Brands for Good,[54] are working together to "use marketing, communications and brand influence to make sustainable living accessible, aspirational and rewarding" and to transform marketing at scale to do this.

This makes the measuring and tracking of ESG or sustainability/CSR communications tricky. A growing number of ESG and employee engagement platforms are emerging. The Sustainable Brands' Ad Sustainability Awareness Platform (ASAP) measures the impact of purpose-driven campaigns on the actions and behaviors of customers. WeSpire leverages behavioral science to help companies design, run, and measure ESG and sustainability/CSR campaigns. And Benevity provides an all-in-one corporate purpose platform supporting engagement with employees, customers, and nonprofits.

Trend 5: Greenwashing in 2022

Greenwashing, or misrepresenting environmental claims to appear to be environmentally conscious for marketing reasons without making tangible environmental efforts, has been around for many years. According to environmental

54. Brands include Procter & Gamble, PepsiCo, Visa, and Nestlé Waters.

news outlet GreenBiz, from June to December 2022, regulators in the United States, Britain, Norway, and the Netherlands collected millions of dollars from companies found to be making false environmental claims.[55]

Without a set of global requirements for how to communicate ESG efforts and to avoid greenwashing, many companies follow the ESG frameworks (GRI, SASB, TCFD) and rater requirements (ISS, MSCI, Sustainalytics) described earlier in this chapter. In our experience, corporate ESG/Sustainability/CSR teams are becoming more cognizant of the legal ramifications of overstating ESG information, and today ESG/Sustainability/CSR Reports are often reviewed by both internal and external legal counsel. In our experience, potential legal liability of ESG claims is often newer for marketing teams who are using more unregulated channels, such as social media and websites to tout environmental and social efforts.

Regulations continue to evolve in an attempt to eradicate greenwashing, most notably the European Union's 2005 Unfair Commercial Practices Directive[56]; France's 2021 Climate Law, which will require specific environmental and social labeling for certain goods and services sold when the law takes effect[57]; and the SEC's proposed rule to require funds labeled as "ESG" to invest at least 80 percent of their assets in a manner that aligns with ESG strategy.[58]

As of December 2022, two potential opportunities for greenwashing in the ESG space, in our opinion, are with net zero commitments and woke-washing (when a company is advertising values they do not themselves follow).

Net Zero Commitments

While net zero simply means getting as close to zero greenhouse gas emissions as possible, there are differences in how a company can and should message this (is the company striving for "net zero" or "carbon neutral," for instance?) and can and should approach this (using carbon offsets or not—which is in itself an instance where greenwashing can be perceived, using renewable energy credits or not, setting a science-based target, setting a science-based target certified by the Science Based Targets initiative, to name a few).

In our opinion, to be credible, all net zero commitments must have a detailed plan behind them that lays out how they will be achieved and the interim targets that will be reached. According to a study by NewClimate Institute and Data-Driven EnviroLab, the number of net zero pledges from cities, regions, and companies roughly doubled between late 2019 and October 2020, with more than 1,500 companies now having set these targets.[59] Though net zero targets are on the rise, the same study found that only 8 percent of companies' net zero targets

55. See https://www.greenbiz.com/article/what-know-about-europes-new-anti-greenwashing-laws.

56. See https://commission.europa.eu/law/law-topic/consumer-protection-law/unfair-commercial-practices-law/unfair-commercial-practices-directive_en.

57. See https://www.sgs.com/en/news/2022/05/safeguards-05822-new-environmental-labeling-decree-in-france.

58. See https://www.sec.gov/news/press-release/2022-91.

59. See https://newclimate.org/sites/default/files/2020/10/NewClimate_NetZeroReport_October2020.pdf.

include interim targets to chart an actual decarbonization pathway.[60] As the report goes on to note, "Interim targets offer clarity and guidance on how particular targets should be implemented. They provide the transparency necessary to ensure accountability."

We also see credible net zero targets as those that include all relevant emissions, including Scope 3 emissions. A different NewClimate Institute and Carbon Market Watch study looked at the net zero plans of multinational corporations with combined 2020 revenues of more than $3 million. It found that only three firms out of the twenty-five analyzed demonstrated a clear commitment to reduce all emissions by more than 90 percent.[61] The average emissions reduction planned across the twenty-five corporations was less than 20 percent.[62] One cause for this is that several of the companies were omitting Scope 3 emissions, which are produced across a company's entire value chain and often make up the vast majority of emissions, from their net zero goal. As an example, the analysis found that while Google claims to be carbon neutral since 2007 and plans to be carbon free by 2030, Scope 3 emissions, making up 60 percent of Google's GHGs in 2020, were excluded from its carbon neutrality claim and it is unclear whether Scope 3 emissions are included in its net zero claim.[63]

In 2022, we saw the first examples of net zero lawsuits. In August 2022, Santos, one of Australia's largest oil and gas companies, was accused of "greenwashing" its energy claims. The Australasian Centre for Corporate Responsibility (ACCR), a shareholder activist group, sued Santos for "engaging in misleading or deceptive conduct relating to its clean energy claims and its net zero plan in its 2020 annual report, investor day briefing, and in its 2021 Climate Change Report."[64] Earlier in the year, TotalEnergies was sued by Greenpeace France, Friends of the Earth France, and Notre Affaire à Tous. The claimants say TotalEnergies mislead consumers about its efforts to fight climate change and broke European consumer law by suggesting it could reach net zero carbon emissions by 2050 while continuing to produce fossil fuels.[65]

These lawsuits follow other notable greenwashing suits, including the one against Washington Gas Light Company for allegedly violating Washington, DC's consumer protection laws when labeling its gas as clean and sustainable.[66] And the one People for the Ethical Treatment of Animals (PETA) brought against shoe company Allbirds for advertising with eco-friendly phrases while not measuring their full carbon footprint.[67]

---

60. *Ibid.*

61. See https://newclimate.org/sites/default/files/2022-06/CorporateClimateResponsibilityMonitor2022.pdf.

62. *Ibid.*

63. *Ibid.*

64. See https://www.abc.net.au/news/rural/2022-08-31/santos-accused-of-greenwashing-by-accr-in-federal-court-case/101385728.

65. See https://www.reuters.com/business/sustainable-business/environmental-groups-sue-totalenergies-over-climate-marketing-claims-2022-03-03/.

66. See https://www.clientearth.org/latest/latest-updates/news/we-re-joining-legal-action-against-greenwashing-ads-by-a-dc-gas-company/.

67. See https://www.classaction.org/media/dwyer-v-allbirds-inc.pdf.

Woke-Washing

Similar to greenwashing, woke-washing is when an organization uses a cause for financial gain without making real contributions.[68] Companies are increasingly under pressure to take a stance on social issues. According to public relations giant Edelman's 2022 Trust Barometer, an annual survey of 36,000 people from twenty-eight countries, 81 percent of those surveyed felt CEOs should be personally visible when discussing work their company has done to benefit society and 60 percent expect their CEO to speak publicly about controversial social and political issues.[69] The same survey found that 58 percent of consumers buy or advocate for brands based on their beliefs and values.[70]

While corporations may feel pressure from employees and consumers to externally champion social causes, launching marketing campaigns that do not accurately reflect a company's social progress can often backfire. As an example, International Women's Day is a time to celebrate women's achievements and raise awareness against bias. It is also a time when many companies post about their commitments to women and diversity on social media. In 2022, a Twitter bot called @PayGapApp began quote-tweeting every corporate message that used the International Women's Day hashtag #IWD2022 with the organization's mean gender pay gap.[71] The bot's tweets, with gender pay gaps reported as 50+ percent in some cases, made national and international news.[72] As another example, in response to Pepsi's controversial advertisement with model Kendall Jenner at a simulated protest, the company pulled the marketing campaign and issued a public apology.[73]

In addition to negative press and reputation damage, overstating social commitments may have future legal ramifications. While we have not found a corporate lawsuit based specifically on woke-washing, investigations and lawsuits that focus on misleading marketing in the social space continue. After 2022's Black History Month concluded, the National Advertising Division investigated Niantic Labs, a software company, and DoorDash, a food delivery service, to substantiate the claims of committing sizable charitable contributions to social justice causes.[74]

In October 2021, Hershey's and the Rainforest Alliance were sued by the Corporate Accountability Lab in a consumer protection case alleging false and

68. See https://www.forbes.com/sites/forbestechcouncil/2021/06/15/woke-washing-the-glass-cliff-and-the-need-for-a-better-answer-in-diversity-leadership/?sh=159300b65ea0.

69. See https://www.edelman.com/sites/g/files/aatuss191/files/2022-01/2022%20Edelman%20Trust%20Barometer%20FINAL_Jan25.pdf.

70. *Ibid.*

71. See https://twitter.com/PayGapApp.

72. See https://fortune.com/2022/03/09/twitter-paygapapp-bot-international-womens-day-gender-pay-gap-figure-shaming/.

73. See https://www.nytimes.com/2017/04/05/business/kendall-jenner-pepsi-ad.html.

74. See https://www.retailconsumerproductslaw.com/2022/03/nad-makes-clear-that-woke-washing-is-false-advertising/.

deceptive marketing representations.[75] The suit claims that labeling products as "responsibly produced" while benefitting from child labor is misleading to consumers.[76] As another example, class-action lawsuits against food and beverage companies hit a record high in 2020, including a lawsuit against Tyson's "all natural chickens" and "safe work environment" claims.[77]

The SEC has also continued its push in holding corporations accountable for false and misleading statements. In April, the SEC charged Vale S.A., a Brazilian mining company, with making false and misleading claims about the safety of its dams prior to a dam collapse that killed more than 200 people.[78] According to Gurbir S. Grewal, Director of the SEC's Division of Enforcement, "Many investors rely on ESG disclosures like those contained in Vale's annual Sustainability Reports and other public filings to make informed investment decisions. By allegedly manipulating those disclosures, Vale compounded the social and environmental harm caused by the Brumadinho dam's tragic collapse and undermined investors' ability to evaluate the risks posed by Vale's securities."[79] In May 2022, the SEC then charged BNY Mellon for misstatements and omissions about ESG considerations in its investment decisions, and BNY Mellon settled with a $1.5 million penalty.[80]

75. See https://corpaccountabilitylab.org/calblog/2021/11/2/cal-files-suit-against-hershey-and-rainforest-alliancenbsp.

76. *Ibid.*

77. See https://www.nytimes.com/2021/09/07/science/food-labels-lawsuits.html.

78. See https://www.sec.gov/news/press-release/2022-72.

79. *Ibid.*

80. See https://www.sec.gov/news/press-release/2022-86.

CHAPTER 9

Privacy Considerations for ESG: A Matter of Trust

Chantal Bernier and Amanda Branch

Introduction

ESG and data privacy intersect fundamentally and specifically in relation to social commitment and to the governance structure to implement it. Fundamentally, as individuals entrust their personal data to organizations, ESG calls for the respectful use and protection of the data. These organizations are legally and ethically beholden to use the data for purposes consistent with those for which the data were initially provided and to protect the personal data at the level that would be reasonably expected. Specifically, ESG and data privacy come into play, most saliently, when personal data are collected to fulfill ESG, such as gathering sensitive data to ensure diversity and inclusion, when data are monetized to provide a free and therefore equal access to the Internet, or when data are optimized for the public good, but beyond the objectives for which the data were provided, for example, in the case of research.

In this chapter, focusing on privacy as ESG, we describe the evolving socioeconomic context of the right to privacy, the legal requirements around the protection of that right in the private sector, and how the right to privacy serves, or competes, with objectives under ESG. To do so, we must take stock of the evolving context around privacy.

Growing Awareness and Assertiveness around the Right to Privacy

Privacy is the right to self-determination over one's personal data. In that sense, it can be put at odds with an organization's desire to collect and monetize personal information or even to process it for beneficial purposes other than those for which the data were collected. At the same time, it is well recognized that organizations need to process personal data to fulfill their functions and even to grow, innovate, and further legitimate business interests.

Consumers are increasingly aware of the value their personal data hold and of organizations' means to accumulate it, at the risk of their privacy. In addition, due to the rise in high-profile data breaches, consumers are acutely aware of the security risks of the accumulation of personal data. Social expectations about the protection of personal data grow correspondingly.

Consumers' expectations with respect to the handling of their personal information have also increased as a reaction to the legislative revolution triggered by Europe with the introduction of the *General Data Protection Regulation* (GDPR),[1] adopted in 2016 and in force since 2018. Becoming the "gold standard," the GDPR started a significant global transformation in privacy law with a number of jurisdictions around the world adopting privacy laws based on that model.

The Growing Business of Personal Data

In parallel, consumers are increasingly using e-commerce platforms, ordering products and services, as well as socializing online, shifting from a predominantly in-person experience to one that takes place entirely online. For example, you can now buy your groceries online, visit your doctor virtually, and handle all your banking online. This shift to a more virtual world has been accelerated by the effects of the COVID-19 pandemic, and the public health measures, like stay-at-home orders, put in place to curb the spread of the virus.

The growing number of privacy laws and increased global regulatory oversight, the unprecedented volume of personal data online through online interactions each day, the power of data analytics, and the frequency of data breaches have resulted in privacy becoming a central focus for organizations. Strong privacy practices are often used as a competitive advantage and a way to attract consumers by representing the organization's ethical and responsible use of personal data.

It is not only consumer awareness that is growing. Companies are coming under more scrutiny from interested stakeholders, such as investors and business customers, as to how they use personal data and what governance protocols they have to protect it.

Privacy intersects with ESG in a number of key ways, including, significantly, the potential impact on an organization's ESG score. ESG offers a way for companies to measure and demonstrate performance in this area as related to the Environmental, Social, and Governance practices. Specifically, Data Privacy intersects in relation to the ethical use of data and therefore Social and Governance are key considerations that we examine in this chapter.

---

1. REGULATION (EU) 2016/679 OF THE EUROPEAN PARLIAMENT AND OF THE COUNCIL of April 27, 2016, on the protection of natural persons with regard to the processing of personal data and on the free movement of such data, and repealing Directive 95/46/EC (General Data Protection Regulation at https://eur-lex.europa.eu/legal-content/EN/TXT/PDF/?uri=CELEX:32016R0679).

Legal and Regulatory Requirements

With respect to social considerations, privacy legislation attempts to balance the individual's right to privacy as the right to control the collection, use, and disclosure of one's personal information versus the legitimate interests of an organization to use that personal information for various purposes.

Throughout the world, privacy law is changing rapidly in reaction to the evolving context of data privacy risks. As mentioned above, many jurisdictions are following the direction of the EU and implementing GDPR-style legislation in their own country, state, or territory. While privacy legislation is largely jurisdiction-specific, around the world it turns upon the same principles. Here, we refer to the *OECD Guidelines on the Protection of Privacy and Transborder Flows of Personal Data*[2] (OECD Guidelines) as the common underpinning of privacy law around the world and highlight how they relate to ESG. The EU GDPR,[3] the UK GDPR,[4] the *California Consumer Privacy Act* (CCPA),[5] and the *Canadian Personal Information Protection and Electronic Documents Act* (PIPEDA)[6] are among the privacy laws that reflect the OECD Guidelines.

The following privacy principles from the OECD Guidelines dictate the legal requirements for organizations in the protection of the right to privacy.

Collection Limitation Principle

No More Collection than Is Necessary

Companies tend to think the more data, the better. The law, however, limits the collection and storage of data to what is strictly necessary to fulfill the purposes identified upon collection. If an organization can complete its processing activities without data, then it should not collect it in the first place. It should be clear to individuals what information is required for the operation of the services and what information is "optional" (e.g., "nice to have" but not necessary). The former may be collected with implied consent, such as providing payment information to complete a transaction, but the latter requires express consent, such as accepting to subscribe to the organization's newsletter. Once the data is no longer needed, it should be deleted or rendered anonymous. Again, in respecting the trust of the individuals who provided their data, rendering it anonymous must result in the irreversible disassociation of the identifiers from the substantive data.

---

2. *OECD Guidelines on the Protection of Privacy and Transborder Flows of Personal Data*, 2013, at https://www.oecd.org/sti/ieconomy/oecdguidelinesontheprotectionofprivacyandtransborderflowsofpersonaldata.htm.

3. European Union General Data Protection Regulation, https://gdpr-info.eu/.

4. See https://www.legislation.gov.uk/ukpga/2018/12/contents/enacted.

5. See https://leginfo.legislature.ca.gov/faces/codes_displayText.xhtml?division=3.&part=4.&lawCode=CIV&title=1.81.5.

6. See https://laws-lois.justice.gc.ca/ENG/ACTS/P-8.6/index.html.

Obtaining Meaningful Consent

Consumers not only want to trust an organization with their personal information, they also want to retain some level of control over it with respect to ongoing use and disclosure. Consent mechanisms are meant to provide that control by obtaining meaningful consent.

A goal of meaningful consent is to allow individuals the opportunity to make choices relating to their personal information. The right to privacy being the right to control one's personal data—consent (express or implied)—is the pivotal element of privacy law. Organizations must obtain meaningful consent to the collection, use, and disclosure of personal information, and must do so with privacy policies and notices in clear and plain language that is easy to understand and tailored to their target audience. The policy must ensure customers understand the consequences of providing their personal information.

How to frame and obtain consent can be a complex determination. The appropriate form of consent, express or implied, opt-in or opt-out, depends on the situation and the sensitivity of the personal information at issue. Express consent is given explicitly through a positive action.

As a best practice, express consent should be used whenever possible and generally must be used where the personal information collected is considered sensitive (i.e., financial or health-related information or information relating to a vulnerable population, including children). Implied consent may be appropriate in certain circumstances where the information collected is less sensitive. If providing individuals with the opportunity to opt out, then this should be apparent at the time of consent. Referring back to ESG, the organization should consider the social expectations of privacy in each context and respect them in determining to seek express or implied consent.

Data Quality Principle

Personal information must be kept accurate, complete, and up-to-date as necessary for the purposes for which it is to be used. The extent to which personal information must be kept accurate, complete, and up-to-date depends on the context in which it will be used. For example, an organization should not routinely update personal information, unless that updating is necessary to fulfill the purposes for which the information was collected.

When an individual successfully demonstrates the inaccuracy or incompleteness of personal information, the organization must amend the information as required, including by correcting, deleting, or adding information. Where appropriate, the amended information must be transmitted to third parties having access to the information in question.

Purpose Specification Principle

As a corollary to meaningful consent, the purposes for collection of personal information must be clearly identified upon collection. In line with the principle on limitation of collection, the purposes must be such that a reasonable person would find them appropriate. Identification upon collection is key to the individual's exercise of control over one's personal information.

Consent must be obtained for each purpose. It follows that any new purpose requires fresh consent. The purposes should be defined as clearly and narrowly as possible and overbroad language should be avoided.

Use Limitation Principle

As a matter of ESG and by law, organizations must respect the individual's terms of consent. That means personal information may only be used for the purposes for which the individual provided it, or for purposes consistent with the purposes for which it was collected.

Information must also only be used on a lawful basis. What is a "lawful basis" varies by jurisdiction but generally includes consent, contract, legal obligation, and other legitimate interests. Information also should not be retained beyond what is necessary to fulfill the originally stated purpose(s). Organizations are required to create a data retention policy that sets out their business needs, the length of time each type of data will be retained, and how it will be deleted or anonymized when it is no longer needed.

Security and Safeguarding

Organizations are expected to safeguard the information within their control using measures that are commensurate to the sensitivity of the information. This requires more than mere technological assessments. Specific data security risks should be identified, whether in relation to the location of data storage, the physical configuration of the office and telework, or the industrial sector it belongs to in relation to the level of targeting of that sector in cyberattacks.

Once a risk assessment has been performed, and the level of sensitivity of the information has been determined, personal data must be protected from unauthorized access and accidental or unlawful situations of destruction, loss, alteration, communication, or any type of improper or unlawful processing, by administrative, technological, organizational, and physical measures, as applicable.

Openness Principle

Organizations' openness about their personal information management practices is certainly a matter of ESG. Without transparency, though descriptions are clear and easy to understand, individuals cannot provide meaningful consent to the processing of their personal data. These descriptions must also be readily available.

Organizations can use a public-facing privacy notice which describes privacy practices to users, such as the types and categories of data collected, the purpose for which the data was collected, the lawful basis for collection, how the information will be used, to whom the information will be disclosed and for what purpose, whether the information will be sold, information about its retention practices, any transfers of information for processing, and information about which jurisdictions the information may be processed in. The privacy notice should also include, in easy-to-understand language, the name or title and contact information of the person who is responsible for the organization's privacy policies and practices, how individuals can gain access to their personal information, and how an individual can submit complaints.

Too often, privacy notices are long, complex, and difficult for the average user to understand, defeating the purpose of transparency. Individuals should not be expected to decipher complex legal language in order to learn about an organization's privacy management practices and make informed decisions on whether or not to provide consent. "Modular" privacy notices—for example, those with an outline where each title can be expanded to full text—allow organizations to provide comprehensive information, scalable to the individual's interest for more or less information on each privacy practice.

Organizations are encouraged to provide information about their privacy practices in a number of different ways, such as in person, in writing, by telephone, and online, through a link to a text or to a video or just-in-time notices. The objective is to present users, at the time a particular piece of information is collected, with a brief explanation of why that information is needed and how it will be used.

Individual Participation Principle

The individual participation principle entails, in the GDPR, the UK GDPR, the CCPA, PIPEDA, and most privacy law regimes, that individuals have the right to access the personal information an organization holds about them, to have it rectified, and to challenge an organization handling it, subject to certain specific situations.

The right to access is inherent to the fact that individuals merely entrust their personal information to an organization for a specific use. It remains theirs and subject to their right to control it. It should be clear to individuals how they are able to exercise this right, for example, by including this information in a privacy notice. Organizations should be able to explain where the information was obtained, how the information was used, and to whom it has been disclosed. Depending on the jurisdiction, organizations may be required to respond to an access request within a certain time frame. Where legal limitations apply restricting access, for example, where providing access would reveal personal information about another individual without consent, then the organization must provide the justification.

Individuals also have the right to correct or amend any incorrect, incomplete, or out-of-date data an organization holds about them. If personal information is amended, the organization should, where appropriate, send the revised information to any third parties that have access to the information.

An individual must be able to challenge an organization's compliance with privacy legislation. Accordingly, organizations must inform consumers about their avenues of recourse, such as the organization's internal complaints process, the complaints process of the industry association, or the right to lodge a complaint with a regulatory body. This requires organizations to develop a complaint handling and investigation procedure, with policies and guidelines for its implementation, and assign the responsibility to an individual in the organization who has the required skills to review the complaint and address it. Organizations should acknowledge receipt of the complaint, keep the individual updated throughout, and record the nature of the complaint as well as the decision to ensure consistency around the complaints process and across similar issues. Individuals must be notified of the outcome, including any steps taken to arrive at the conclusion.

Accountability Principle

The accountability principle is also inherent to the right to control one's personal information and to the fact that the information is merely provided to the organization in trust, with the duty to demonstrate compliance with the terms of consent. Differences exist between privacy laws as to the specific requirements of the accountability principle, but around fundamental rules:

- Organizations must have in place appropriate policies and procedures that promote good privacy practices and that describe the manner in which they protect privacy.
- In some jurisdictions, they must all designate someone who is accountable for their personal information management program (e.g., a privacy officer or data protection officer).[7] In others, only organizations where processing personal information constitutes a higher risk are under the obligation to appoint a data protection officer.[8] Under any regime, it constitutes a key component of an effective privacy program.
- The GDPR creates a requirement to maintain an internal record of all processing activities.[9]
- Finally, organizations remain accountable for information while it is in the custody of a sub-processor which requires adopting contractual measures to ensure that compliance through service agreements.[10] The GDPR creates the obligation for organizations to only use service providers who can comply with the GDPR.[11] PIPEDA expressly states that organizations remain responsible for data in their custody even when it is transferred to a service provider requiring the organization to impose contractual clauses or other means to ensure comparable data protection.[12] Under the CCPA, third-party management removes an organization's liability for a violation by a service provider as long as, at the time of disclosing the personal information, it did not have actual knowledge, or reason to believe, that the service provider intended to commit such violation.[13]

7. Such as Canada's *Personal Information Protection and Electronic Documents Act* (PIPEDA, clause 4.1.2 Schedule 1).

8. Article 37, *General Data Protection Regulation*.

9. Article 30. GDPR.

10. Clause 4.1.3 of Schedule 1 of PIPEDA and Article 28 GDPR.

11. Article 28 GDPR.

12. Clause 4.1.3 Schedule 1 PIPEDA.

13. Section 1798.145 (h) CCPA.

Voluntary Standards and Guidelines

Germane to the accountability principle, adopting voluntary standards and guidelines demonstrates commitment to the protection of privacy. Personal data handling practices can impact an organization's reputation, trustworthiness with consumers, and ESG score. Many organizations choose to voluntarily adopt standards or guidelines not only as a way to reduce their exposure and risk but also as a way to demonstrate their commitment to protecting personal data to stakeholders, customers, and consumers.

There are a number of voluntary standards relating to the protection and reporting requirements for personal information:

- *Global Reporting Initiative* (GRI),[14] a third-party framework, used by companies to assess their ESG performance, has released the GRI 418: Customer Privacy standards (the "Standard"). This Standard can be used by an organization of any size, type, sector, or geographic location that wants to report on its impacts related to this topic. The Standard includes requirements, recommendations, and guidance on the topics of customer privacy and breaches of customer privacy.
- *The National Institute of Standards and Technology Cybersecurity Framework (NIST Framework)*[15] is a framework meant to address and manage cybersecurity risk in a cost-effective way based on business and organizational needs. The framework is meant to drive organizations to consider cybersecurity activities and risk as part of the organization's overall risk management processes.
- *ISO Standards*,[16] particularly ISO 27018, establish a code of practice for the protection of personally identifiable information in public clouds acting as personal information processors. The objective of ISO 27018 is to create a common set of security categories and controls which can be implemented by a cloud service provider acting as a data processor.

Voluntary standards are typically reflective of established industry standards and best practices. They are drafted in a way that is easy for organizations to understand and use, and they provide frameworks that are customizable for each organization. They can also help companies organize their compliance efforts by using a risk-based approach so that organizations can determine where the biggest risk lies and take steps to prioritize significant compliance gaps. Finally, voluntary standards can be an effective way to communicate with all stakeholders, including internal and external stakeholders, and reflect an organization's commitment to upholding societal expectations of privacy.

Because these standards are voluntary, compliance is at the discretion of the organization. In some instances, however, organizations may be required by contract to comply with certain standards.

---

14. See https://www.globalreporting.org/.
15. See https://www.nist.gov/cyberframework.
16. See https://www.nist.gov/cyberframework.

Governance and Compliance

The Key Components of Governance for Compliance

As described under the accountability principle, privacy law includes governance requirements. A clear governance structure to implement policies to properly manage personal information under an organization's control also benefits the organization. It provides an additional way to explain to various stakeholders how it views respect for privacy holistically and to demonstrate that privacy considerations are integrated into every aspect of the business.

Effective data protection requires more than just an understanding of privacy principles. It requires organizations to implement a robust privacy program which incorporates the protection of personal information at every step of the process. A privacy compliance program that will be meaningful and helpful in the context of ESG has two steps:

- First, an organization must have quality, documented privacy policies that demonstrate an understanding of applicable law. These policies should reflect a thoughtful and purposeful balance between compliance with applicable legislation and practices that are understandable and meaningful to employees, connected to an organization's industry and operations, and tailored to the specific practices of the organization.
- Second, the organization must be ready to demonstrate compliance with its own privacy policies with a clear implementation plan, defining respective responsibilities and mechanisms for compliance assurance. Policies must be "living" documents, socialized throughout the organization, followed and monitored, and updated from time to time.

A Concrete Example

Privacy regulators have highlighted the "social" principle of data minimization and the "governance" principles of accountability, transparency, and third-party data management issues. A recent investigation illustrates the critical importance of effective data protection governance.[17]

The investigation focused on a mobile app which continually tracked and recorded the movements of users every few minutes of every day, even when the app was not in use, without knowledge or consent. While the app asked for permission to access the mobile device's geolocation function, it misled users into thinking location information would be used only when the app was in use. Unbeknownst to the users, and therefore in violation of their trust, the company contracted with a third-party location service supplier using the app location data to infer where users lived, worked, whether and when they visited the organization's competitors and whether they were traveling, going against every

17. Office of the Privacy Commissioner of Canada (OPC) PIPEDA Findings #2022-001 at https://www.priv.gc.ca/en/opc-actions-and-decisions/investigations/investigations-into-businesses/2022/pipeda-2022-001/.

socially reasonable expectation of privacy, and collecting the data constituted a loss of privacy that was not proportional to the benefits. Proportionality is a key consideration in following ESG principles, particularly in the digital economy where it can be easy to implement highly invasive tracking. If there are less privacy-invasive means available for collecting information, then the organization should pursue these avenues instead.

The investigation report underscores the importance of third-party management, data processing agreements (DPAs), and internal compliance mechanisms. As noted above, an organization is responsible for personal information in its possession or custody, including information that has been transferred to a third party for processing, and the organization shall use contractual or other means to provide a comparable level of protection while the information is being processed by a third party.

The company investigated had partnered with a third-party processor in order to infer addresses of users. The contract between the parties was vaguely and broadly drafted, and left the door open for the third party to use the data in ways other than its original consented-to purposes, including the possibility that the third party could use the data for its own purposes.

ESG entails that, when engaging with third-party processors, they be held to the same ESG standards as the organization, through written contracts in place with accurate definitions, unambiguous limitations, and clearly delineated responsibilities to ensure that the modalities to which individuals have meaningful consent are respected. Terms like "personal information" or "de-identified information" should be defined and in a manner consistent with privacy legislation. The contract must clearly provide adequate protection for the personal information while being processed by a third party and use must be restricted to the purposes for which the individuals have provided their information, as a matter of honoring their trust.

In this case, accountability and transparency called for a robust privacy management program to ensure the app and any future products or services were compliant with applicable privacy legislation, including a privacy impact assessment (PIA) when contemplating any new app or any new app practices to ensure they respect the individual's terms of trust in providing their personal information.

Practice Tools

The "G" in ESG points to the critical practice tool for privacy law compliance: a corporate privacy program. Below are some practical steps an organization should take when preparing its privacy compliance program.

- ***Putting the structure in place***
  - *Buy-in at the top:* As for all ESG initiatives, the moral grounding for the protection of data privacy rests with the engagement of the highest levels of the organization to reflect its importance and to embed

it in the corporate culture. Compliance with data privacy obligations must apply throughout the organization, as risks exist throughout the organization. This can only be secured with the creation of a culture of protection of data privacy.

- *Designate an individual responsible for privacy compliance within the organization:* Whether required by law, or not, an individual should be tasked with developing privacy policies and procedures for the approval of senior management, disseminating the policies and procedures throughout the organization, providing employee training, and monitoring ongoing compliance. This individual should also be responsible for responding to consumer or user requests.

- ***Understanding personal information collection and integrating privacy principles throughout the product life cycle***
  - *Data mapping:* To have an effective privacy program, an organization must understand what data it holds, where it is located, and what data flows are in place. A comprehensive assessment should be undertaken to identify what data is collected, where it is stored, and who has access to it within the organization. This analysis should also extend to subcontractors and third parties to which data has been transferred. This data mapping exercise allows the organization to understand what is currently happening with personal data and compare its current practices to what its "ideal state" looks like. This allows an organization to more effectively assess its potential exposure to privacy risks and can allow it to identify corresponding mitigation measures and prioritize areas of concern.
  - *Privacy by Design:* Privacy must be considered from the outset and at all stages of the design and implementation process. This is often referred to as "Privacy by Design," an approach that seeks to ensure the protection of personal information by integrating privacy issues from the very beginning of the development of products, services, business practices, and so on, and keeping privacy considerations integrated throughout the entirety of the development process.
  - *Data Protection Impact Assessments (DPIAs) or PIAs:* The GDPR creates the obligation to conduct a DPIA (PIA in North America) where the intended data processing may result in a high risk to the rights of individuals.[18] Even where it is not required by law, new initiatives or changes to existing initiatives that are privacy impactful should be the object of a DPIA or PIA. The DPIA must be conducted before any data processing activity takes place. Organizations may wish to develop a DPIA template for consistency and to ensure that all relevant considerations are taken into account for each project. Whether a legal requirement or not, DPIAs constitute a best practice to assess risk and manage privacy risk, implement effective Privacy by Design, and ensure compliance with a benchmark to measure it.

18. Article 35 GDPR.

- ***Documented data protection policies***
  An organization should have documented data protection policies. These policies should align with applicable law and any relevant ESG metrics or certification requirements. All policies should be regularly updated, including to reflect any changes in applicable law, and the practices described within the policies should be monitored and audited on a regular basis. An organization should have the following written policies:
  - *Data retention policy:* A business should be collecting only the data needed to fulfill the purpose for which it was collected, and such data should be retained only as long as required to satisfy this purpose. This will also limit the amount of information available to unauthorized third parties and will help minimize the potential exposure and risk to customers, clients, and employees. Documenting the purpose for which the information is collected keeps it within the boundaries of what would be legally recognized as necessary. Determining retention times with their justification and how the information will be disposed of once the retention period ends provides staff the guidelines to retain or destroy personal information. Limiting the collection and retention of data is also beneficial in the event that the business experiences a security breach: minimizing collection and retention minimizes the databases and therefore risk exposure.
  - *Information management and security policies:* These policies should set out the requirements related to the organization's encryption standards, security review, hardware/device security, physical and environmental security, online security, and system monitoring, together with any employee-specific requirements (e.g., password requirements, limitations of access).
  - *Business continuity/disaster recovery plan:* This plan should set out the steps an organization will follow in the event of a disaster of any kind (e.g., any unplanned incident or emergency). The plan should outline the steps that will be taken during and after an emergency that affects information systems, with a view to minimizing the effect on business operations and minimizing the risk to personal information. For example, in the event of a physical disaster, hard copies of documents could be scattered around and made available to the public. An organization should consider how hard copies of documents should be secured and how they would be recovered following a disaster. By way of another example, if secure channels are down, personal information may need to be processed by less secure channels. The organization should consider what these channels may be and how to best mitigate any potential risk to personal information while processing through backup channels.
  - *Breach response plan:* It is of crucial importance that organizations have a plan in place *before* a security incident occurs. If (or when!) an incident occurs, an organization will have to react quickly, and it can be difficult to think clearly and strategically during a crisis. It is wise to have plans in place before an incident arises. The policy should include a definition of what constitutes a security incident, a list of key

decision makers, and the process for contacting them, together with clear instructions on how incidents will be escalated and addressed. The policy should also set out the company's data breach notification and reporting obligations under applicable data protection laws to help ensure that the organization meets any legislative notification or reporting timelines.

  - *Data breach management:* Data breach management is an integral part of a privacy framework, as well as external frameworks (GRI and NIST, described above). Breaches can have a serious impact on a business, its stakeholders, its public perception, its value, and the level of consumer trust. In order to ensure the organization is able to react to a breach, it must have policies and procedures in place, as well as ongoing monitoring and recording of any breach incidents. Under law, failure to report breach incidents where required can result in significant, impactful fines. Furthermore, organizations may be exposed to a class action risk from affected individuals whose personal information was impacted by the breach.
  - *Employee personal information handling policies:* Employees are both an organization's first line of defense in protecting personal information and its weakest point. Through social engineering, employees may be fooled into providing unauthorized access to an organization's databases and some employees are complicit with outside threat actors or simply make mistakes that jeopardize the security of personal information. These policies should document the organization's specific rules and procedures for collecting, using, and disclosing personal information in the course of employees' responsibilities. The policy should set out any requirements for handling the personal information of customers and other third parties, how employees may be monitored or audited, what constitutes a "data breach" incident, and how it should be escalated. Employees should be trained on these policies, so they know how to react in the event a privacy incident occurs.

- ***Specific risks assessments***
  Following the data mapping process and the creation of the various privacy policies, actual privacy practices should be compared against documented policies to identify whether there are compliance gaps. If the actual practices do not align with the written policies, then the individual responsible for privacy compliance should, alone or with key stakeholders, be in charge of remediating compliance efforts. Clear roles and responsibilities as well as timelines for compliance are critical to success.
- ***Third-party management***
  As mentioned under the accountability principle, an organization's obligations toward the individuals who entrust it with their personal information do not end when the information is transferred to a service provider, as may be needed for the realization of the service agreement. Under any law, ESG entails that the organization entrusted with the personal information protects it through the continuum of processing. This is achieved through due diligence in hiring and proper DPAs.

- *Due diligence in outsourcing:* Being responsible for the personal information in their care and control, even when that information is in the possession of a third party, organizations must adopt guidelines on the choice of service providers, pay close attention to the information handling practices of their service providers as well as that of their subcontractors, and refrain from transferring personal information without proper warranties that it will protected at the level that was represented to the individual.
- *Data Processing Agreements.* To ensure that personal information is handled in accordance with applicable privacy laws, the organization's privacy policies and its commitments to the individuals who entrusted it with their personal information require a written contract, usually called a Data Processing Agreement. Whether required by law or not, as mentioned above under the accountability principle, DPAs constitute best practice, identifying the data transferred, specifying authorized use by the processor, and, if applicable, where both parties may interact with the individual, the modalities of consent, respective data security responsibilities, conditions on hiring subcontractors, including a process by which the transferring organization may approve or reject subcontractors, and data retention, deletion, or return once the processing of information is complete. With respect to enforcement, the DPA should provide for proactive and continual monitoring of service providers as well as noncompliance and indemnification obligations—apportioning the risk and responsibility between the parties.

The Case for ESG

Abuse of trust is obviously irreconcilable with ESG, but the basis of trust is not always clear in the context of highly complex technology that supports business models essentially predicated upon personal information or in the context of processing personal information for ESG purposes. How much personal information is it reasonable to collect to pursue beneficial purposes? What is the reasonable expectation of privacy on the Internet? When is it violated? To what extent can personal information be monetized to allow free access to the Internet? We address the issues through three case studies.

Case Study #1: Using Sensitive Personal Information in Diversity and Inclusion Efforts

A focus of the "social" aspect of ESG is how a company manages its relationships, both internally and externally, including working conditions, health, safety, and diversity. ESG certifications may include questions about the diversity of an organization's workforce, including statistics on how many women and minorities are in leadership and executive positions. To understand the composition of its workforce, an organization may wish, or may be required, to collect data about ethnicity, religious affiliation, race, gender, sexual orientation, or disabilities.

A number of different laws may intersect when it comes to diversity and inclusion, including human rights laws and privacy legislation. Some privacy laws restrict the processing of sensitive categories of data, including ethnicity, sexual orientation, race, and religious beliefs, while other privacy legislation requires express consent from individuals prior to the processing of this sensitive information. Collecting this sensitive personal information requires careful consideration from the organization.

Privacy Principles Applicable to This Analysis

Purpose Specification

The organization should start with an analysis of the scope and the purposes for collecting, using, and disclosing the diversity information as well as its challenges to protect privacy. In context, is it realistic to keep the information anonymous? Will the information be used only internally to help understand and advance diversity and inclusion efforts? Will it be aggregated to be disclosed broadly to the public as part of an Annual Report? Will it be disclosed to clients if they request the organization completes a diversity and inclusion survey? All these questions call for privacy measures to be applied.

Once the organization has determined the purposes for which the information will be collected, it should decide how it can best accomplish its goals in the least privacy intrusive way possible. For example, the organization may be able to achieve its reporting goals or metrics through the collection of anonymous self-reported information and the disclosure of aggregated statistics. Anonymous data should be processed where possible to help protect individual privacy and guard against potential misuse of this data. Using anonymous data may also help respondents feel more comfortable responding to the survey, resulting in increased voluntary participation.

If anonymous data is insufficient for the organization's legitimate and reasonable purposes, then the organization must provide employees with a full explanation of the purposes for which the data will be collected, why it is important that the employee provides a response, how the data will be used and disclosed, and any methods the organization is using to safeguard the information.

Collection and Disclosure Limitation

It must be made clear to employees that disclosure of diversity data is optional. If the employee withdraws consent, then the organization must immediately cease using the data, including removing it retroactively from any databases and notifying any third parties who have received the data that consent has been withdrawn.

Diversity and inclusion questionnaires should seek only the personal information necessary to assess diversity and inclusion. Within the organization, policies and procedures relating to the diversity information must be implemented. Access to the diversity information should be restricted on the basis of need-to-know to perform relevant duties. A retention policy should be developed, keeping in mind that the information should only be kept for so long as is reasonably necessary to fulfill the original stated purpose. Organizations should consider whether aggregated, rather than anonymized, data would meet their goals. For example, if the purpose is to compare progress year over year, this may be suitably achieved through the use of aggregated statistics and not the retention of sensitive personal information.

Case Study #2: Using Personal Information for Marketing and Advertising

One type of social contract is based on a bargain of personal information in exchange for some kind of desirable benefit. More and more, individuals are willing to give up a certain amount of personal information, so long as they receive something of perceived value in exchange, such as loyalty coupons, discounts, or free products. These exchanges of personal information have become commonplace, taking the form of customer loyalty programs and user agreement for websites and mobile phone applications to name a few. More importantly, they constitute a business model.

In the first privacy investigation regarding a social network, in 2009,[19] the regulator started from the premise that the legality of use of personal information for advertising on a free social networking site is actually its business model, which reduces the reasonable expectation of privacy on the site. As a society committed to free, and therefore equal access to the Internet, we must accept a certain amount of advertising as the only source of revenue for a free service. That being said, the level of advertising and the encroachment upon privacy must not exceed what is necessary to provide the free service.

More recently, the CCPA was adopted, in large part, with a view to regulate the use of personal information for advertising. It creates the right for consumers to "direct" a business not to sell their personal information to third parties,[20] which is the mechanism to deliver ads on the internet, through an opt-out function. ESG dictates the rapport between the organization and individuals in relation to providing free access in return for advertising, but within reasonable expectations of privacy.

19. OPC PIPEDA Report of Findings #2009-008 at https://www.priv.gc.ca/en/opc-actions-and-decisions/investigations/investigations-into-businesses/2009/pipeda-2009-008/.

20. Section 5 amending section 1798.120 of the Civil Code.

Privacy Principles Applicable to This Analysis

Collection Limitation and Openness

Organizations must be entirely transparent about the extent and nature of their use of personal information to serve ads. This entails full disclosure in the privacy notice and options for individuals to provide a greater or lesser level of personal information in return for proportionate services.

Individual Participation

Upon request, an individual should be able to obtain the list of third parties with whom the organization shares personal information to serve ads.

Accountability

An organization sharing personal information with third parties to serve ads is responsible for ensuring that those third parties respect the terms of the privacy notice describing the type and level of use of personal information for advertising. For example, if the privacy notice commits to refraining from tracking searches that reveal sensitive information, such as health subjects, the organization must ensure, through contractual clauses and technological mechanisms, that all third parties advertising on its platform comply with this commitment.

Safeguarding

The obligation to safeguard personal information is proportionate to the sensitivity of the personal information. Organizations must realize that profiles used to target ads, in the level of detail they reveal about an individual, constitute sensitive information. They must be safeguarded appropriately.

Case Study #3: Secondary Use of Personal Information

"Secondary use" of personal information refers to the use of information for a different purpose than the purpose for which it was originally collected.

There can be a tension between individual rights of privacy and the desire to use personal information for various reasons, including the advancement of social good. For example, medical information can be used to monitor the health of the population, identify populations at high risk of disease, and inform public health policies. In health care, secondary use may arise when health survey data sets which were initially collected for a specific research purpose are reused to answer a different research question.

There are a number of social benefits associated with using data for a secondary purpose. In the health field, benefits include the avoidance of duplication, a reduced burden on participants, or the application of a new hypothesis that was not available at the time the data were initially collected. Privacy concerns arise when data are used for a secondary purpose, including the possibility that individuals could be identified or reidentified through the potential linking of information.

Privacy Principles Applicable to Secondary Use

Consent

An individual has the right to know how their personal information is being used and an organization must make reasonable efforts to ensure the customer is advised of the purposes for which their personal information will be used. At the time of collection, individuals should be given the opportunity to express preferences about the future use of their information, including use for potential research projects.

Limitation of Collection and Openness

While it is legitimate for an organization to perform research whether scientific, social, or for marketing, it must be open about its use of personal information in that regard. If the information must remain identified through the secondary use process—for example, to ensure traceability—then express consent is required for that use. If the information is de-identified and used internally, for purposes consistent with the operations of the organization, most privacy laws recognize this use as consistent with the original purposes and therefore not requiring new consent. If the information can be anonymized, meaning the irreversible disassociation of identifiers from substantive information, then the information is no longer personal information and may be used for secondary uses, of any kind, including through disclosure, without consent.

Safeguarding

The use of personal information for secondary uses can yield sensitive personal information as it is processed for a very specific explorative research purpose. For that reason, it must be safeguarded with commensurate data security measures.

Summary and Takeaways

With now years of managing the unprecedented privacy risks brought by information technology and new business models, some best practices and key strategies emerge as an inherent to ESG:

- Creation of a culture of Data Privacy as a duty to honor the trust of individuals to whom the data relate is the foundation of compliance. This may be achieved through staff discussions around corporate privacy policies as part of the values of the organization.

- Annual data security training required to maintain access to the organization's networks significantly strengthens the effectiveness of the organization's safeguards.
- Identifying where service providers store data and assessing whether the countries to which the data is transferred offer comparable protection prevents putting personal data at risk of breach through cyberattacks or State interference. Developing considerations and guidelines supports the due diligence process before transferring personal information to third parties.
- Data mapping is critical to the application of safeguards appropriate to the level of sensitivity of the data as well as monitoring to prevent or detect breaches. In addition, in case of a breach, data mapping guides the forensic investigation to quickly determine the extent of the breach and the nature of the data breached to assess whether it triggers the legal obligation to notify individuals and report to regulators.
- A detailed breach response plan, with pre-established checklists for information to be included in breach records and for determining whether the breach is of such gravity to trigger legal obligations to notify and report, as well as a clear decision-tree for breach response, allows just-in-time application of remediation measures and, central to ESG, serves as a moral compass for the organization at a critical time.

As the subtitle of this chapter states, respecting the right to privacy intersects with ESG as a matter of trust. Personal data is not relinquished but entrusted with an organization, and privacy principles articulate the measures to honor that trust. They are premised upon the fundamental right to control one's personal data, subjecting all data processing to the exercise of meaningful consent. Consent is meaningful where it is informed by transparent data management practices and by the clear identification of the purposes of collection. These rules can only be implemented with the proper governance structure that ensures compliance with the terms of consent, throughout the continuum of use of the data, including the transfer to third-party processors.

As ESG may be described as the implementation, by an organization, of social expectations, more than ever, with the shift to business models essentially predicated upon the use of personal data, respecting privacy is essential to ESG.

CHAPTER **10**

ESG and Non-financial Disclosure

Travis Miller

Introduction

Non-financial disclosure of environmental, social, and governance (ESG) information falls into two categories. There is a vast amount of regulated disclosure requirements on companies in the ESG space. Rules administered by the Environmental Protection Agency (EPA) and Occupational Safety and Health Administration (OSHA), for example, require disclosure across a wide spectrum of issues from environmental emissions to injury rates. Companies in the United States frequently report ESG information to dozens of federal, state, and local regulators.

This chapter focuses on nonregulated, or voluntary, ESG disclosures. Although there is a long history of companies providing information on environmental and social performance through marketing and philanthropic communications, we focus specifically on the emergence of standardized disclosures that has occurred since the mid-1980s. The rise of voluntary, formal reporting on environmental and social aspects of the company and its performance has occurred in parallel with the rise of frameworks, guidelines, and standards to assist companies in their disclosure. The goal of these frameworks and standards is to promote more consistent and complete reporting of these issues in order to drive greater comparability between the practices of different companies.

The chapter looks briefly at the history of voluntary disclosure frameworks, specifically how different drivers and levers have influenced the evolution of these frameworks. We then look at the dominant standards and guidelines in the marketplace today. This is not intended to be an exhaustive list of standards in voluntary disclosure as there are dozens if not hundreds. Rather, we focus on those standards that have gained considerable traction in the marketplace. While each standard fills a particular niche in the ESG world, there are multiple points of complementarity and subsequent collaboration between standards developers today. Finally, the chapter will explore some of the trends in voluntary disclosure and ESG data that have emerged in the early 2020s and how these trends may continue to change the landscape of non-financial ESG disclosure in the future.

Evolution of Voluntary Disclosures

While sharing information on environmental or social benefits of the company stretches back well over 100 years, the modern movement by companies to discuss their environmental and social responsibility to a wide swath of society saw a turning point around the first Earth Day celebration in 1970. The founding of Earth Day marked a rising awareness among society (and consumers) of the importance of environmental protection and the role of business in either depleting or preserving the environment. Subsequent events in the 1980s, such as the Exxon Valdez oil spill and the cyanide gas leak in Bhopal, highlighted corporate diligence to society while also driving home the idea to companies that environmental performance held potentially large financial risks.

In the 1980s and 1990s, companies began to publish nonregulated and non-financial information in the public domain on environmental and social responsibility. These disclosures were frequently largely marketing pieces and advertising claims on the positive efforts undertaken by the company to protect people and the environment. These reports were frequently a mix of select performance data, anecdotes on corporate initiatives, and information on corporate philanthropy efforts (donations of cash and time for non-business-related social and environmental efforts). Reports were issued under a range of titles, including "Corporate Citizenship," "Corporate Social Responsibility," and "Corporate Environmental" reports.

External stakeholders, particularly advocacy groups, civil society groups, and nongovernmental organizations (NGOs), were keen for these company reports to be more consistent in the type and nature of the disclosed information. In particular, these organizations hoped for a more consistent, and objective, approach to identifying the environmental and social information that should be included in voluntary reporting. They also wanted to encourage companies to avoid greenwashing by promoting more complete and transparent reporting of both the positive efforts of the company and the risks to society and the environment that were the result of the company's activities. A small number of socially minded investors such as negative screening and socially responsible investment (SRI) managers also supported this movement toward more consistent and transparent disclosure.

The Global Reporting Initiative (GRI) was founded in 1997 as a direct response to this stakeholder pressure on the heels of the Exxon Valdez spill. It was the first global guideline for non-financial, voluntary social, and environmental reporting.[1] While initially focused on the environment, the GRI quickly adopted

1. See GRI website, https://www.globalreporting.org/Information/about-gri/Pages/default.aspx.

a "triple bottom line" approach to reporting by including social and economic aspects in addition to environmental aspects. The GRI was a comprehensive approach to voluntary reporting. First, it encouraged companies to create higher quality reporting by outline principles such as clarity, timeliness, accuracy, and comparability. It also sought to counter greenwashing by emphasizing principles such as balance, completeness, and transparency. For process, the GRI provided guidance on how companies could assess and define those issues that were material to either the company's stakeholders or to the business itself. Finally, the GRI provided a menu of potentially material indicators with recommendations on metrics to promote more consistent reporting.

The GRI arose from the interests of a broad set of stakeholders to corporate behavior and so the resulting guideline for voluntary reporting reflected the idea that companies should consider a wide range of stakeholder interests when deciding which indicators were material. The result was a growth in voluntary disclosure under the banner of "sustainability" reporting—an acknowledgment of the interrelated nature of business, environmental, and social performance. As corporate disclosure, and the associated performance data and descriptions of management approach, advanced, it became increasingly clear that some aspects of environmental and social management may have financial implications. The result was a rise in interest among mainstream investors interested in assessing potential financial risk exposure from "non-financial" data. Over the course of the 2010s, mainstream investor interest in sustainability information surged. A particular focus emerged on those aspects of sustainability that could have a relationship with financial performance of the company along with a shift in the lexicon to include governance issues as these are seen as frequently material to financial performance. The result was an increasing reference to "ESG," which emphasizes those aspects of sustainability most related to investor interests.

Standards setters such as the Sustainability Accounting Standards Board (SASB) were formed to address the growing interest of investors in ESG.[2] In 2011, when SASB was launched, there was relatively little empirical information on the relationship between "non-financial" ESG information and financial performance. As a result, SASB approached the challenge through consensus by asking a wide range of stakeholders what the most "financially-material" aspects of sustainability were in their opinion. SASB published the results as a set of sector standards. These standards are intended to not only narrow sustainability to the most financially relevant indicators but also consolidate disclosures by companies to investors around a more manageable set of indicators. As discussed below, SASB continues to be at the forefront of ESG disclosure to investors through its recent collaborations and partnerships as part of the Value Reporting Foundation and now the International Sustainability Standards Board.

Investors have continued to be the predominant lever pushing for greater levels of information on ESG aspects. Of particular note was the desire among investors to not only understand performance against potentially financially

2. See https://www.sasb.org/.

material ESG indicators in line with standards such as SASB but also understand the specific financial implications of ESG risks and how companies were responding to control and mitigate those risks through the business strategy. At the tip of this spear was climate change, which by the start of the twenty-first century was seen as a clear threat to the global economy and all companies around the world. The result was an effort by the Financial Stability Board (FSB) to create a guideline for companies to report on climate risks to the business. FSB formed a Task Force on Climate-Related Financial Disclosures (TCFD) which released its guidelines for reporting in 2017. The TCFD Guideline was a landmark in ESG disclosure as it created the first explicit expectation to link ESG management and performance to the business strategy and financial performance of the company.

The evolution of non-financial, or voluntary, disclosure has not occurred in a vacuum. Regulators have been active participants in the standards development and are now building on or referencing these voluntary standards and guidelines in the development of new rules for regulated disclosure. This topic is addressed in another chapter.

Current State of Voluntary Disclosures

Sustainability Accounting Standards Board, the Value Reporting Foundation and the International Sustainability Standards Board

The Sustainable Accounting Standards Board (SASB) has produced a set of seventy-seven industry-specific standards designed to address the environmental and social issues that are most significant within a particular sector. The sector-based approach is targeted at companies to allow them to identify the issues most salient to their particular business activities. This approach acknowledges that many ESG issues will be relevant across sectors such as climate change or inequality, but that the majority of issues will be more sector-specific. A consumer goods company, for example, would rightly focus more time and energy on toxics in products rather than emissions or pollutants.

The SASB sector standards have garnered a great deal of support and traction, particularly by asset owners, asset managers, and financial regulators. In 2020, Larry Fink, CEO of Blackrock, wrote in his annual letter to company CEOs that there is an expectation that companies would report pursuant to the SASB standards. Because of the focus of SASB on investor-relevant information, it has become a dominant standard in the investor-led ESG space.[3]

However, the objectives of SASB also create limitations to the standard. In its attempt to focus metrics down to the most clearly financially material and salient issues to drive comparability, SASB intentionally leaves issues "off the table." Many of these excluded issues are material to noninvestor stakeholders

3. See https://sustainability-academy.org/sasb-tcfd-are-becoming-more-dominant-among-esg-investors/.

and some may even have financial relevance, but the evidence or demonstrability of that linkage is insufficient to warrant inclusion in the SASB standards. The heavy emphasis on financial materiality in the SASB standard can also result in a strong preference for more short-term ESG impacts, leaving issues that may have significant long-term consequences to the business out of the standard.

SASB itself has evolved over recent years. In 2021, the Value Reporting Foundation (VRF) was founded. The VRF is the product of a merger between SASB and the International Integrated Reporting Council (IIRC). The IIRC, which itself was founded in 2010, sought to promote and guide companies to produce investor reports that integrated financial and non-financial information under the multi-capitals. In theory, companies would assess the value of financial, manufactured, social, human, intellectual, and environmental capitals that it either accessed or depended on to give investors a balanced view of the dependence, impacts, and benefits created. The merger of SASB and the IIRC into the VRF presents the promise of an investor-oriented standard that can look ESG information that is both directly financially material and indirectly financially material through dependence on external capitals. For example, socioeconomic inequality is generally not directly material to the financial performance of a company, but communities with high inequality can create a drag on a company's ability to recruit talent.

Most recently, VRF and the Climate Disclosure Standards Board (CDSB—an initiative of CDP, described below) announced that they would collaborate and consolidate to create the board for a new initiative: the ISSB. The announcement, released from the Glasgow Conference of Parties on Climate Change (COP26), was from the International Financial Reporting Standards (IFRS) Foundation which is backstopping the ISSB and will serve as a conduit between the ESG standards and mainstream accounting and financial reporting standards.[4] The Global Reporting Initiative will also be collaborating with the ISSB after an announcement made in 2022.[5]

The intense collaboration and consolidation of ESG disclosure standards speaks to the interest of a large swath of investors. Comparability across diverse portfolios is a key priority for large asset managers, institutional investors, and sovereign wealth funds. Although some material ESG information may be left out of the standards, the consensus among these investors is that comparability will provide better data over time and better insight into relative risks in the short term.

Global Reporting Initiative

The Global Reporting Initiative (GRI) was formed to help companies, governments, and other organizations better understand and communicate their impact on sustainability issues such as climate change, human rights, governance, and

4. See https://www.ifrs.org/news-and-events/news/2021/11/ifrs-foundation-announces-issb-consolidation-with-cdsb-vrf-publication-of-prototypes/.

5. See https://www.globalreporting.org/about-gri/news-center/ifrs-foundation-and-gri-to-align-capital-market-and-multi-stakeholder-standards/.

social well-being. GRI launched its first guideline in 2000. After several iterations, GRI launched a formal standard for sustainability reporting in 2016 (subsequently updated in 2021).[6] The GRI standard continues to have considerable appeal among reporting companies. According to the GRI, "of the world's largest 250 corporations, 92% report on their sustainability performance and 74% of these use GRI's standards."[7]

On face value, GRI and SASB are distinguished by the relative emphasis on investors to determine materiality. While SASB explicitly points to mainstream investors as the arbiter of "what is material," and makes reference to a U.S. Supreme Court case defining materiality explicitly in terms of the "reasonable investor," the GRI Standard approaches materiality as a multi-stakeholder concept. That is, GRI allows companies to define material issues based on an assessment of their own stakeholders, which might include customers, employees, communities, policymakers, etc. However, in practice, the two standards have substantial overlap. This is in part because our understanding of which ESG factors may be financially material continues to evolve and, in general, grow. It is also because the interests of many stakeholders, such as customers and employees, frequently align with the interests of shareholders. The result is that GRI has been and continues to be an active collaborator with SASB, the VRF, and now the ISSB in the setting of investor-oriented standards.

Task Force on Climate-related Financial Disclosures

The Financial Stability Board (FSB) formed the Task Force on Climate-related Financial Disclosures (TCFD) in 2015 to develop a consistent framework for companies to use in making voluntary climate-related financial disclosures for investors, lenders, and others.[8] The TCFD's recommendations, published as a guideline in 2017, articulate four core themes. The guidelines call for disclosures that (1) describe the organization's governance with regard to climate-related risks and opportunities; (2) explain how climate-related risks and opportunities could impact the company's business, financial condition, and strategy; (3) discuss how the organization identifies, assesses, and manages climate-related risks, including through scenario analyses; and (4) use metrics and targets to evaluate and manage these risks and opportunities.[9]

The TCFD guideline looks at three distinct types of climate risk. First, that organizations might face climate-related transition risks such as policy and legal developments, technological improvements that disrupt markets, risks associated with changing customer perceptions of the organization's business, and risks associated with the physical impacts of climate change. The second type of climate risk outlined by the TCFD is physical risk (sometimes referred to as adaptation risk). Physical risks could include property damage or damage to assets due

6. See https://www.globalreporting.org/about-gri/mission-history/.
7. See https://www.globalreporting.org/information/sustainability-reporting/Pages/gri-standards.aspx.
8. See https://www.fsb-tcfd.org/about/.
9. TCFD Final Report, *supra* note 176.

to rising sea levels or extreme weather. Physical risk can also include disruption to business continuity as a result of resource scarcity or supply-chain disruptions. The third type of risk is from costs associated with emissions or mitigation risk. For some sectors in particular, there is a risk that a cost will be assessed on certain types of climate emissions, for example, as a tax. Finally, the TCFD highlights that companies also might find opportunities resulting from their climate strategies, including opportunities around energy efficiency, resource reuse, and the development of new products and markets.

Like SASB, the TCFD guideline has grown in popularity among companies. This is because the recommendations provide a useful structure to help companies build strategies to manage and report on the effects of climate change. Others have also expressed support for the TCFD recommendations. In the same 2020 letter where he supported adoption of the SASB standards, Larry Fink declared that BlackRock would be reporting under the TCFD and that there would be an expectation for companies in which Blackrock invests to follow the recommendations.

Unlike SASB and GRI, the TCFD recommendations are not a standard. They do not provide prescriptive indicators or metrics and do not give a threshold of "adequate" or "qualifying" disclosure. In other words, the TCFD does not give a standard that would necessarily promote comparability in disclosures. The failure to specify a core set of climate change metrics and to mandate reporting methodologies limits the TCFD's value as a benchmarking tool. As such, the TCFD is of limited use to investors seeking to compare companies on the basis of their climate change risks and opportunities. It is unsurprising therefore that investors are seeking a combined approach to disclosure that would adopt the specific metrics of climate change under SASB alongside the more descriptive risk analysis and financial impacts of the TCFD recommendations.

Of course the TCFD is also limited to climate risks leaving many environmental risks and all social risks out of scope unless they are explicitly tied to climate impacts. Recently, there has been increased interest for equivalent recommendations on disclosure for other broad, global ESG risks such as biodiversity and ecosystem services (Task Force on Nature-Related Financial Disclosures[10]) and socioeconomic inequality (Task Force on Inequality-Related Financial Disclosures[11]). Both of these efforts are still in early stages at the time of writing, but they demonstrate the quickly expanding expectations of stakeholders to better understand the financial implications of ESG information.

CDP

The CDP (formerly the Carbon Disclosure Project) organizes a disclosure platform that tracks the impact of companies, municipalities, and other entities in three distinct spaces: climate, forests, and water.[12] Companies voluntarily report

10. See https://tnfd.global.
11. See https://thetifd.org.
12. See https://www.cdp.net.

information to the CDP based on an annual questionnaire. More than 7,000 companies and 620 cities currently report information to the CDP platform as of 2019.[13] The CDP's climate change metrics (although covering only about 2,000 of the 7,000 reporting companies) are especially highly valued. Indeed, most analyses of corporate GHG emissions derive from CDP metrics. The CDP analyzes the data it has gathered with reference to climate change and other critical environmental risks and opportunities—and shares the resulting analyses and scores with investors and other stakeholders.

As of 2021, the CDP had aligned its questionnaire to the recommendations of the TCFD so that companies reporting climate information to the CDP would also be compiling information against the TCFD recommendations. Moreover, the CDSB, which is an initiative of the CDP, announced in 2021 that it would partner with SASB under the auspices of the IFRS Foundation to form the board for the ISSB. Therefore, CDP continues to play an important role not only in data collection but also in the dissemination of the standards used to guide the collection of that data.

Like TCFD, the CDP addresses only a piece of the overall ESG disclosure picture. CDP also does not provide consistent methodological requirements for its metrics or independently verify the data reported on its platform because CDP is not a standard like SASB or GRI.

UN Sustainable Development Goals (SDGs)

In 2016, the United Nations adopted seventeen Sustainable Development Goals (SDGs) ranging from climate change to poverty and hunger. While the SDGs are not a disclosure standard or even a guideline for reporting, they do define the global objectives that companies and society can aim for. The SDGs also provide granular detail under each of the seventeen goals in the form of 169 defined policy targets.[14] While the target audience for the SDGs is primarily policymakers, the applicability for companies is evident as the SDGs define a directionality for sustainability and ESG activities. Therefore, many companies have begun to map their activities to the SDGs.[15] Some have mapped their existing activities or material issues to the SDGs. Others have documented opportunities for their business inherent in the solutions to these global goals and have disclosed on business activities to take advantage of these opportunities and trends. Still other companies have set targets aligned to the achievement of the seventeen goals and the 169 policy objectives. In the end, though, the SDGs do not set expectations on metrics or strategies, and therefore it is up to individual companies to determine for themselves what goals to set, how to track progress, what metrics to report, and what methodologies to adopt.

---

13. *Id.*
14. Sustainable Development Goals, United Nations, https://sdgs.un.org/goals.
15. *Id.*

World Economic Forum (WEF)

The World Economic Forum (WEF) issued its own recommended ESG metrics in September 2020 in response to what it perceived as a gap in the ESG disclosure space. Specifically, while investor-focused metrics were consolidating and standardizing, the same was not true for multi-stakeholder sustainability disclosures. The WEF identified an opportunity to drive more consistent and consolidated voluntary disclosure of sustainability information that was responsive to a wider range of stakeholders. The guideline, referencing the idea of "stakeholder capitalism," seeks to establish a common set of metrics that acknowledges the importance of a wide group of stakeholders, and their expectations on business, but aligning the metrics against the UN SDGs.[16] The WEF guideline includes four "pillars": (1) principles of governance, (2) planet, (3) people, and (4) prosperity.[17] The WEF guidelines contend that responsibility to society and the planet should be core business principles and so ambitions such as ending poverty and hunger are legitimate business strategies alongside financial performance.

Trends in Voluntary Disclosure

Movement toward Standardization and Alignment with Regulation

The merger and collaboration of SASB, IIRC, CDSB (and CDP), GRI, and the IFRS Foundation points to one of the predominant trends in voluntary reporting today: consolidation toward a dominant investor ESG standard. In this case, the "dominant standard" refers to an ESG disclosure standard that most asset managers and asset owners prescribe to when collecting comparable information across portfolios on ESG information. It is likely that the ISSB will emerge as this dominant standard. Part of the reason for the importance of the ISSB is the coordination with financial disclosure regulators in the European Union (EU) which are looking to reference and build upon the ISSB in the evolution of financial reporting requirements. We have already seen this in references from regulators in the EU and the United States pointing to standards such as SASB and the recommendations of the TCFD (which will be reflected in the ISSB through CDSB) when drafting proposed rules.

However, a "dominant standard" should not be confused with the only standard nor even the only approach to ESG data collection. Investors, like all stakeholders, represent a wide range of opinions and interests. There is an understanding that standardization of some ESG information is only part of the overall puzzle. Investors will also continue to seek information on less structured

---

16. World Economic Forum, Measuring Stakeholder Capitalism: Toward Common Metrics and Consistent Reporting of Sustainable Value Creation, 12 (2020), http://www3.weforum.org/docs/WEF_IBC_Measuring_Stakeholder_Capitalism_Report_2020.pdf.

17. *Ibid.*

risks, information on risks and opportunities where the correlation with financial performance is less well understood, and information that is not priced in the marketplace.

Nevertheless, consolidation toward a dominant standard will have many benefits for companies and investors. For investors, it will drive more comparable data across a broader proportion of companies. It will also likely lead to improvements in data collection and quality, which has been an ongoing challenge in ESG.[18] For companies, the movement toward a dominant standard will streamline the collection of information for a subset of ESG information. Climate emissions and risk, water conservation, biodiversity impacts, etc. are likely to be described against the prescribed metrics of a dominant standard eliminating the duplication of this information for multiple stakeholders and the associated variances in scope and boundary.

Integration of Financial Risk Information

In addition to more consistent metrics, there is movement toward a more consistent approach to assessing the financial impacts of a core set of ESG indicators. The TCFD represents the vanguard in this thinking. While metrics provided comparability, the ideas of the TCFD look for more contextual analysis of how climate change can impact on the business and how the business strategy can be designed to mitigate these risks (or take advantage of these opportunities). Moreover, the TCFD is structured to assess climate risks in the context of the core business and against different scenarios of climate change and so mitigating these risks follows the same pattern as any other enterprise-level risk. Finally, the TCFD seeks a translation of these climate-related risks into financial implications such as asset write-downs, lost revenues, changes in market share, etc. This translation of risk to financial impact, which is a frequent assessment for other financial risks, will create a new set of information for investors to weigh in investment strategies.

The TCFD is laying the path for our understanding of other global, chronic ESG risks such as ecosystem services and socioeconomic inequality. The message to companies should be clear: that contextual analysis of external risks to the business, under different scenarios, and with reference to the specific financial impacts on the business, will grow in the future. Investors will drive that push and it will be incumbent on companies to understand the most appropriate process to understand and disclose this information.

Sector-Led Frameworks

As discussed above, many ESG issue areas are not universal but are best defined in the context of certain sectors. For example, climate change is a different risk to the oil and gas sector than it is for the concrete and construction materials

18. Daniel C. Esty & Todd Cort, *The Data Challenges Which Remain in* Sustainable Investing: Revolutions in Theory and Practice (Cary Krosinsky and Sophie Purdom eds. 2008).

sector. Moreover, some ESG risks are quite specific to certain sectors, such as the risks associated with data privacy to the software and mobile telecommunications sectors.

Companies within sectors are viewing the consolidation of standards and are quite keen to ensure that they have a voice in the standards development, not only to help guide the approach of the standards setters, but also to help refine the material issues and metrics selected by the standards setters. Sector organizations are being proactive in identifying and defining the material issue areas themselves in advance of standards setters. For example, IPIECA (an oil and gas trade group), along with the American Petroleum Institute (API) and International Association of Oil & Gas Producers (IOGP), has published several iterations of an industry guideline for voluntary reporting in sustainability.[19] The Global System for Mobile Communications Association (GSMA) has also been working to standardize metrics and assessments for sustainability for the telecommunications sector.[20] These sector-based initiatives see opportunity in standards to consolidate data collection as well as risk should the standards settle on metrics that are not material or overly onerous to member companies.

Expansion of Unstructured Data

Standards, guidelines, and framework represent the tip of the proverbial iceberg when it comes to ESG data. Beyond the core metrics and common ESG risks lies an enormous and complex system of novel factors for markets. From the uncertainty around ecosystem collapse and resource depletion to the potential for social instability and political upheaval, global ESG factors represent a wide range of unstructured data that can be interpreted differently by different market players resulting in inconsistent pricing. Moreover, these factors are changing rapidly, almost on a daily basis, as we see the impacts of ESG factors (severe weather, droughts, pandemics, conflicts, technology, etc.) on society and economies unfold. The forces driving these changes are accelerating and irreversible.

All of this unstructured data is emerging in the context of massive digitalization that is revolutionizing how data are collected and analyzed. Digital, unstructured data will disrupt the fundamental processes by which analysis of information is conducted. Investors will have greater flexibility and the ability to customize data at lower costs. This will allow a drastic change in the way that investors access and integrate ESG information. Technology will also play a role in finding solutions within the marketplace—for example, identifying the most efficient and impactful investments to drive decarbonization. This nexus between ESG, technology, and finance will evolve and shape the future.

This revolution is already underway. Companies such as Arabesque, Persefoni, CSRHub, Sustainalytics, MSCI, Refinitiv, Goby, Covalance, and dozens of others are capitalizing on the mining and organization of unstructured

---

19. See Sustainability Reporting Guidance, IPIECA, https://www.ipieca.org/our-work/sustainability/performance-reporting/sustainability-reporting-guidance/.

20. See Sustainability, GSMA, https://www.gsma.com/aboutus/sustainability-at-the-gsma.

ESG information for investors. It is a race to find new data that could be meaningful and/or to analyze these vast and complex data sets into decision-useful information on which investors can make meaningful investment strategies. While there has been some merger and acquisition of these data companies, the proliferation far exceeds the pace of consolidation and so it seems that ESG data will continue to expand into the future.

Conclusion

From relatively simple beginnings, voluntary sustainability or ESG disclosure has exploded into a massive industry. What began as an effort to promote transparency and better understanding of corporate behavior has transformed into a race for both better information and new information. However, the evolution of ESG disclosure has followed a recognizable pattern across the board. First has been a push for greater transparency against a variety of stakeholder priorities. Second has come a consolidation and standardization information through a dominant standard or guideline. Third has come an acknowledgment, reference, and adoption by regulators. We saw this evolution in the first efforts to understand stakeholder sustainability information through the GRI and subsequent regulations like the Dodd–Frank Act. We see it occurring today in the standardization of core, financially material ESG information which is leading to financial disclosure rules. Finally, we see the early stages in the proliferation of unstructured digital information.

For companies trying to navigate the voluntary ESG reporting space, the variety of standards, frameworks, and guidelines can be daunting. The voluntary reporting frameworks discussed above are a few examples in a patchwork of different reporting regimes. Not included are the hundreds of lesser known reporting frameworks, brand certifications, labels, ratings, and rankings looking at one or more aspects of ESG information. To help companies navigate the different reporting frameworks, various initiatives have been launched by thought leaders, advisory firms, academics, and membership organizations. Most notable among these are two tools provided by the World Business Council for Sustainable Development (WBCSD). The WBCSD's Reporting Exchange is an online platform that aggregates nearly 2,000 mandatory and voluntary ESG reporting standards and frameworks in seventy countries.[21] The WBCSD's ESG Disclosure Handbook provides further guidance for companies as they approach their ESG reporting processes.[22] The Disclosure Handbook is designed to help companies navigate the disclosure process, giving consideration to the informational demands of multiple stakeholders and the array of reporting standards.[23]

21. See *The Reporting Exchange*, World Business Council for Sustainable Development (2019), https://www.wbcsd.org/Programs/Redefining-Value/External-Disclosure/The-Reporting-Exchange.

22. See *ESG Disclosure Handbook*, World Business Council for Sustainable Development (April 2019), https://www.wbcsd.org/Programs/Redefining-Value/External-Disclosure/Purpose-driven-disclosure/Resources/ESG-Disclosure-Handbook.

23. *Id.*

A few lessons can be gleaned from our current state of voluntary ESG disclosure. First, some consolidation is on the horizon, specifically for large-scale investors that is expected to ease some of the burden of reporting. Second, the remaining requests for information will have to be sorted and prioritized by the company itself, ideally using a form of materiality assessment. Third, the majority of ESG information collected by stakeholders in the future will not be disclosed by the company. Rather it will be disclosed *about* the company by civil society, advocacy groups, journalists, employees, and others. Therefore, it will be incumbent on companies to integrate responsible business practices to prevent ESG risks rather than trying to control the flow of information.

CHAPTER 11

ESG and Regulated Disclosures

Gabriella Mickel

"Sunlight is said to be the best of disinfectants; electric light the most efficient policeman."

—Justice Louis Brandeis[1]

Introduction

This chapter provides a practical introduction to regulated ESG disclosures[2] for legal professionals in the United States. Part I provides an overview of the types of ESG disclosures. Part II highlights current and emerging disclosure regulations. The survey of regulations in Part II illustrates the variety of actual and potential structures and sources of ESG disclosure regulations. Part III reviews ESG disclosure-related enforcement, litigation, and pressures to help legal professionals understand incentives and risks.

1. Louis Dembitz Brandeis, Other People's Money and How the Bankers Use It 92 (1914).

2. Disclosure, generally, is the act of making all relevant information about a company known to the public. This includes both positive and negative information that could impact an investor's decision-making. The purpose of disclosure is to provide transparency and ensure that investors have access to all of the information they need to make informed decisions about a company's business. ESG (environmental, social, and governance) disclosures refer to the information that companies provide about their environmental, social, and governance practices and performance. This includes information about a company's environmental impact, labor practices, supply chain management, diversity and inclusion efforts, and other factors that can impact its long-term sustainability and success. ESG disclosures are often provided in a company's annual report, sustainability report, or other public documents.

Part I: Types of ESG Disclosures

To orient the reader in the world of regulated ESG disclosures, this section explains that (1) ESG disclosures fall on a spectrum that ranges from voluntary to mandatory, and (2) ESG disclosure initiatives often take either a comprehensive or issue-specific approach. Due to the lack of comprehensive regulation of ESG disclosures in the United States, the majority of ESG disclosures made by U.S. companies are voluntary. Many voluntary disclosure frameworks are broad, as are some mandatory disclosure frameworks outside the United States. In the United States, policymakers have opted to create a piecemeal "regime" of issue-specific ESG disclosure regulations. This section describes these differences.

The Spectrum of Voluntary to Mandatory

In the face of serious pressure to disclose accurate and adequate ESG information,[3] companies are increasingly choosing to voluntarily disclose ESG information. In 2019, 90 percent of S&P 500 companies voluntarily published stand-alone ESG reports, up from 86 percent in 2018 and 20 percent in 2011.[4] In addition, more than 90 percent of S&P 500 companies voluntarily disclosed some type of ESG information on their websites.[5] For example, General Motors maintains a webpage to voluntarily disclose ESG information in various formats: a sustainability report that offers narrative descriptions, an ESG "data center" that offers quantitative information, and a supplement that includes disclosures aligned with popular voluntary frameworks.[6] Voluntarily disclosing information extends companies' significant discretion; however, this discretion has resulted in serious frustrations. Voluntary ESG disclosures often lack uniformity (even between similar companies) and accuracy.

In an attempt to address these issues, dozens of organizations have created voluntary reporting standards and frameworks.[7] Unfortunately, these too often fall short. As Yale Professors Dan Esty and Todd Cort pointed out, these organizations often send companies burdensome ESG questionnaires, soliciting information that is not material with no guarantee that the resulting metrics will be accurate.[8] Since anti-fraud provisions of federal securities law apply to both voluntary and mandatory disclosure, voluntarily disclosed information is

3. *Infra* pt. III(C).

4. Governance & Accountability Inst., Inc., 2020 Flash Report Russell 1000 4 (2020), http://ga-institute.com/fileadmin/ga_institute/images/FlashReports/2020/Russell-1000/G&A-Russell-Report-2020-FINAL.pdf?vgo_ee=FrExUIWwdl6Gmv2sBvsRqBwUnRnlmwiuCIJkd9A7F3A%3D.

5. Sol Kwon, State of Integrated and Sustainability Reporting 2018 27 (Heidi Walsh ed., 2018), https://corpgov.law.harvard.edu/2018/12/03/state-of-integrated-and-sustainability-reporting-2018/.

6. GM Sustainability, https://www.gmsustainability.com/ (last visited Dec. 30, 2022) (GRI, SASB, TCFD, UN SDG, and UNGC).

7. *Infra* pt. II(C)(c).

8. Dan Esty & Todd Cort, *Toward Enhanced Corporate Sustainability Disclosure: Making ESG Reporting Serve Investor Needs*, 16 VA. L. & Bus. Rev. 423 (2022) ("[T]he data collected and metrics generated by the rating companies are of widely varying quality and aggregated in such disparate ways that investors have little confidence in their comparability, integrity, and utility. As a result of this cacophony of questionnaires, companies are overwhelmed—and investors still do not have the methodologically consistent and investment-grade information that they need to properly integrate sustainability risks and opportunities into their portfolio analyses.").

regulated *by the government*[9] insofar as it should not be materially false or misleading by itself or render any of the required disclosure materially false or misleading.[10] Nonetheless, a U.S. Government Accountability Office (GAO) study found 86 percent of institutional investors remain skeptical of voluntary ESG disclosures. In part, these issues support the call for more government regulated, mandatory reporting.

Mandatory ESG disclosure regulations that affect U.S. companies arise internationally and within the United States at both the federal and state levels. For example, the SEC requires disclosure related to executive and employee pay,[11] and the state of California requires certain retailers and manufacturers doing business in California to disclose information related to slavery and human trafficking in their supply chain.[12] There are also private governance efforts, such as stock exchange rules and contractual provisions, that mandate and regulate ESG disclosures.[13] Failing to develop an understanding of privately regulated ESG disclosures, and only focusing on disclosures regulated by governments, would leave legal professionals significantly disadvantaged when advising clients.

Furthermore, while it is tempting to categorize regulated ESG disclosures as strictly voluntary or mandatory, in reality, ESG disclosures fall on a spectrum. As the former Acting Director of the SEC's Division of Corporation Finance, John Coates, pointed out:

> People often think of mandatory disclosure in a way that suggests that there is nothing more than an on/off switch between mandatory and voluntary disclosure. Our existing disclosure regime, however, is already more nuanced than that, and there is no reason an ESG disclosure system would need to be less nuanced.[14]

Even disclosures required by the federal government in the United States often provide flexibility in their mandate. For example, some mandatory disclosures are only required if the information is material.

Additionally, flavors of voluntary and mandatory disclosures often address different needs. Mandatory ESG disclosures help ensure corporate accountability around ESG and provide material information to stakeholders. Researchers have noted that "[m]andatory ESG disclosure increases the availability and quality of ESG reporting, especially among firms with low ESG performance."[15] Some com-

9. For a discussion of private governance and how organizations and companies privately regulate voluntary disclosures, see *infra* pt. III(C).

10. See, generally, Thomas Lee Hazen, *Treatise on the Law of Securities Regulation §§ 7.1, 12.19* (6th ed. 2009).

11. *Infra* pt. II(A)(b)(iv).

12. *Infra* pt. II(B)(a).

13. *Infra* pt. II(C).

14. Statement, John Coates, Acting Director, Division of Corporation Finance, SEC, ESG Disclosure—Keeping Pace with Developments Affecting Investors, Public Companies and the Capital Markets (Mar. 11, 2021), https://www.sec.gov/news/public-statement/coates-esg-disclosure-keeping-pace-031121; Lisa M. Fairfax, *Dynamic Disclosure: An Exposé on the Mythical Divide between Voluntary and Mandatory ESG Disclosure* (forthcoming 2023).

15. Philipp Krueger et al., *The Effects of Mandatory ESG Disclosure around the World* (European Corporate Governance Institute—Finance Working Paper No. 754/2021; Swiss Finance Institute Research Paper No. 21-44).

panies view their voluntary sustainability reports "as a place to publish relevant ESG information that may not necessarily be material under the SEC definition and is therefore not included in regulatory filings."[16] Voluntary disclosures are often more expensive than mandated disclosures. For a practical example, compare General Motor's 10-K to its aforementioned voluntary disclosures.[17]

Comprehensive v. Issue-Specific Disclosure Initiatives

Another orienting distinction in the world of ESG disclosures is the difference between disclosure initiatives that take a more comprehensive approach or a more issue-specific approach. The following comparison illustrates the difference. The Financial Stability Board's Task Force on Climate-Related Financial Disclosures (TCFD) specifically focuses on climate-related risks. The group develops recommendations on the types of information that companies should disclose to support investors, lenders, and insurance underwriters in assessing risks related to climate change. The TCFD is an issue-specific disclosure initiative. Now, compare the French requirements for ESG-related disclosures. Since 2017, companies must provide disclosures on forty-two ESG metrics or explain why they will not disclose, a "comply or explain" model.[18] The French initiative is a comprehensive disclosure initiative.

Part II: Current and Emerging Disclosure Regulations

In many jurisdictions, regulators are building off developed disclosure regimes and beginning to require companies and other entities[19] to disclose ESG information. This section highlights key regulations, initiatives, and frameworks, established or emerging, to give the reader an introductory survey of regulated ESG disclosures. Written with practitioners in mind, this section contains real-world examples to illustrate the results of these regulations. While these examples are informative and interesting, they should not be taken as examples of best practices.

Federal

At the federal level, the existing piecemeal regime for public companies mandates few ESG disclosures and does so in a variety of ways. Regulations often

16. U.S. Gov't Accountability Off., GAO-20-530, Disclosure of Environmental, Social, and Governance Factors and Options to Enhance Them 18 (2020), https://www.gao.gov/assets/710/707967.pdf.

17. GM, Form 10-K (2021), https://investor.gm.com/static-files/6ac492ca-6a4f-462e-9de8-0e2a7d471327.

18. Esty & Cort, *supra* note 8, at 441.

19. To what company entities do disclosure initiatives apply? Like any good lawyer would say, "it depends." Disclosure initiatives specify.

permit variations in how companies respond to mandates, including, for example, only disclosing items if they are material. The regime also contains "comply and explain" requirements that allow for flexibility, thus stopping short of mandating the requirement and instead allowing companies to offer information in lieu of compliance.[20]

Overview

For practitioners new to securities law, this section provides a brief overview of the general federal disclosure system. The SEC, a federal, independent administrative agency, manages the majority of reporting requirements where ESG-related disclosures are, or could be, included. The SEC receives about 3,000 filings per day, most of which are disclosures that are available to the public for free.[21] The SEC's filing requirements include:

- Securities Act of 1933: Companies that offer securities to the public must file registration statements that disclose material facts for investors.
- Securities Exchange Act of 1934 (commonly referred to as the "Exchange Act")[22]: Public companies must file annual reports on Form 10-K,[23] quarterly reports on Form 10-Q,[24] special information reports on Form 8-K,[25] and proxy statements.[26] SEC Regulations S-K[27] and S-X[28] detail the line-item disclosures required in these reports. Regulation S-K focuses on qualitative descriptions, whereas Regulation S-X focuses on financial statements.
- Exchange Act: Self-regulatory organizations, such as securities exchanges and the Financial Industry Regulatory Authority (FINRA), must file rule changes.

The above list is nonexhaustive. For example, the Investment Company Act of 1940 and the Investment Advisers Act of 1940 also trigger filing requirements. However, the list highlights key existing filing requirements that do, or could, trigger ESG-related disclosures.

A foundational understanding of materiality is key to understanding securities law and many ESG-related disclosure issues. A fact is material if "there is a

20. For example, Item 407(d)(5) of Regulation S-K, 17 C.F.R. § 229 (2021) (requiring a company that does not have an audit committee to explain why).

21. "EDGAR, the Electronic Data Gathering, Analysis, and Retrieval system, is the primary system for companies and others submitting documents under the Securities Act of 1933, the Securities Exchange Act of 1934, the Trust Indenture Act of 1939, and the Investment Company Act of 1940." *About EDGAR*, SEC, https://www.sec.gov/edgar/about (last visited Dec. 29, 2022).

22. SOX and Dodd–Frank enhanced many of the requirements.

23. 17 C.F.R. § 249.310 (2021).

24. *Id.* § 249.308a.

25. *Id.* § 249.308.

26. Schedule 14A, 17 C.F.R. § 240.14a-101 (2021) (proxy statement disclosures); 17 C.F.R. § 240.14a-3(b) (2021) (annual report to shareholders).

27. 17 C.F.R. § 239 (2021).

28. 17 C.F.R. § 210 (2021).

substantial likelihood a reasonable investor would consider it important in making a securities-related decision."[29] The concept of materiality is incorporated into securities laws by SEC rule, case law, and statute. For example, the Securities Act of 1933 prohibits material misstatements and omissions in connection with the offer or sale of securities,[30] and the Exchange Act imposes liability for material misstatements and omissions in filings with the SEC.[31] While it is tempting to believe that all ESG information is material, even if it were, not all material information must be disclosed. Disclosures must only be made when there is a duty to disclose.[32] Notably, especially in the context of ESG disclosures, the SEC is not legally prohibited from requiring specific disclosures that may not be material.

As a final point here, securities law is not the only source of disclosure requirements from the federal government. Indeed, many environmental statutes mandate disclosures. For example, the Emergency Planning and Community Right-to-Know Act (EPCRA) established the Toxics Release Inventory (TRI). The TRI makes information about industrial management of toxic chemicals available to the public. The TRI is a mandatory program, and companies that meet the reporting criteria must disclose information annually. Nonetheless, most federal disclosure requirements arise from securities law.

A Few Existing Rules

Conflict Minerals Rule

In 2012, pursuant to Section 1502 of the Dodd–Frank Wall Street Reform and Consumer Protection Act of 2010, the SEC issued the Conflict Minerals Rule.[33] The rule requires reporting companies[34] to make specialized disclosures on Form SD, typically with an attached conflict minerals report,[35] and conduct related diligence when a product contains a conflict mineral: cassiterite; columbite-tantalite (coltan); wolframite; tin, tantalum, and tungsten (often referred to as the "three Ts"); and gold. Form SD, and usually the attached conflict minerals report, must be "filed."[36] The rule also requires reporting companies to post certain conflict minerals disclosures on their websites, a link to which must be provided on

29. TSC Industries, Inc. v. Northway, Inc., 426 U.S. 438 (1976).

30. Securities Act of 1933 § 17(a)(2), 15 U.S.C. § 77q(a)(2).

31. Securities Exchange Act § 18(a), 15 U.S.C. § 78r(a).

32. See Matrixx Initiatives, Inc. v. Siracusano, 563 U.S. 27, 44 (2011) ("Moreover, it bears emphasis that §10(b) and Rule 10b-5(b) do not create an affirmative duty to disclose any and all material information. Disclosure is required under these provisions only when necessary 'to make . . . statements made, in the light of the circumstances under which they were made, not misleading.'"); ZVI Trading Corp. Employees' Money Purchase Pension Plan & Tr. v. Ross (In re Time Warner Inc. Sec. Litig.), 9 F.3d 259, 267 (2d Cir. 1993) ("[A] corporation is not required to disclose a fact merely because a reasonable investor would very much like to know that fact. Rather, an omission is actionable under the securities laws only when the corporation is subject to a duty to disclose the omitted facts.").

33. 17 C.F.R. § 240.13p-1 (2021).

34. A company subject to Section 13 or 15(d) of the Exchange Act is a reporting company.

35. SEC, Form SD, https://www.sec.gov/files/formsd.pdf.

36. Federal securities laws impose liability for material misstatements and omissions in information that is "filed" with the SEC. "Furnished" information does not carry the same liability.

the Form SD. The U.S. Secretary of State may designate additional minerals but is not currently expected to do so. Armed groups in the eastern region of the Democratic Republic of the Congo continue to commit severe human rights abuses while profiting from the exploitation of conflict minerals.

Notably, two states have created laws to supplement this rule. California requires any public company contracting with the State of California to comply with the Conflict Minerals Rules.[37] Maryland prohibits state agencies from obtaining supplies or services from companies that violate the Conflict Minerals Rules.[38]

Real-World Example: Intel's Form SD and Conflict Mineral Report.[39]

Disclosure of Payments by Resource Extraction Issuers[40]

In a decade-long effort to implement Section 13(q) of the Exchange Act,[41] which Congress enacted as part of the Dodd–Frank Act, the SEC finalized rules in 2020 requiring "resource extraction issuers"[42] to disclose the type and total amount of payments made to foreign governments or the U.S. federal government for the purpose of the commercial development of oil, natural gas, or minerals in their annual report on Form SD. The rules require issuers to disclose non-de minimis payments, including payments made by a subsidiary or entity controlled by the issuer, that fall within the payment types specified in Item 2.01(d)(9) of Form SD. The rules contain three exemptions—two conditional and one nonconditional. The conditional exemptions are for when an issuer is unable to provide the required disclosure without violating the laws of the jurisdiction where the project is located, and for when the terms of an existing contract prohibit the required disclosure. The nonconditional exemption is for smaller reporting companies and emerging growth companies. Compliance is required starting with the fiscal year ending no earlier than March 16, 2023, and disclosures must be "furnished" to the SEC no later than 270 days following the end of the most recently completed fiscal year.

---

37. California's Senate Bill 861 (2011 CA S.B. 861 (NS)).

38. Maryland's House Bill 425 (2012 MD H.B. 425 (NS)).

39. Intel, Form SD (2021), https://www.intel.com/content/dam/www/central-libraries/us/en/documents/form-sd-and-conflict-minerals-report.pdf.

40. 17 C.F.R. §§ 240, 249(b) (https://www.sec.gov/rules/final/2020/34-90679.pdf); see also Press Release, SEC Adopts Final Rules for the Disclosure of Payments by Resource Extraction Issuers (Dec. 16, 2020), https://www.sec.gov/news/press-release/2020-318.

41. The U.S. District Court for the District of Columbia vacated the SEC's 2012 final rules in July 2013.

42. "Every issuer that is required to file an annual report with the Commission on Form 10-K (17 CFR 249.310), Form 20-F (17 CFR 249.220f), or Form 40-F (17 CFR 249.240f) pursuant to Section 13 or 15(d) of the Exchange Act (15 U.S.C. 78m or 78o(d)) and engages in the commercial development of oil, natural gas, or minerals must furnish a report on Form SD (17 CFR 249b.400) within the period specified in that Form disclosing the information required by the applicable items of Form SD as specified in that Form."

Consideration of Diversity in Director Selection[43]

Regulation S-K Items 401(e)(1) and 407(c)(2)(vi) require disclosures about consideration of diversity in director selection. Item 401(e) requires the reporting company to briefly discuss the "specific experience, qualifications, attributes, or skills that led to the conclusion that a person should serve as a director, briefly discuss the specific experience, qualifications, attributes or skills that led to the conclusion that the person should serve as a director."[44] Item 407(c)(2)(vi) requires a description of whether and how the nominating committee (or the board) considers diversity in identifying nominees for director. In 2019, the SEC clarified compliance and disclosure interpretations to encourage reporting companies to disclose how self-identified diversity characteristics of directors factor into director selection decisions.[45]

Real-World Example: General Electric's Proxy Statement ("Governance section").[46]

Pay Ratio Rule[47]

In 2015, the SEC adopted a final rule, resulting in Item 402(u) of Regulation S-K, to require public companies to disclose the ratio of the compensation of their principal executive officer (usually the CEO) to the median[48] compensation of their employees. The SEC permits reporting companies to calculate the median employee's annual total compensation flexibly. Companies are allowed to use statistical sampling and other reasonable estimates to compile the information. Mandated by Dodd–Frank, the rule helps inform shareholders when casting their advisory "say on pay" votes.

Real-World Example: McDonald's 2022 Proxy Statement (Section titled "Additional Compensation Matters")[49] disclosed a ratio of 2,251:1.

43. Item 407(c)(2)(vi) of Regulation S-K. (Disclosure required of "whether, and if so how, the nominating committee (or the board) considers diversity in identifying nominees for director" and "if the nominating committee (or board) has a policy with regard to the consideration of diversity in identifying director nominees, describe how the policy is implemented, as well as how the nominating committee (or the board) assess the effectiveness of its policy.")

44. 17 C.F.R. § 249 (2021).

45. SEC, Compliance & Disclosure Interpretations (2020), https://www.sec.gov/divisions/corpfin/guidance/regs-kinterp.

46. GE, Notice of Annual Meeting and Proxy Statement (2022), https://www.ge.com/sites/default/files/ge_proxy2022.pdf.

47. 17 C.F.R. § 249 (2021).

48. The median calculation must exclude the pay of the principal executive officer.

49. McDonald's, Notice of Annual Shareholders' Meeting and Proxy Statement (2022), https://www.sec.gov/Archives/edgar/data/63908/000120677422001058/mcd3962181-defc14a.htm#mcd3962181-predef14aa006.

Human Capital

Prior to 2018, when the pay ratio rule took effect, companies were not required to disclose any specific information about their nonexecutive workforce, except for the total number of employees.[50] However, in August 2020, the SEC adopted amendments to certain disclosure requirements in Regulation S-K. The regulation (Item 101—Description of business) now calls for:

> A description of the registrant's human capital resources, including the number of persons employed by the registrant, and any human capital measures or objectives that the registrant focuses on in managing the business (such as, depending on the nature of the registrant's business and workforce, measures or objectives that address the development, attraction and retention of personnel).[51]

The regulation requires disclosure of "only information material to an understanding of the business taken as a whole."

Real-World Example: Adobe Form 10-K (Section titled "Human Capital").[52]

A Few Proposed Rules

The Enhancement and Standardization of Climate-Related Disclosures for Investors

In 2022, the SEC proposed new and amended rules for financial and non-financial disclosure regarding climate-related risks and opportunities.[53] Disclosures required by the proposal would be included in periodic reports (Forms 10-K, 10-Q, and 20-F) and registration statements (Forms S-1, S-3, F-1, and F-3). Some of the disclosure requirements include physical or transitional climate-related risks that are reasonably likely to have a material impact; Scope 1, Scope 2, and, for larger companies if they are material, Scope 3 emissions; any net zero targets or goals; and climate-specific governance disclosure. The SEC's proposed disclosure requirements incorporate concepts and vocabulary developed by the TCFD. The rule is likely to face significant legal challenges.[54]

---

50. For a great article on human capital, see George S. Georgiev, *The Human Capital Management Movement in U.S. Corporate Law*, 95 Tul. L. Rev. 639 (2021).

51. 17 C.F.R. § 249 (2021).

52. Adobe, Form 10-K 16–18 (2021), https://www.adobe.com/pdf-page.html?pdfTarget=aHR0cHM6Ly93d3cuYWRvYmUuY29tL2NvbnRlbnQvZGFtL2NjL2VuL2ludmVzdG9yLXJlbGF0aW9ucy9wZGZzL0FEQ-kUtMTBLLUZZMjEtRklOQUwucGRm.

53. The Enhancement and Standardization of Climate-Related Disclosures for Investors, 87 Fed. Reg. 21334 (proposed Apr. 11, 2022) (to be codified at 17 C.F.R. §§ 210, 229, 232, 239, 249).

54. See, for example, *SEC Proposes Climate Disclosure Regime*, Davis Polk (Mar. 22, 2022), https://www.davispolk.com/insights/client-update/sec-proposes-climate-disclosure-regime.

New and Enhanced Cybersecurity Disclosure Rules

In 2022, the SEC proposed new and enhanced rules for disclosures regarding cybersecurity. The SEC proposed three primary changes:

1. Amend Form 8-K, which is used to announce important events, to require current disclosure of material cybersecurity incidents;
2. Add Item 106 to Regulation S-K to require disclosure of cybersecurity-related information;[55] and
3. Amend Item 407 of Regulation S-K to require disclosure of whether any board members have expertise in cybersecurity and, if so, the nature of such expertise.

The proposed rule builds on interpretive guidance from 2011 and 2018.

Proposed Amendments to Rules and Forms under the Advisers Act and Investment Company Act

In 2022, to help investors avoid greenwashing, the SEC proposed amendments to rules and forms under the Advisers Act and Investment Company Act to require certain investment advisers and funds to disclose information about their ESG investment practices.[56] The proposal defines three types of funds:

- *Integration Funds:* Funds that integrate ESG factors alongside non-ESG factors in investment decisions would be required to describe how ESG factors are incorporated into their investment process.
- *ESG-Focused Funds:* Funds for which ESG factors are a significant or main consideration would be required to provide detailed disclosure, including a standardized ESG strategy overview table.
- *Impact Funds:* A subset of ESG-Focused Funds that seek to achieve a particular ESG impact would be required to disclose how it measures progress on its objective.

The level of detail of the disclosures would depend on which of the three definitions a fund meets. Additionally, there would be similar disclosure requirements for investment advisers through proposed changes to the brochure in Part 2A of Form ADV.

---

55. According to the proposed rule, Item 106 would require registrants to: (1) provide updated disclosure in periodic reports about previously reported cybersecurity incidents; (2) describe its policies and procedures, if any, for the identification and management of risks from cybersecurity threats, including whether the registrant considers cybersecurity risks as part of its business strategy, financial planning, and capital allocation; and (3) require disclosure about the board's oversight of cybersecurity risk, management's role in assessing and managing such risk, management's cybersecurity expertise, and management's role in implementing the registrant's cybersecurity policies, procedures, and strategies.

Cybersecurity Risk Management, Strategy, Governance, and Incident Disclosure, 87 Fed. Reg. 16590 (proposed Mar. 23, 2022) (to be codified at 17 C.F.R. §§ 229, 232, 239, 240, 249).

56. Enhanced Disclosures by Certain Investment Advisers and Investment Companies about Environmental, Social, and Governance Investment Practices, 87 Fed. Reg. 36654 (proposed Jun. 17, 2022) (to be codified at 17 C.F.R. §§ 200, 230, 232, 239, 249, 274, 279).

State

The development of a piecemeal ESG regulated disclosure regime in the United States reflects a key difference between federal and state regulation—federal securities law focuses on disclosure, while state law often affects corporate conduct, rights, and obligations. As evidenced by the following examples, this general difference does not mean states have completely shied away from filling gaps in the federal disclosure regime.[57]

California Transparency in Supply Chains Act (Effective January 2012)

The Transparency in Supply Chains Act applies to all retailers and manufacturers doing business in California with annual gross revenue exceeding $100,000.[58] The Supply Chains Act does not require that companies actually make any effort to eliminate slavery and human trafficking.[59] Covered businesses only need to report what efforts, if any, are being made to eliminate slavery and human trafficking in their supply chain.[60] The information must be posted on the retail seller's or manufacturer's website with a conspicuous and easily understood link to the required information.[61] If the retail seller or manufacturer does not have a website, consumers can request the disclosure and the retailer or manufacturer must provide the written disclosure within thirty days.[62] The Supply Chains Act itself provides an exclusive remedy for violations—an action brought by the California Attorney General for injunctive relief.[63] In addition, consumers have brought actions informed by Supply Chains Act disclosure statements.[64]

Real-World Example: Target's *CA Transparency in Supply Chains Act* webpage.[65]

---

57. A comprehensive discussion on relevant preemption issues would be too long to include here, particularly because this chapter is not limited to a discussion of ESG disclosures solely in the context of securities. For a start, see, for example, Merrill Lynch, Inc. v. Dabit, 547 U.S. 71 (2006); Guice v. Charles Schwab & Co., 674 N.E.2d 282 (N.Y. Ct. App. 1996); Dahl v. Charles Schwab & Co., 545 N.W.2d 918 (Minn. 1996).

58. Cal. Civ. Code § 1714.43(a)(1) (West 2021).

59. *See* Barber v. Nestle USA, Inc., 154 F. Supp. 3d 954, 959 (C.D. Cal. 2015).

60. Cal. Civ. Code § 1714.43(c) (West 2021).

61. *Id.* § 1714.43(b).

62. *Id.* § 1714.43(b).

63. *Id.* § 1714.43(d).

64. See, for example, *Barber*, 154 F. Supp. 3d at 962. While the *Barber* plaintiffs were unsuccessful, the Unfair Competition Law (UCL) (Cal. Bus. & Prof. Code §§ 17200 to 17210), False Advertising Law (FAL) (Cal. Bus. & Prof. Code §§ 17500 to 17509), and Consumers Legal Remedies Act (CLRA) (Cal. Civ. Code §§ 1750 to 1784) could provide a basis for similar litigation in the future. For more discussion on disclosure-informed litigation, see *infra* pt. III.

65. *CA Transparency in Supply Chains Act*, TARGET, https://help.target.com/help/subcategoryarticle?childcat=CA+Transparency+in+Supply+Chains+Act&parentcat=Compliance#:~:text=California%20Transparency%20in%20Supply%20Chains%20Act%20(SB%20657)&text=Under%20the%20law%2C%20large%20manufacturers,trafficking%20within%20their%20supply%20chains (last visited Dec. 30, 2022).

Delaware Certificate of Adoption of Transparency and Sustainability Standards Act (2018)

The Delaware Certificate of Adoption of Transparency and Sustainability Standards Act created a voluntary certification program. To receive a certification, companies adopt principles, guidelines, and standards for operating in a sustainable and responsible manner. To maintain certification, companies must then publicly publish the standards and assessment measures it has adopted on its website and, at least annually, publicly disclose an evaluation of its performance. To incentivize participation, the Act even attempts to limit liability—"[n]either the failure by an Entity to satisfy any of its Standards, nor the selection of specific Assessment Measures . . . shall, in and of itself, create any right of action on the part of any person or entity or otherwise give rise to any claim for breach of any fiduciary or similar duty owed to any person or entity."

Public Company Boards of Directors Diversity

As shareholders and stakeholders continue to demand further diversity on boards, some states have adopted nonbinding statements of encouragement, while other states have enacted legislation imposing disclosure obligations or mandating quotas.[66] Colorado enacted a house resolution encouraging public companies in Colorado to have gender diverse boards. In 2018, California became the first state to enact a gender quota for boards of directors. In 2020, California followed with a similar "underrepresented communities" quota. Both quotas have faced significant legal challenges. Illinois has both a statement of encouragement and a reporting mandate. In 2019, Illinois enacted a law to require any publicly held company headquartered in Illinois to include diversity information in its annual reports submitted to the Illinois Secretary of State. The information will be made available to the public. In addition to the reporting requirement, Illinois passed a house resolution encouraging public companies in Illinois to have gender diverse boards.

Private Governance

Public governance refers to the systems and processes by which a government or other public entity makes and implements decisions for a specific jurisdiction or territory. Private governance refers to the systems and processes by which private organizations make and implement decisions that affect their operations and stakeholders. Private governance is carried out by private organizations that operate within the boundaries set by public laws and regulations. Privately

66. For more on gender quotas, see Darren Rosenblum, *Diversity and the Board of Directors: A Comparative Perspective*, in Research Handbook on Comparative Corporate Governance (Afsharipour & Gelter, eds., 2020); Westlaw, Board Diversity Requirements: State Law Chart, Practical Law Checklist w-035-7795 (2022); Deloitte, Missing Pieces Report: The Board Diversity Census of Women and Minorities on Fortune 500 Boards (6th ed., 2021), https://www2.deloitte.com/content/dam/Deloitte/us/Documents/center-for-board-effectiveness/missing-pieces-fortune-500-board-diversity-study-sixth-edition.pdf.

governed does not necessarily mean voluntary, and voluntary does not mean unregulated. Regulations, frameworks, and rules for ESG disclosure managed via private governance can be as influential as government regulations, frameworks, and rules. Just as one should not create a false dichotomy between mandatory and voluntary disclosures, one should not create a false dichotomy between public and private governance. Voluntary disclosures can help fill gaps left by the piecemeal "regime" of issue-specific ESG disclosure regulations, serve as laboratories of disclosure experimentation,[67] and are often more accessible.[68] Private governance, such as companies leveraging contract law to require disclosures, can reach companies (think small, private, and international companies) and require disclosures that public governance may not. The governance of these voluntary disclosures by private organizations is a form of regulation that legal professionals should not ignore.

Stock Exchange Rules

Many companies have, or strive to have, their equity securities listed on a prestigious stock exchange. Thus, stock exchanges wield significant power over the governance of public corporations, and they often exercise that power through listing standards. In the United States, listing standards are subject to approval of the SEC under § 19(b) of the Securities Exchange Act of 1934, as amended.[69] Due to this relationship, the SEC is said to have "raised eyebrow" power, informal influence, over exchange rulemaking.[70] Stock exchanges have begun using this power to require ESG disclosures, especially governance-related disclosures.[71]

Under Nasdaq's Board Diversity Rule, companies must have at least two diverse directors or explain why they do not.[72] The two diverse directors must include one who self-identifies as female and one who self-identifies as either an underrepresented minority or LGBTQ+. Companies provide this disclosure in its proxy statement or its information statement (or if the company does not file a proxy, its Form 10-K or 20-F), or on the company's website. The aim of comply-or-explain rules and regulations, such as Nasdaq's Board Diversity Rule, is to give shareholders, and other stakeholders, enough information to make a reasonable evaluation of the company's position on the issue.[73]

---

67. Fairfax, *supra* note 14, at 322–23 ("Voluntary disclosure enables corporations to experiment around disclosure practices, and thus serves as a critical source of learning about the most appropriate disclosure practices.").

68. Despite the push for plain language disclosures, reading mandatory filings, such as a 10-K, is often a drag compared to the often visually appealing voluntary reports.

69. 15 U.S.C. § 78s.

70. Donald E. Schwartz, *Federalism and Corporate Governance*, 45 Ohio St. L.J. 545 (1984).

71. For a comparison of the corporate governance listing requirements of the NYSE and NASDAQ, see Comparative Corporate Governance Standards Chart: NYSE vs. Nasdaq by Practical Law Corporate & Securities.

72. NASDAQ, NASDAQ'S BOARD DIVERSITY RULE: WHAT NASDAQ-LISTED COMPANIES SHOULD KNOW (2022), https://listingcenter.nasdaq.com/assets/Board%20Diversity%20Disclosure%20Five%20Things.pdf.

73. For more on gender quotas, see Darren Rosenblum, *Diversity and the Board of Directors: A Comparative Perspective*, in RESEARCH HANDBOOK ON COMPARATIVE CORPORATE GOVERNANCE (Afsharipour & Gelter, eds., 2020).

The New York Stock Exchange (NYSE) requires listed companies to adopt and disclose corporate governance guidelines. The guidelines must include director qualification standards (such as independence), responsibilities, access to management, compensation, and more. The NYSE requires companies to post these guidelines on the company's website and to disclose in its proxy statement or Form 10-K that the guidelines are available on the website with a link to the location on the website.

Real-World Example: Apple's 2021 Proxy Statement—"Apple's key governance documents, including our Corporate Governance Guidelines, are available at investor.apple.com/leadership-and-governance."[74]

Short of creating hardline rules, stock exchanges have also begun issuing ESG disclosure guidance to listed companies. Nasdaq published the ESG Reporting Guide in 2019. The NYSE published *Best Practices for Sustainability Reporting* in 2021.[75] Nasdaq and the NYSE also maintain a repository of ESG resources on their websites for listed companies.

Contract Provisions

As pressure and incentives to disclose ESG information increase, even companies themselves are beginning to fill disclosure-related regulatory gaps with private governance tools. For example, some companies are using supply chain contract provisions to obtain ESG information from suppliers.[76] The Chancery Lane Project, a U.K.-based organization that creates model contract provisions that "deliver climate solutions," noted that their most popular provision is one that requires GHG reporting obligations throughout the supply chain.[77] Provisions such as these can reach private companies that may not be subject to the SEC's pending climate disclosure rule.

Voluntary Reporting Organizations

Dozens of organizations, such as the aforementioned TCFD, have created voluntary reporting standards and frameworks. Some of the most popular have

74. Apple, Notice of 2021 Annual Meeting of Shareholders and Proxy Statement 14 (2021), https://www.sec.gov/Archives/edgar/data/320193/000119312521001987/d767770ddef14a.htm; *Leadership and Governance*, Apple, https://investor.apple.com/leadership-and-governance/default.aspx (last visited Dec. 30, 2022), where you can download guidelines; Apple, Corporate Governance Guidelines (2022), https://s2.q4cdn.com/470004039/files/doc_downloads/gov_docs/Corporate-Governance-Guidelines.pdf.

75. *New York Stock Exchange ESG Guidance: Best Practices for Sustainability Reporting*, NYSE, https://www.nyse.com/esg-guidance#reporting-frameworks-and-standards (last visited Dec. 20, 2022).

76. Michael P. Vandenbergh, Model Environmental Supply Chain Contracts (forthcoming in Contracts for Responsible and Sustainable Supply Chains: Model Clauses, Legal Analysis, and Practical Discussion (David Snyder & Susan Maslow, eds.)), https://papers.ssrn.com/sol3/papers.cfm?abstract_id=4241316.

77. *The Net Zero Standard for Suppliers*, The Chancery Lane Project, https://chancerylaneproject.org/climate-clauses/the-net-zero-standard-for-suppliers/ (last visited Dec. 20, 2022); Email from Josh Hopkins, Secondee from Clyde & Co to TCLP, to Gabriella Mickel (Nov. 11, 2022) (on file with Author).

noted their intention to work together to create a comprehensive and uniform reporting framework to address the issues of incomparability and fragmentation.[78] However, this uniformity and cohesion has not yet manifested. Two of the most popular organizations are the Global Reporting Initiative (GRI) and the Sustainability Accounting Standards Board (SASB).[79]

The GRI is an independent, international standard setting institution. GRI Standards, one of the most widely used systems for disclosing ESG performance, provide a comparable, interconnected system of qualitative and quantitative disclosures. The standards are organized by (1) universal standards that apply to all organizations, (2) sector-specific standards for forty high-impact industries, and (3) topic standards (e.g., waste, tax, health, and safety). Companies use these standards for comprehensive sustainability reporting or more narrowly for issue-specific disclosure. GRI guides reporting organizations to select topics in consultation with their stakeholders that reflect their most significant ESG impacts.

SASB Standards[80] identify the subset of environmental, social, and governance issues most relevant to financial performance and enterprise value for seventy-seven industries. Each standard has about six disclosure topics and thirteen accounting metrics. About two-thirds of the accounting metrics in the SASB Standards are quantitative. The disclosure topics range across five "sustainability"[81] dimensions: environmental, social, and human capital; business model and innovation; and leadership and governance. The GRI and SASB standards are free and publicly available for use.

Certifications and Ratings

Companies sometimes choose to voluntarily disclose ESG information in exchange for a certification or rating. One popular example is the B Corp Certification offered by the nonprofit organization B Lab,[82] not to be confused with the legal designation of a benefit corporation.[83] While requirements for B Corp certification vary based on company revenue and size,[84] generally, companies fill out an

---

78. CDP, Climate Disclosure Standards Bd., Glob. Reporting Initiative, Int'l Integrated Reporting Council & Sustainability Acct. Standards Bd., Statement of Intent to Work Together Toward Comprehensive Corporate Reporting, Integrated Reporting 2–3 (2020), https://www.integratedreporting.org/resource/statement-of-intent-to-work-together-towards-comprehensive-corporate-reporting/.

79. For more information, see GRI & SASB, A Practical Guide to Sustainability Reporting Using GRI and SASB Standards (2021), https://www.globalreporting.org/media/mlkjpn1i/gri-sasb-joint-publication-april-2021.pdf.

80. "Effective August 1, 2022, the Value Reporting Foundation—home to the SASB Standards—consolidated into the IFRS Foundation, which established the first International Sustainability Standards Board (ISSB). SASB Standards are now under the oversight of the ISSB." *About*, SASB, https://www.sasb.org/about/ (last visited Dec. 25, 2022).

81. Sustainability is broadly defined by SASB.

82. *About B Corp Certification*, B Lab, https://www.bcorporation.net/en-us/certification (last visited Dec. 25, 2022).

83. Over forty states that have proposed or passed legislation acknowledge benefit corporations. Benefit corporations are a type of for-profit corporate entity. Typically, states require benefit corporations to have the purpose of creating a general public benefit.

84. B Lab, *supra* note 79.

initial assessment with various ESG disclosure requirements and must resubmit information every three years. The B Lab Certification team then reviews the information, certifies the company as a "Certified B Corporation," and creates a webpage with the company's scores and disclosures.

Real-World Example: Vital Proteins LLC's B Lab webpage.[85]

International and Foreign

Disclosure laws have interjurisdictional effects. Over sixty countries have mandatory reporting requirements for listed companies.[86] These disclosure requirements impact U.S. companies. There are also global efforts related to ESG disclosures. Many of the examples highlighted below are not explicit ESG disclosure frameworks but are used by companies and other organizations in developing disclosures. In addition, some could also be listed in the section "Private Governance."

UN Global Compact

The UN Global Compact is a nonbinding pact meant to encourage businesses to adopt sustainable and socially responsible policies and to report on their implementation. Participants commit to the Ten Principles, which fall under anticorruption, labor, environment, and human rights.[87] After the initial commitment, participants must complete the annual Communication on Progress, which requires the completion of a questionnaire to prompt disclosures and the submission of an electronic statement by the Chief Executive Officer expressing continued support for the UN Global Compact.[88]

Organisation for Economic Co-operation and Development (OECD)

The OECD is an international organization that develops guidelines--nonbinding principles and standards for responsible, multinational business conduct. The OECD Guidelines for Multinational Enterprises include disclosures.[89] In addition to disclosure of financial and non-financial material information, the guidelines also encourage a second set of disclosures in areas where reporting

---

85. *Vital Proteins LLC*, B Lab, https://www.bcorporation.net/en-us/find-a-b-corp/company/vital-proteins-llc (last visited Dec. 25, 2022).

86. World Bus. Council for Sustainable Dev. & Climate Disclosure Standards Bd., Insights from the Reporting Exchange: ESG Reporting Trends (2018), https://www.cdsb.net/sites/default/files/cdsbreport_1_esg.pdf.

87. *Principles*, UN Global Compact, https://www.unglobalcompact.org/what-is-gc/mission/principles (last visited Dec. 25, 2022).

88. UN Global Compact, Questionnaire Communication on Progress (2022).

89. OECD Guidelines for Multinational Enterprises 27 (2011), https://www.oecd.org/daf/inv/mne/48004323.pdf.

standards are still evolving such as ESG issues.[90] The OECD Due Diligence Guidance for Responsible Business Conduct also encourages disclosures related to the due diligence process.[91] The OECD continues to be an influential player. For example, due diligence under both the U.S. Conflict Minerals Rules and the analogous EU regulation must be conducted using the OECD framework.

United Nations Sustainable Development Goals (SDGs)

In 2015, the United Nations adopted seventeen sustainable development goals (zero hunger, gender equality, climate action, etc.) with 169 associated targets as part of its 2030 Agenda for Sustainable Development. Numerous ESG assessment frameworks have incorporated the goals. A 2018 report by KPMG noted that 40 percent of the world's largest 250 companies acknowledged the SDGs in their corporate reporting. The GRI and the United Nations Global Compact have even released a guide on integrating SDGs into corporate reporting.[92] The report lists the goals and targets with corresponding disclosure prompts from a variety of frameworks (GRI, SASB, CDP, UN Global Compact).

European Union—Corporate Sustainability Reporting Directive

In 2022, the Council of the European Union gave its final approval to the corporate sustainability reporting directive (CSRD). For non-European companies, the requirement to provide a sustainability report applies to all companies generating a net turnover of EUR 150 million in the EU and which have at least one subsidiary or branch in the EU exceeding certain thresholds.[93] The CSRD also applies to companies with securities listed on an EU-regulated market, regardless of whether the issuer is registered in the EU or a non-EU country. Thus, some U.S. companies will be required to provide broader and more detailed ESG disclosures.

Part III: ESG Disclosure-Related Enforcement, Litigation, and Pressure

As the frameworks for ESG disclosures develop, so do mechanisms for enforcement of ESG disclosures. Companies and their lawyers should be mindful of increasing enforcement and litigation when making ESG disclosures. The SEC

---

90. *Id.* at 29–30.

91. OECD Due Diligence Guidance for Responsible Business Conduct (2018), http://mneguidelines.oecd.org/OECD-Due-Diligence-Guidance-for-Responsible-Business-Conduct.pdf.

92. GRI, Integrating the SDGs into Corporate Reporting: A Practical Guide (2022), https://www.globalreporting.org/public-policy-partnerships/sustainable-development/integrating-sdgs-into-sustainability-reporting/.

93. Press Release, Council of the EU, Council Gives Final Green Light to Corporate Sustainability Reporting Directive (Nov. 28, 2022), https://www.consilium.europa.eu/en/press/press-releases/2022/11/28/council-gives-final-green-light-to-corporate-sustainability-reporting-directive/.

has begun using the existing regulatory framework for ESG disclosure-related enforcement, as it works on building out that framework with new proposed rules. In addition to actions initiated by the SEC, companies are also facing consumer claims, as well as securities fraud and breach of fiduciary duty claims.

SEC Enforcement Actions

Both the SEC Division of Enforcement and Division of Examinations have recently increased scrutiny of ESG disclosures. In March 2021, the SEC announced the new Climate and ESG Task Force within the Division of Enforcement. The Task Force aims to develop initiatives to proactively identify ESG-related misconduct, as investor reliance on climate and ESG-related disclosure and investment increases. The Task Force is searching for "potential violations including material gaps or misstatements in issuers' disclosure of climate risks under existing rules, and disclosure and compliance issues relating to investment advisers' and funds' ESG strategies."[94] Additionally, the SEC's Division of Examinations prioritized the review of ESG disclosures for accuracy and adequacy.[95] The Division of Examinations intends to continue to focus on ESG-related advisory services and investment products, such as mutual funds, exchange-traded funds, and private fund offerings, to discourage greenwashing. Recent enforcement actions taken by SEC elucidate the role of the new Climate and ESG Task Force and highlight the SEC's focus on ESG.

SEC regulations require mutual funds to use a document called a prospectus to disclose information about the fund to investors. The prospectus must include information such as the fund's investment objectives or goals, its strategies for reaching those goals, the principal risks of investing in the fund, the fund's fees and expenses, and its past performance. In 2022, the SEC charged BNY Mellon Investment Adviser, Inc., for misstatements and omissions about ESG considerations in certain mutual fund prospectuses. According to the order and SEC press release,

> BNY Mellon Investment Adviser consented to the entry of the SEC's order finding that it violated Sections 206(2) and 206(4) of the Investment Advisers Act of 1940 and Rules 206(4)-7 and 206(4)-8, and Section 34(b) of the Investment Company Act. Without admitting or denying the SEC's findings, BNY Mellon Investment Adviser agreed to a cease-and-desist order, a censure, and to pay a $1.5 million penalty. The SEC's order also noted that BNY Mellon Investment Adviser

94. *Spotlight on Enforcement Task Force Focused on Climate and ESG Issues*, SEC, https://www.sec.gov/spotlight/enforcement-task-force-focused-climate-esg-issues (last visited Dec. 30, 2022).

95. In April 2021, the Division of Examinations released a Risk Alert titled The Division of Examinations' Review of ESG Investing. SEC, Priorities 12–13 (2021), https://www.sec.gov/files/2022-exam-priorities.pdf; *Risk Alert*, SEC, https://www.sec.gov/files/esg-risk-alert.pdf (last visited Dec. 24, 2022).

promptly undertook remedial acts and cooperated with Commission staff in its investigation.[96]

BNY Mellon is not alone, the SEC also charged Vale S.A., a publicly traded Brazilian mining company and one of the world's largest iron ore producers, with making false and misleading claims about the safety of its dams prior to a collapse that killed 270 people and led to a loss of more than $4 billion in Vale's market capitalization.

The Vale charge highlights a particularly important consideration for legal professionals working with clients who make ESG-related disclosures--the SEC is not only looking at mandatory ESG disclosures. In its complaint, the SEC noted Vale's statements in its mandatory periodic filings and its voluntary sustainability reports and ESG webinar.[97] A 2020 ESG disclosure study done by GAO confirms this point. The SEC evaluates a company's mandatory filings by examining information outside of the filings, including information voluntarily disclosed.[98] Indeed, anti-fraud provisions of the federal securities laws apply to voluntary disclosures--press releases, websites, sustainability reports, etc.

Other Litigation

Liability does not only stem from federal securities laws, potential liability also stems from other laws, such as federal and state consumer protection laws. While litigation is often not successful, companies should consider litigation costs and reputation risks. This section highlights a few ESG-disclosure-related lawsuits.[99]

In re Danimer Scientific, Inc.[100]

In 2022, investors filed a federal securities class action suit against Danimer Scientific, Inc. The company claimed that its products were made of "a naturally occurring bioplastic that effectively biodegrades in both anaerobic environments, such as a waste treatment facility, and aerobic environments, such as an ocean." After *The Wall Street Journal* published an article questioning Danimer

96. Press Release, SEC Charges BNY Mellon Investment Adviser for Misstatements and Omissions Concerning ESG Considerations (May 23, 2022), https://www.sec.gov/news/press-release/2022-86; Order Instituting Administrative and Cease-And-Desist Proceedings, https://www.sec.gov/litigation/admin/2022/ia-6032.pdf.

97. Complaint & Demand for Jury Trial, Securities and Exchange Commission v. Vale S.A., No. 22-cv-2405 (E.D.N.Y. Apr. 28, 2022) ("Vale's public statements, including through SEC periodic filings on Forms 20-F and 6-K in 2017 and 2019, sustainability reports issued in 2017 and 2018, and a December 2018 ESG webinar, touted the stability declarations and reassured investors that its dams were stable and safe."), https://storage.courtlistener.com/recap/gov.uscourts.nyed.479268/gov.uscourts.nyed.479268.1.0.pdf.

98. U.S. GOV'T ACCOUNTABILITY OFF., GAO-20-530, PUBLIC COMPANIES: DISCLOSURE OF ENVIRONMENTAL, SOCIAL AND GOVERNANCE FACTORS AND OPTIONS TO ENHANCE THEM 9 (2020), https://www.gao.gov/assets/710/707967.pdf.

99. For more, see Ramirez v. Exxon Mobil Corp., 334 F. Supp. 3d 832 (N.D. Tex. 2018); Oracle, Qualcomm, and others have been the target of shareholder derivative lawsuits asserting (1) breaches of the duty of care and loyalty based on alleged insufficient commitment to diversity and (2) misleading disclosures regarding these companies' commitment to diversity and compliance with antidiscrimination laws.

100. See In re Danimer Scientific, Inc., Securities Litigation, 1:21-cv-02708 (E.D.N.Y., May 14, 2021).

products titled "Plastic Straws that Quickly Biodegrade in the Ocean, Not Quite, Scientists Say," the stock price dropped. It dropped again after subsequent reports supported the doubts raised by the WSJ article. The investors claimed Danimer's SEC filings, press releases, and other market communications were materially false and misleading. The WSJ article even states that "many claims about Nodax are exaggerated and misleading, according to several experts on biodegradable plastics." Danimer filed a motion to dismiss in May 2022.

Most claims relating to a company's ESG disclosures tend to be brought under Section 11 of the Securities Act of 1933, which covers material misstatements and omissions in securities offering documents, and under Section 10(b) of the Securities Exchange Act of 1934 and Rule 10b-5, the principal anti-fraud provisions. The investors in this action utilize Section 10(b) of the Securities Exchange Act of 1934 and Rule 10b-5, as well as Section 20(a) of the Securities Exchange Act of 1934, which establishes that "controlling persons" can be vicariously liable for Rule 10b-5 violations.

Nat. Consumers League v. Walmart Stores, Inc.

In 2019, Walmart Stores, Inc., The Children's Place, Inc., and JC Penney Corporation, Inc. settled a lawsuit filed by the National Consumers League (NCL). The NCL alleged the companies violated sections of the District of Columbia Consumer Protection Procedures Act because they did not follow through on the corporate social responsibility statements listed on their websites. In denying the companies' motion to dismiss, the court narrowed in on the companies' promises to audit suppliers' compliance with the listed standards.[101] After the claim survived the motion to dismiss, the companies settled.[102]

The threat of potential litigation should not dissuade companies from making ESG disclosures. Instead, companies should include appropriate disclaimers and work to ensure disclosures are accurate and precise. Indeed, the consequences of not disclosing information may often outweigh risks.

External Pressure

The consequences of noncompliance or even of producing underwhelming disclosures do not stop at enforcement actions and litigation. Companies without accurate and adequate ESG disclosures will continue to face external pressures from policymakers and stakeholders such as shareholders, investors, and employees. In the 2022 proxy season, shareholder resolutions focused on diversity, climate change, and the environment made up the bulk of successful proxy votes.[103] Shareholders will likely continue to leverage their ability under Exchange

101. Order Denying Motion to Dismiss, https://nclnet.org/wp-content/uploads/archive-page-media/2016-07-22_Denying_Joint_Motion_to_Dismiss.pdf.

102. *Statement on resolution of lawsuit against Walmart, JC Penney, and The Children's Place*, NCL (Jan. 25, 2019), https://nclnet.org/archive-pages/resolution_walmart/.

103. Ellen Meyers, *Investors Rally behind Climate, Diversity Proposals as Proxy Season Ebbs*, Roll Call (Jul. 21, 2022), https://rollcall.com/2022/07/21/investors-rally-behind-climate- diversity-proposals-as-proxy-season-ebbs/.

Act Rule 14a-8 to submit shareholder resolutions requesting more comprehensive ESG disclosures. The shareholders are not alone in their efforts to pressure companies to do better. Institutional investors continue to push for more robust ESG commitments, communications, and performance.[104] State Street Global Advisors' CEO Cyrus Taraporevala announced that, beginning in 2022, State Street is implementing new proxy voting guidelines that will require companies in major indices in the United States to make TCFD-aligned climate disclosures.[105] In January 2021, BlackRock CEO Larry Fink released his annual letter to CEOs, in which he asked companies to disclose a net zero plan. BlackRock also again requested companies disclose against the TCFD and SASB standards. Even the New York State Comptroller sent letters to companies in 2019 requesting that they "develop robust transition plans and business strategies that are to be aligned with a two-degree and below two-degree future." Internally, employees are increasingly concerned with the ESG activities of their employers,[106] and employee activism is on the rise to back up the concern.[107]

Conclusion

The importance of ESG disclosures is growing as (1) more reporting entities recognize that these factors can impact value and (2) many investors and other stakeholders continue to seek information about whether companies align with their values. Publicly and privately governed and mandated ESG disclosures are becoming increasingly prevalent and are expected to continue to be so in the future. As a result, it is crucial for legal professionals to stay informed about developments in this rapidly evolving field in order to effectively represent and advise their clients.

---

104. Kiran Vasantham and David Shammai, Institutional Investor Survey 2020 (Morrow Sodali, 2020), https://morrowsodali.com/uploads/insights/attachments/83713c2789adc52b596dda1ae1a79fc2.pdf.

105. *CEO's Letter on Our 2022 Proxy Voting Agenda*, State Street (Jan. 12, 2022), https://www.ssga.com/us/en/individual/mf/insights/ceo-letter-2022-proxy-voting-agenda.

106. Herbert, Smith, Freehills, Future of Work Adapting to the Democratized Workplace 12 (2019), https://hsfnotes.com/employment/2019/12/02/future-of-work-adapting-to-the-democratised-workplace/.

107. *Id.* ("Over 80% of companies predict a rise in workforce activism").

Index

Page numbers followed by "n" indicate footnotes.

About the Editors

Travis Miller is the Head of Supply Chain Compliance and Social Responsibility for Google. He is responsible for supply chain strategy related to global compliance and social responsibility programs and initiatives. He serves as the Chair of Supplier Responsibility Steering Committee responsible for advising senior executives on emerging regulatory trends, impacts on core business operations, and coherent strategy to address risk to business continuity and sustainability goals. He formerly served as General Counsel of Assent, has written two additional books on CSR law and supply chain compliance, and has founded numerous start-ups dealing with international trade and regulatory compliance.

Dr. Todd Cort works at the intersection of sustainability and investor value. Over the course of twenty years, in consulting and academia, he has applied a scientific and economic lens to corporate social and environmental responsibility (or sustainability) in order to identify the tools, mechanisms, metrics, and indicators that create the greatest value for investors, businesses, and society. He has worked extensively with companies and investors across industrial sectors. His experience ranges from "on the ground" implementation of sustainability programs to corporate-level communication and investor strategy development. He has also worked extensively on integrated programs to meet regulatory requirements while promoting awareness and understanding of sustainability priorities through communications and engagement with communities, regulators, policy makers, and internal stakeholders. He is currently a faculty member at the Yale School of Management with courtesy appointment at the Yale School of the Environment. He serves as Faculty Co-Director for the Yale Center for Business and the Environment (CBEY) and the Yale Initiative on Sustainable Finance (YISF). He serves on a variety of advisory boards, including the JUST Capital Scientific Advisory Board and the PRIME Coalition Academic Advisory Committee. He is also currently a Board Member and Treasurer for Save the Sound, a regional environmental nonprofit serving communities around Long Island Sound.

About the Contributors

Chantal Bernier is Co-chair, Global Privacy and Cybersecurity Group, and is a member of Dentons' Canadian Privacy and Cybersecurity and Government Affairs and Public Policy practice groups. She comes to Dentons after nearly six years as Assistant and Interim Privacy Commissioner of Canada. In that capacity, she led national and international privacy investigations in the public and private sectors, as well as privacy audits, privacy impact assessment reviews, technological analysis, and privacy policy development and research.

Amanda Branch expertly guides clients through the evolving global landscape of privacy and marketing law. Having worked both in private practice and as in-house counsel, she provides business-focused and practical legal advice to help clients creatively manage risk. She advises on all areas of privacy and marketing law, including cross-border transfers, anti-spam legislation, and branding. She is frequently asked to speak about hot topics in privacy law and has authored several publications about privacy and advertising law issues.

Sarah Carpenter is Director of Corporate Responsibility at Assent. She provides direction to Fortune 500 companies on human rights due diligence and ESG strategies with a focus on supply chain impacts. She also leads Assent's B-Corp Certified corporate sustainability program. Following the 2013 Rana Plaza collapse in Bangladesh, she supported the United Nations International Labour Organization's work promoting labor rights reform in the garment industry. She has worked for a range of rights-based nongovernmental organizations, including Plan International and the Canadian Network on Corporate Accountability. She is the current chair of the Slavery and Trafficking Risk Template Working Group of the Social Responsibility Alliance.

Ann Condon is the Interim President of the Institute for Sustainable Communities and a guest lecturer at Yale University. She has long been a leader in global environmental and social governance. During her thirty-four-year career with General Electric Company (GE), she built robust global compliance programs focused on the environment, health, and safety (EHS); supply chain ethics; sustainability; and chemical and product stewardship. Her team worked closely with GE's businesses on resource efficiency and life cycle management, showing how reducing GE's environmental impact could bring business value, demonstrate GE technology, and put GE in a leadership position. The team supported GE's Ecomagination initiative with regulatory, technical, and life cycle expertise; setting and achieving the Ecomagination operating goals; and coordinating climate and chemical management policy. She is a graduate of the University of Connecticut and George Washington University's National Law Center.

David Hackett is Senior Counsel at Baker & McKenzie LLP where he advises senior management, legal departments, and boards of major corporations and nonprofits on compliance, risk, environmental, and sustainability matters. He has exceptional experience managing U.S. and international compliance and environmental projects, including the evaluation and development of effective compliance and sustainability programs. He also has extensive experience litigating major civil and criminal environmental matters. He sits on multiple nonprofit boards and additionally advises many civic and nonprofit organizations across the globe. Following his tenure with the Environmental Enforcement Division of the U.S. Department of Justice, he joined the Firm where he has played a formative role in the establishment of the Firm's compliance, environmental, climate, and ESG practices. At Baker McKenzie, he has served as the managing partner of North America, a member of the Global Executive Committee, and Chicago office managing partner. He is a graduate of Haverford College and the University of Pennsylvania Law School.

Shyla John, Principal, brings over twelve years of combined experience in sustainability, corporate responsibility, and communications to the NPV team. She supports Fortune 500 clients in managing and implementing their CR programs across a variety of areas, including ESG strategy development, stakeholder engagement, report development, and communications. She works across multiple industries, including food and beverage, oil and gas, consumer products, finance/banking, and ICT, as well as organizations in the nonprofit sector. She previously served as a Senior Sustainability Consultant for DNV GL's Sustainability Advisory Services team and worked as a consultant in Europe, Mexico, and the United States. She began her career as an integrated marketing executive managing marketing and public relations campaigns for large consumer brands. She holds a BA in Sociology from the University of California, Los Angeles (UCLA), and an MBA from ESADE Business School.

Caleb Lee is a sophomore at Yale University studying Ethics, Politics, and Economics, and Statistics and Data Science. He is actively researching ESG data analytics and software tools to develop novel financial models for integration of ESG factors into investment decision-making. He is the Vice President of Global Research and Consulting, a pro-bono consulting group at Yale where he helps nonprofits of all scales to achieve their missions and increase their impact through research, analysis, and strategic recommendations. As the head of an investment team at the Urban Philanthropic Fund, he not only prioritizes sustainable investment strategies but also champions social impact investments. He works closely with partners, such as EmergeCT and Winning Ways CT, to support formerly incarcerated individuals and their families as they reintegrate into society. In addition, he serves on the Executive Board of the Yale Policy Institute and is a senior editor of the Yale Politic. In particular, he researches and works with incarcerated individuals and pursues prison justice. Outside of work, he enjoys singing and touring the world with his acapella group the Yale Society of Orpheus and Bacchus, playing tennis, and exploring the Planetarium and Observatory on campus.

Gabriella Mickel is a joint degree student (JD/MEM) at the Elisabeth Haub School of Law at Pace University and the Yale School of the Environment.

Sarah Gudernatch Smith is a Principal Consultant and co-owner of NPV Associates. She co-leads NPV's reporting and disclosures practice and has worked with clients including The Walt Disney Company, Chevron, Dell, and Norton among others. She is a seasoned writer and editor and has significant experience in messaging, reporting, communications, and stakeholder engagement. Both in her career and at home with her two young children, she believes in compassion and dialogue, renewable energy and composting, and getting things done. Prior to her work in sustainability, she served as a Communications Manager in the nonprofit sector. She received her MS in Sustainability Management from Columbia University and BA in Political Science from Providence College. She is a SA8000 certified auditor and LEED GA certified.

Jamen Tyler is Managing Director at StoneTurn where she assists private and publicly traded companies and nonprofits with Enterprise, Global, and Targeted Risk Assessments; Reviewing Compliance Programs and Implementing Program Enhancement; Post-Incident Response and Remediation; M&A Due Diligence and Post-Acquisition Integration and Risk Assessments; Review of Internal Structure and Governance; Development of Compliance Policies, Procedures, and Communications; and Compliance Training.

Andrew Waitman is a renowned entrepreneur, executive, and investor with a successful track record of building and scaling technology companies. He is widely recognized as a leader in the technology industry and has been instrumental in the growth of many start-ups. He co-founded and became the Managing Partner of Celtic House Venture Partners, which, under his stewardship, became one of Canada's most successful venture firms with Fund IIA sporting one of the highest (Top 10) IRRs ever. In 2008, he joined Pythian, a leading provider of data management services, where he served as CEO growing the business from under $5M to over $50M in revenue in under five years. In 2014, he joined the founding team at Assent and as CEO grew the business from under US$1M in ARR to over

US$100M and more than 1,000 team members in 2023. Today, he is a sought-after advisor and investor in the tech industry, providing guidance and support to start-ups and established companies alike.

Annabelle Xing is a sophomore at Yale University studying Computer Science and Economics with certificates in Advanced Chinese Language Studies and Energy Studies. She is passionate about steering financial capital toward socially impactful channels and has worked on various carbon financing and sustainability investment projects with real estate investment trusts, private equity firms, and venture capital funds. Recently, she has been researching the role of ESG investment strategies in personal and corporate finance globally.